Introduction to Extended Reality (XR) Technologies

Scrivener Publishing
100 Cummings Center, Suite 541J
Beverly, MA 01915-6106

Publishers at Scrivener
Martin Scrivener (martin@scrivenerpublishing.com)
Phillip Carmical (pcarmical@scrivenerpublishing.com)

Introduction to Extended Reality (XR) Technologies

Edited by

Manisha Vohra

Scrivener Publishing

WILEY

This edition first published 2025 by John Wiley & Sons, Inc., 111 River Street, Hoboken, NJ 07030, USA and Scrivener Publishing LLC, 100 Cummings Center, Suite 541J, Beverly, MA 01915, USA

For more information about Scrivener publications please visit www.scrivenerpublishing.com.

Wiley Global Headquarters
111 River Street, Hoboken, NJ 07030, USA

For details of our global editorial offices, customer services, and more information about Wiley products visit us at www.wiley.com.

Library of Congress Cataloging-in-Publication Data

ISBN 978-1-119-85722-8

Front cover images courtesy of Adobe Firefly
Cover design by Russell Richardson

Set in size of 11pt and Minion Pro by Manila Typesetting Company, Makati, Philippines

Printed in the USA

10 9 8 7 6 5 4 3 2 1

Contents

Preface

Extended Reality Technologies, abbreviated as XR technologies, are rapidly growing and rank among the top technology trends. XR essentially comprises Augmented Reality (AR), Virtual Reality (VR), and Mixed Reality (MR). These technologies extend reality by combining the virtual and real worlds or by blending them to create an enhanced experience.

Augmented Reality (AR): It overlays digital information onto the actual real world. The user's experience of the real world is enhanced with digital elements such as animations and other details.

Virtual Reality (VR): It creates a simulated 3D environment generated using computers. Users can interact with this virtual environment using special devices such as headsets.

Mixed Reality (MR): This blends virtual and real-world environments. In Mixed Reality, objects from the real world and virtual objects can coexist and interact with each other in real time.

Extended Reality Technologies offer significant advantages. They have the potential to revolutionize how people perceive and experience the virtual environment. Because of their capabilities, XR technologies can transform various sectors where they are applied. For example, in fields such as education, healthcare, business, entertainment, and gaming, these technologies can act as game changers and prove highly beneficial.

This book, "Introduction to Extended Reality (XR) Technologies", discusses and explains the fundamentals, concepts, and various other aspects of XR technologies. It is designed to be useful for both academic and industry audiences. Along with discussing the fundamentals and concepts, this book also highlights the different applications of XR technologies, including real-world examples.

The organization of the book, which provides an overview of each chapter, is as follows:

Chapter 1 explores the term Extended Reality (XR), which is rapidly growing in popularity. Extended Reality technologies comprise Augmented Reality (AR), Virtual Reality (VR), and Mixed Reality (MR), all of which hold great importance. These technologies are being widely adopted across different industries. For example, VR, which was once considered primarily useful in the entertainment industry, is now proving beneficial in sectors like education and healthcare. XR technologies are reaching new heights across various fields. This chapter defines XR and presents a brief conceptual overview. It discusses the different elements of XR, including its history and applications.

Chapter 2 delves into the evolving nature of Extended Reality (XR) technologies, highlighting their growing presence across different sectors. There are numerous possibilities with XR. This chapter provides a detailed understanding of XR, offering insights into its important historical milestones. It also explains the characteristics and benefits of XR technologies.

Chapter 3 examines how Extended Reality (XR) technologies are becoming a significant topic of discussion in today's technological landscape. These technologies are being implemented in numerous sectors due to their benefits and possibilities. This chapter provides a brief description of different XR technologies, along with their applications, supported by examples.

Chapter 4 focuses on the introduction of Augmented Reality (AR) and Virtual Reality (VR), highlighting their characteristics, components, and recent research applications. The chapter explores how advancements in technology have paved the way for VR, AR, and Mixed Reality (MR), which integrate real-world physical objects with virtual ones. It emphasizes 3D visualization as a key feature of AR/VR technology and discusses its vital role in various sectors. Additionally, the chapter examines the growing market for AR/VR technologies and their potential to address real-world challenges.

Chapter 5 discusses Augmented Reality (AR), Virtual Reality (VR), and Mixed Reality (MR) technologies, which are integral components of XR. These technologies possess extraordinary capabilities and are growing rapidly. This chapter provides an overview of AR, VR, and MR, discussing their history, advantages, and potential to revolutionize sectors through diverse applications.

Chapter 6 explores the possibilities of Augmented Reality (AR) and Virtual Reality (VR) technologies, which are key elements of XR. The chapter discusses their applications across various sectors, supported by examples, and highlights the immense opportunities these technologies offer.

Chapter 7 examines the application of Extended Reality (XR) technologies in the aviation sector. As a vital and expansive field, aviation requires smooth and efficient work processes, which XR can help facilitate. This chapter discusses various XR technologies and their applications in aviation, using examples from literature reviews to highlight their benefits.

Chapter 8 explores how Extended Reality (XR) technologies can help revitalize the tourism sector, which was severely impacted by the COVID-19 pandemic. Tourism contributes to job creation and economic development while promoting cultural exchange and local products. This chapter discusses the role of XR in tourism marketing, promotion, and publicity, emphasizing its potential to recover and enhance the sector.

Chapter 9 highlights the role of Augmented Reality (AR) and Virtual Reality (VR) in the healthcare sector, particularly in disease diagnosis and surgical preplanning. The chapter discusses AR and VR applications in medical imaging, radiology, and biomedical engineering, emphasizing their ability to provide efficient solutions and enhance medical education and equipment design.

Chapter 10 explores the growing applications of Virtual Reality (VR) technology in healthcare. As a cutting-edge tool, VR is being used for training sessions, rehabilitation, operation planning, and more. This chapter examines VR's benefits, challenges, and potential for future research in the healthcare sector.

Chapter 11 focuses on the application of Augmented Reality (AR) and Mixed Reality (MR) in education. The chapter discusses examples of AR and MR technologies and their potential benefits for students and educators, emphasizing how XR can revolutionize the education sector by providing innovative tools for learning.

Chapter 12 discusses the concept of Extended Reality (XR) as a universal term encompassing immersive technologies like VR, AR, and MR. The chapter explores how XR integrates the physical and digital worlds, benefiting industries such as medicine and education. It highlights key developments, industry players, and real-world applications, supported by examples from the literature. The chapter concludes by discussing the exponential growth of XR technologies and their future potential.

This book will be an informative and valuable resource for gaining comprehensive knowledge about Extended Reality Technologies. The editor sincerely thanks Martin Scrivener, the team at Scrivener Publishing, and all the chapter contributors for their efforts in making this book possible. It will serve as a useful guide for becoming well-acquainted with Extended Reality Technologies.

Manisha Vohra
December 2024

Section 1

INTRODUCTION TO EXTENDED REALITY

1

Extended Reality: A Conceptual Description

N. Rajamurugu[1]* and S. Yaknesh[2]

[1]Department of Aerospace Engineering, KCG College of Technology, Chennai, India
[2]Department of Aerospace Engineering, Chandigarh University, Punjab, India

Abstract
Extended reality (XR) is a term which is growing rapidly in popularity. Extended reality technologies comprise of augmented reality (AR), virtual reality (VR), and mixed reality (MR) and have great importance. They are widely adopted in different industries—for example, VR, which was widely considered to be useful in the entertainment industry, is now being considered to be useful in education industry, healthcare industry, etc. XR technologies are reaching great heights across different industries. In this chapter, XR is defined, and a brief conceptual description of XR is presented. The different elements of XR, including its history, applications, etc., are discussed in the chapter.

***Keywords*:** Extended reality (XR), augmented reality (AR), virtual reality (VR), mixed reality (MR), environment, immersive

1.1 Introduction

Technologies help the world across different sectors in different ways. There are so many technologies present such as cloud computing, Internet of Things (IoT) digital twin, blockchain, etc. Each plays an important role across different sectors. Among the wide number of technologies present, there are particular technologies which are currently gaining a lot of popularity like the XR technologies.

XR is also called X reality or extended reality. Herein X is representing any spatial computing technologies which are presently existing or which may exist in the future like AR, VR, MR, and the areas interpolated among

**Corresponding author*: n.rajamurugu@gmail.com

Manisha Vohra (ed.) Introduction to Extended Reality (XR) Technologies, (3–16) © 2025 Scrivener Publishing LLC

them [1]. XR technologies are evolving rapidly. They provide the users with a lot of advantages and are hence making their place across different sectors. Let us first understand what XR, which is discussed below, is.

1.2 What is XR?

XR comprises of AR, VR, and MR. XR means all real environments and virtual environments brought together, wherein human and machine interaction takes place via interactions that have been generated by hardware and computer technology [1].

Let us now understand VR, AR, and MR. Starting with VR, in simple words, it is a simulation generated by a computer of a three-dimensional environment which appears to the user to be real. VR's aim is to convince the user that the virtual environment is as real as the physical reality. MR is a hybrid system. In MR, both physical elements and virtual elements are present [4].

An environment is created by VR technology in which the user feels as well as seems to be moving within a virtual world that is created by a computer in a way just like how people move within or inside a natural environment; while immersed in the virtual world, the real world that actually surrounds the user cannot be perceived by the user. Talking about AR, it is opposite to this; AR lets the user view the real world and augments it with superimposed virtual objects. So, it can be stated that while reality is replaced by VR, AR supplements it; an environment is created in which real objects as well as virtual objects harmonically coexist [5].

All the computer technologies which promote the generation of virtual environments that let the user have an interaction with them is called VR or, in other words, it is what VR refers to.

Over the time period of the past 10 years, utilizing computer-generated reality concept to support daily practice has become ever more mature, and this is all thanks to the advancement of hardware as well as software. In the product design area, many different previous studies have tried adopting VR technologies in various stages of product development [16].

Application of VR in medical education is an important area. Virtual simulation platforms over the period of the last decade have been growingly developed. These platforms have proved to be helpful in further increasing the ability of medical students to gather information during medical history collection and also to make their diagnostic problem-solving skills better [22].

Getting back to the AR discussion, AR is the amalgamation of elements from the real world and the virtual world. AR offers the possibility of mixing two environments and combining them—the physical environment and the digital environment—in real time via the use of emerging technologies which are also easily accessible, like smartphones or tablets [2].

Along with computer-generated images (CGI), real-world scenes are combined by AR. Presently, AR is a modern media which is very advanced and is engaged in a growing number of industries [17].

The author in [34] defines AR as systems which possess different characteristics. They are as follows:

1) The first characteristic is combining real and virtual.
2) The second characteristic is being real-time interactive or, in other words, being interactive in real time.
3) The third characteristic is being registered in 3D [34].

So, the items above are the different characteristics which AR systems possess according to the author in [11].

Pokemon Go and Google Glass are two extremely familiar examples of AR [11]. During the time period of over a decade, technology like AR has matured [18].

In different areas like the industrial area, AR can be utilized in different ways—for example, how AR can be used to support the preparation of kit in the context of material supply to assembly; the insight of this is given in the paper [24].

AR has proved to be a good solution for the manufacturing-related area,—solution which is having innovation and is having a great effect as well in helping to solve some difficult problems to simulate, assist, and make the manufacturing processes better prior to them being conducted—thus ensuring that things like design, machining, etc., are correctly done for the first time without the requirement of consequent re-working and any modifications. In various applications, in manufacturing as well as in many other fields, AR has been exhibited to be a solution [18].

In recent years, augmented reality smart glasses (ARSG) have been identified as a very powerful technology which supports shop-floor operators who are working on different tasks like maintenance, assembly, quality control, and material handling [15].

A subsequent rise in VR and VR applications which leverage smartphone technology has been seen with the growing popularity of smartphones and their adoption [32].

In recent times, quite considerably, the maturity of VR and AR devices has grown. For the consumer market, there is the availability of reasonably low-priced and powerful VR and AR devices, all thanks to technical advancement for this [31].

Coming to MR, it is a fusion of the physical world and the digital world which explores the relationship between human, computer, and environmental interactions [4]. The simplest way of viewing a MR environment is the one in which both real and virtual world objects are presented together within a single display [35]. MR, in general, can be used in different applications such as in [21]. A MR-based user interface for the quality control inspection of car body surfaces has been proposed so as to improve the ergonomics and also the productivity of workers [21]. Similarly, MR can be used in more different applications.

The description above helps to understand what is VR, AR, and MR. Now, coming back to VR technology, it is not very new, but the developments in the recent times in immersive technologies, specifically with respect to interactions and visualization, have made VR come across as attractively growing to scholars. Recent VR head-mounted displays (HMDs), like Oculus Rift, HTC Vive, etc., let the users experience a high degree of immersion. According to the authors in [6], immersion describes user involvement in an environment that is virtual and during which the awareness—real-world awareness and awareness of time—often becomes disconnected, thus providing a sense of being in the task environment instead. HMDs for mobile devices are available, which are low-budget like Google Cardboard, Samsung Gear VR, etc., which let each one to get the experience of immersive virtual environments. The present devices also offer interaction capabilities [6].

There are three different types of VR systems. They are as follows:

- Non-immersive
- Immersive
- Semi-immersive

The simplest as well as the cheapest type of VR applications which utilize desktops to reproduce images of the world are non-immersive systems [7].

With the help of different sensory outputs devices like HMDs for the enhancement of the stereoscopic view of environments via movement of the user's head and audio and haptic devices, the immersive systems provide a complete simulated experience [7].

Semi-immersive systems such as Fish Tank VR, which are semi-immersive, are between immersive and non-immersive systems. The systems like Fish Tank VR provide a stereo-image of a 3D scene which is viewed on a monitor by utilizing a perspective projection that is coupled to the head position of the observer [7].

VR devices: The manner in which a user communicates with the computer is decided by the input devices [9].

Talking about the output devices, the ones which are responsible for the presentation of a virtual environment and its phenomena to the user are output devices. The output devices contribute to the generation of an immersive feeling at most. They include visual, auditory, or haptic displays.

After input hardware and output hardware, the underlying software is the one which actually plays an important role. The underlying software has the responsibility for the management of I/O devices. It also has the responsibility for analyzing the data which is incoming and for generating proper feedback [9].

AR devices: The main devices for augmented reality are displays, input devices, tracking, and computers.

- Displays: Three major types of displays used in AR are as follows:
  - Head-mounted displays (HMDs)
  - Handheld displays
  - Spatial displays
- Input devices: There are many types of input devices for AR systems. Some systems utilize gloves, while some utilize wireless wristbands. The input devices selected will be based on the application [8].
- Tracking: Tracking devices consist of digital cameras and/or other optical sensors, GPS, accelerometers, solid-state compasses, wireless sensors, etc. [8].
- Computer: The computer does the work of analyzing the visual which is sensed, and it also analyzes other data in order to synthesize and position augmentations [8].

VR, AR, and MR are all very important and have various advantages. Now, the way in which scientists and engineers look at computers in order to perform mathematical simulations, data visualization, and also decision making is changed by VR [23].

VR creates an environment in which virtual spaces and objects replace real-world scenes completely. AR creates an environment where virtual objects are superimposed on a predominantly real-world scene [14]. AR is based on the possibility of adding further information and dimensions to the reality that surrounds us, letting the display of virtual data overlap a real object by just framing it [13]. A participant in VR systems is completely immersed in a virtual environment [20].

AR and VR are two technologies which let students conduct experiments in a safe environment [10]. To support as well as facilitate learning and teaching processes, VR is a powerful tool for it [19]. Numerous industries implemented AR/VR successfully [26].

One of the differences that AR has with VR and MR is that AR is much closer to the environment of the real world, whereas placing of VR is done in one of the most distant points of the context, while MR is placed halfway between them as it incorporates elements of VR and AR [3]. VR/MR tools are considered as trustworthy solutions for training operators of service maintenance [25].

A huge spectrum of hardware and software is encompassed by XR [12].

XR systems are important in different applications, and from the Industry 4.0 point of view they are of importance as well. It is necessary to have a successful integration of XR systems in digital transformation of manufacturing as this will contribute toward the realization of the Industry 4.0 vision.

1.3 History of XR

There are different events and happenings which contributed to the evolution of XR. Below are some of the important events and happenings in the history of XR.

Starting with the stereoscope, the invention of which is done by Charles Wheatstone in 1838, it is considered to be the initial point for the journey of AR as well as VR. He found out that the brain takes one image from each eye and combines them both to create a single 3D image. On the basis of this, he created a stereoscope device which took two images and made a 3D image, and it also added an illusion of depth. Nowadays, stereoscopic displays are utilized in modern VR systems. They provide the digital images with a feeling of depth, boosting the immersion feel.

In 1935, American science fiction author Stanley Weinbaum published Pygmalion's Spectacles, wherein the main character explores a world of fiction via a pair of goggles which lets the users experience virtual senses such as sight, hearing, etc.

In 1938, William Gruber and Harold Graves came up with the View-Master. It was a stereoscopic 3D photo viewer that offered a modern take on the scenic postcard.

Sensorama, the first virtual reality machine, was built by cinematographer Morton Heilig in 1956. To surprise the audience in the film, this film booth integrated 3D, color video with sounds, fragrances, and a vibrating chair. In 1962, Morton Heilig patented Sensorama.

Philco engineers invented the Headsight headset. It was invented in the year 1961. This was the first VR headgear that featured motion tracking technology.

Harvard professor Ivan Sutherland invented an AR headset in 1968. This was the first AR headset. It was named "The Sword of Damocles". It projected computer-generated images which made the user's vision of the world better.

Myron Krueger created the Videoplace. It was created in 1975 [8]. It was artificial reality created by Krueger, a conceptual environment with no existence. Silhouettes of the users, grabbed by cameras, were projected on a large screen in this system, and the participants were able to interact with one another. This was possible due to image processing techniques which let users interact with virtual objects [9].

In the year 1985, the VPL company commercialized the DataGlove and eyephone [7].

At the end of the 1980s, Fake Space Labs created the Binocular-Omni-Orientational Monitor (BOOM). It was a complex system composed of a stereoscopic displaying device. It provided a moving and broad virtual environment and also a mechanical arm tracking [7].

In between 1980 and 1990, the first commercially sold VR devices, the DataGlove and the Eyephone, were made [9].

In 1992, the Electronic Visualization Laboratory of the University of Illinois created the CAVE Automatic Virtual Environment. It is an immersive VR system which is composed of projectors directed on three or more walls of a room [7].

Gunpei Yokoi, a Nintendo designer, created the Virtual Boy in 1995. It was an unsuccessful portable video game device that replicated red and black displays via a visor attached to a handheld controller.

Palmer Luckey, at the age of 18 years, successfully designed a prototype for the Oculus Rift VR headset. This headset brought back the interest in VR with its 90° field of vision (FOV) and also its efficient use of computer processing power. Later, Facebook attained it in 2014.

In 2016, Microsoft's HoloLens headset was introduced. It is an MR device.

In 2017, IKEA Place application was introduced, an AR-based application which allowed customers to preview how furniture would look in their home before purchasing the furniture.

Currently, XR is being widely included in various applications and is evolving rapidly. The discussion above on some of the important events and happenings in the history of XR helps in knowing and understanding the history of XR.

1.4 Hardware Parameters for Extended Reality

Field of view (FOV) and frame per second (FPS) are different hardware parameters, which would affect the overall usability of the systems. Let us discuss them one by one. We will firstly begin by talking about FOV, followed by FPS.

1.4.1 Field of View (FOV)

A screen is needed in an XR system in order to project virtual contents to the users. At any given point of time, how much extent of area is visible to the user would be defined by the FOV parameter of a screen. It has a direct effect on the amount of virtual information which can be rendered. Different screens have different FOVs. The FOVs are of importance as an appropriate FOV is needed to view the entire visual detailing and virtual information inside the virtual environment. A narrow FOV could be less immersive. It could even affect and limit the viewing of visual detailing and virtual information.

Now, we will move toward discussing the next hardware parameter which is FPS.

1.4.2 Frame per Second (FPS)

Frame per second (FPS) is the frequency at which the consecutive frames of images are displayed on a screen. The higher the FPS, the smoother the motion of the content looks. Similar to the FOV, this parameter is more important in VR systems than AR or MR systems. FPS is a parameter which is determined not only by the hardware but also the software. Hence, it makes it important during the development that the virtual scenes should be fine-tuned to obtain desirable FPS.

1.5 Software Used for XR Systems

The XR systems are developed using various software. According to the authors in [27], there are two different approaches here: first is that which is based on open development platform and second is that which is based on the extension of the established commercial software. With open development platform, there is an advantage that it has a completely controlled development process which can be tailored based on individual needs. However, expertise in software engineering is needed. Coming on to the established commercial software extension then, in recent times, established commercial software is the expanding support for XR applications. Due to this, the existing users can create a seamless XR experience without having to put much efforts, but there will be limitations here as the exploration of new XR applications using this kind of software is pursued as the software here, in this case, will be dependent on updates from the software providers [27].

1.6 Applications of XR

XR can be used in different sectors. Some of them are as follows:

- Entertainment
- Healthcare
- Education
- Aviation

1.6.1 Example of Application of AR in Education

In the following example, AR's effect specifically on the learning performance of students in science, technology, engineering, and mathematics (STEM) education is discussed.

Initially, in a traditional manner, a topic is taught by utilizing just simple basic tools which are textbooks, whiteboard, and 3D models. Traditional exercises' set is carried out, which were preliminary prepared, and they are consistent with what study has been done. For this topic specifically, AR test pre-use is carried out. Documentation of results of student's pre-use of AR test is done, data analysis is done, and also evaluations are carried out. After this, AR-enhanced exercises sets are conducted, which are preliminary prepared and are consistent with the material which has been studied. In groups of three, the students carry out work and, a post-use of AR test is conducted. Similar to the procedure in the pre-use of AR test, here also in the post-use of AR case, the test results of the students are documented, analysis of the data is done, and also evaluations are carried out. Then, a comparison of test results of pre-use and post-use of AR is done. In all the groups, each of these steps was performed again for all of the four topics that were taught. To validate this particular experiment, a small size of participants, to be precise comprising of 80 participants, was taken. Later on, in the future, this research can be expanded. A visual as well as a very realistic learning environment is provided by the AR system which is utilized. This kind of learning environment cannot be provided by the traditional manner of teaching. After each topic had been explored two times, i.e., once prior to utilizing an AR tool and once after utilizing AR tool, the post-use AR tests were carried out. For the purpose of creating the test and in the distribution and collection of data, an online tool was used. The online tool utilized here was Results Microsoft Forms. Microsoft Excel, along with its data analysis tools, was utilized to export and analyze the data which was collected from the questionnaires. Data from all the tests carried out, i.e., before AR use and after AR use with each group, were summarized. It can be noticed that in all the three groups, AR tool and AR environment utilization showed improvement in students' understanding of the matter that they studied compared to traditional tools based on text and graph [28].

1.6.2 Example of Application of VR in Education

During the past few years, with the introduction of economic devices which are of high quality and that offer a quality user experience, the use of HMD to view VR environments has grown. The use of HMD-VR within the design and construction industries is increasing. In fact, it has proved to be a powerful visualization tool to help clients understand space. The research carried out by authors in [29] is viewing HMD-VR's potential introduction in the construction education classroom, which is in the context of wood frame construction assemblies. For this purpose, a study was conducted by the authors in [29]. This study conducted utilized commodity HMD-VR headsets. Mobile devices powered the HMD-VR headsets. An immersive HMD VR simulation was developed by this study, which allowed the students to explore a house that was under construction and which was at the stage of framing. To enable students to navigate freely through the environment and, with this, to also enable students to observe the features of the construction were the simulation's purposes. There was a great positive response received from the students as to the use of HMD simulations and its potential for use in the classroom [29]. In the past few years, with the growth of immersive VR, considering its use in teaching robotics in order to make the quality of teaching better in the robotics field is interesting [33].

1.6.3 Example of Application of MR in Education

Inconsistency in teaching is one of common sources of experiencing dissatisfaction among medical students, while heterogeneous access to clinical learning opportunities also remains as another common source of experiencing dissatisfaction among medical students. These were exacerbated during the COVID-19 pandemic by having limited exposure to patients for the purpose of clinical teaching. Now, to overcome these issues, the authors in [30] conducted a proof-of-concept study using MR technology (HoloLens2™) at a London teaching hospital in order to deliver a remote-access teaching ward round. In the year 2020, during the month of June, fourth-year students of Imperial College School of Medicine participated in a teaching ward round which involved HoloLens2™ technology. The authors recruited patients from a teaching hospital in London. The authors based the teaching on learning outcomes from the undergraduate curriculum. The results that the authors received clearly support the feasibility, acceptability, and effectiveness of utilizing MR technology in order to deliver a remote-access, interactive teaching ward round [30]. Hence, MR can be a potential technology to use in education.

AR, VR, and MR—all of these XR technologies—are capable of being applied in the education sector. With the three examples above, it is clear that XR technologies have great potential. They can, without any complexity, be applied for use in the education sector.

1.7 Conclusion

Extended reality (XR) is a term which is growing rapidly in popularity. Extended reality technologies comprise of augmented reality (AR), virtual reality (VR), and mixed reality (MR) and have great importance. They are widely adopted in different sectors or industries—for example, VR which was widely considered to be useful in the entertainment sector is now being considered to be useful in the education sector, healthcare sector, etc. XR technologies are reaching great heights across different sectors or industries. In this chapter, XR is defined, and a brief conceptual description of XR is presented. The different elements of XR including its history, applications, etc., are discussed in the chapter.

References

1. Doolani, S., Wessels, C., Kanal, V., Sevastopoulos, C., Jaiswal, A., Nambiappan, H., Makedon, F., A Review of Extended Reality (XR) Technologies for Manufacturing Training. *Technologies, 8, 4*, 77, 1–20, 2020.
2. Calabuig-Moreno, F., González-Serrano, M.H., Fombona, J., García-Tascón, M., The Emergence of Technology in Physical Education: A General Bibliometric Analysis with a Focus on Virtual and Augmented Reality. *Sustainability*, 12, 2728, 2020.
3. Cabero-Almenara, J., Barroso-Osuna, J., Llorente-Cejudo, C., Del Mar Fernández Martínez, M., Educational Uses of Augmented Reality (AR): Experiences in Educational Science. *Sustainability*, 11, 4990, 2019.
4. Kuleto, V., Stanescu, M., Ranković, M., Šević, N.P., Paun, D., Teodorescu, S., Extended reality in higher education, a responsible innovation approach for generation y and generation z. *Sustainability*, 13, 11814, 2021.
5. Hincapié, M., Caponio, A., Rios, H., González Mendívil, E., An introduction to Augmented Reality with applications in aeronautical maintenance. *13th International Conference on Transparent Optical Networks*, pp. 1–4, 2011, doi: 10.1109/ICTON.2011.5970856.
6. Radianti, J., Majchrzak, T.A., Fromm, J., Wohlgenannt, I., A systematic review of immersive virtual reality applications for higher education: Design elements, lessons learned, and research agenda. *Comput. Educ., 147*, 103778, 2020, doi: https://doi.org/10.1016/j.compedu.2019.103778.
7. Cipresso, P., Giglioli, I.A.C., Raya, M.A., Riva, G., The past, present, and future of virtual and augmented reality research: A network and cluster analysis of the literature. *Front. Psychol., 9*, 2086, 2018, doi: https://doi.org/10.3389/fpsyg.2018.02086.
8. Carmigniani, J., Furht, B., Anisetti, M., Ceravolo, P., Damiani, E., Ivkovic, M., Augmented reality technologies, systems and applications. *Multimed. Tools Appl., 51*, 341–377, 2010.
9. Mazuryk, T., Virtual Reality History, Applications, Technology and Future, 1999.
10. Bucea-Manea-Oni, R., Bucea-Manea-Oni, R., Simion, V.E., Ilic, D., Braicu, C., Manea, N., Sustainability in higher education: The relationship between work-life balance and xr e-learning facilities. *Sustainability*, 12, 5872, 2020.
11. Mcmillan, K., Flood, K., Glaeser, R., Virtual reality, augmented reality, mixed reality, and the marine conservation movement. *Aquat. Conserv. Mar. Freshwater Ecosyst.*, 27, 162–168, 2017.
12. Margetis, G., Apostolakis, K.C., Ntoa, S., Papagiannakis, G., Stephanidis, C., X-Reality Museums: Unifying the Virtual and RealWorld Towards Realistic Virtual Museums. *Appl. Sci.*, 11, 338, 2021.
13. Bozzelli, G., Raia, A., Ricciardi, S., De Nino, M., Barile, N., Perrella, M., Tramontano, M., Pagano, A., Palombini, A., An integrated VR/AR framework

for user-centric interactive experience of cultural heritage: The ArkaeVision project. *Digit. Appl. Archaeol. Cult. Herit.*, 15, e00124, 2019.

14. Shin, D.H. and Dunston, P.S., Identification of application areas for augmented reality in industrial construction based on technology suitability. *Autom. Constr.*, 17, 882–894, 2008.
15. Syberfeldt, A., Danielsson, O., Gustavsson, P., Augmented reality smart glasses in the smart factory: Product evaluation guidelines and review of available products. *IEEE Access*, 5, 9118–9130, 2017.
16. Stylidis, K., Dagman, A., Almius, H., Gong, L., Söderberg, R., Perceived quality evaluation with the use of extended reality. *Proc. Design Soc., Int. Conf. Eng. Design*, 1, 1, 1993–2002, 2019.
17. Kascak, J., Teliskova, M., Torok, J., Baron, P., Zajac, J., Husar, J., Implementation of augmented reality into the training and educational process in order to support spatial perception in technical documentation. *Proc. IEEE 6th Int. Conf. Ind. Eng. Appl. (ICIEA)*, pp. 583–587, 2019.
18. Nee, A.Y.C., Ong, S.K., Chryssolouris, G., Mourtzis, D., Augmented reality applications in design and manufacturing. *CIRP Ann.*, 61, 2, 657–679, 2012.
19. Kaminska, D., Sapinski, T., Wiak, S., Tikk, T., Haamer, R.E., Avots, E., Helmi, A., Ozcinar, C., Anbarjafari, G., Virtual reality and its applications in education: Survey. *Information*, 10, 318, 2019.
20. Gerup, J., Soerensen, C.B., Dieckmann, P., Augmented reality and mixed reality for healthcare education beyond surgery: An integrative review. *Int. J. Med. Educ.*, 11, 1, 2020.
21. Muñoz, A., Mahiques, X., Solanes, J.E., Martí, A., Gracia, L., Tornero, J., Mixed reality-based user interface for quality control inspection of car body surfaces. *J. Manuf. Syst.*, 53, 75–92, 2019.
22. De Ponti, R., Marazzato, J., Maresca, A.M., Rovera, F., Carcano, G., Ferrario, M.M., Pre-graduation medical training including virtual reality during COVID-19 pandemic: A report on students' perception. *BMC Med. Educ.*, 20, 1–7, 2020.
23. Seth, A., Vance, J.M., Oliver, J.H., Virtual reality for assembly methods prototyping: a review. *Virtual Reality*, 15, 5–20, 2011.
24. Hanson, R., Falkenström, W., Miettinen, M., Augmented reality as a means of conveying picking information in kit preparation for mixed-model assembly. *Comput. Ind. Eng.*, 113, 570–575, 2017. 2017/11/01/.
25. Borsci, S., Lawson, G., Broome, S., Empirical evidence, evaluation criteria and challenges for the effectiveness of virtual and mixed reality tools for training operators of car service maintenance. *Comput. Ind.*, 67, 17–26, 2015. 2015/02/01/.
26. Noghabaei, M., Heydarian, A., Balali, V., Han, K., Trend Analysis on Adoption of Virtual and Augmented Reality in the Architecture. Engineering, and Construction Industry. *Data*, 5, 26, 2020.

27. Gong, L., Fast-Berglund, A., Johansson, B., A Framework for Extended Reality System Development in Manufacturing. *IEEE Access*, 9, 24796–24813, 2021, doi: 10.1109/ACCESS.2021.3056752.
28. Petrov, P.D. and Atanasova, T.V., The Effect of Augmented Reality on Students' Learning Performance in Stem Education. *Information*, *11*, 4, 209, 2020, https://doi.org/10.3390/info11040209.
29. Lucas, J.D., Immersive VR in the construction classroom to increase student understanding of sequence, assembly, and space of wood frame construction. *J. Inf. Technol. Construct.*, *23*, 179–194, 2018.
30. Bala, L., Kinross, J., Martin, G., Koizia, L.J., Kooner, A.S., Shimshon, G.J., Hurkxkens, T.J., Pratt, P.J., Sam, A.H., A remote access mixed reality teaching ward round. *Clin. Teach.*, *18*, 4, 386–390, 2021, https://doi.org/10.1111/tct.13338.
31. Eschen, H., Kötter, T., Rodeck, R., Harnisch, M., Schüppstuhl, T., Augmented and Virtual Reality for Inspection and Maintenance Processes in the Aviation Industry. *Procedia Manuf.*, 19, 156–163, 2018.
32. Huang, K.-T., Ball, C., Francis, J., Ratan, R., Boumis, J., Fordham., J., Augmented Versus Virtual Reality in Education: An Exploratory Study Examining Science Knowledge Retention When Using Augmented Reality/ Virtual Reality Mobile Applications. *Cyberpsychol. Behav. Soc. Netw.*, 22, 2, 105–110, 2019, doi: http://doi.org/10.1089/cyber.2018.0150.
33. Román-Ibáñez, V., Pujol-López, F.A., Mora-Mora, H., Pertegal-Felices, M.L., Jimeno-Morenilla, A., A Low-Cost Immersive Virtual Reality System for Teaching Robotic Manipulators Programming. *Sustainability, 10, 4*, 1102, 2018, doi: https://doi.org/10.3390/su10041102.
34. Azuma, R.T., A Survey of Augmented Reality. *Presence: Teleoperators Virtual Environ.*, *6*, 355–385, 1997.
35. Milgram, P. and Kishino, F., A taxonomy of mixed reality visual displays. *IEICE Trans. Inf. Syst.*, 77, 12, 1321–1329, 1994.

2

Characteristics, Benefits, and an Explicative Insight on Extended Reality (XR)

Manisha Vohra

Independent Researcher, India

Abstract

Extended reality (XR) technologies are evolving greatly. They are being included in different sectors. There are various possibilities with XR. This chapter will help to understand the concept of XR. It will provide a brief insight to XR. Also, the important events in the history of XR are discussed. Along with it, its characteristics and the benefits it provides are explained in this chapter.

Keywords: Extended reality (XR), augmented reality (AR), virtual reality (VR), mixed reality (MR), immersive technologies, virtual environment, real world

2.1 Introduction

Extended reality is also referred to as XR. It is a blanket term which includes different immersive technologies like augmented reality (AR), virtual reality (VR), and mixed reality (MR). Extended reality, as the name suggests, is a blanket term which is inclusive of immersive technologies like AR, VR, and MR that can extend the reality by bringing together or blending the real world and the virtual world. Extended reality is not limited to just these three immersive technologies. If any other new immersive technology gets created in the future which can extend the reality via blending the real world and the virtual world or by the creation of a complete virtual

Email: manishavohra94@gmail.com

Manisha Vohra (ed.) Introduction to Extended Reality (XR) Technologies, (17–36) © 2025 Scrivener Publishing LLC

environment, then it will also be counted and included in XR. Hence, it is a blanket term which comprises different immersive technologies.

2.1.1 Augmented Reality

Augmented reality, abbreviated as AR, is an experience wherein there is overlaying of digital information on the real world. This experience lets the user view the real world with different digital details such as animation, images, etc.

Unlike virtual reality which is a simulated three-dimensional environment generated via the help of a computer, augmented reality is where there is overlaying of digital information on the real world. The experience of the real world that the user will have will be enriched.

2.1.2 Virtual Reality

Virtual reality, which is abbreviated as VR, is a simulated three-dimensional environment generated with the help of a computer where the users can interact with the virtual surrounding by using specialized equipment like headset, sensor comprising gloves, etc. Here, in the case of VR, the users find themselves immersed in an environment having simulated realities or, in other words, in a simulated digital environment wherein the users have to utilize a specific headset to interact with the virtual surrounding. A head-mounted display (HMD) could be used.

One of the highly famous VR visual interfaces is HMD. It comprises a stereo pair of small displays which cover the eyes [47].

2.1.3 Mixed Reality

Mixed reality, abbreviated as MR, blends or merges the real-world environment and the virtual environment. Here, in mixed reality, real-world objects and virtual objects can co-exist and interact with each other in real time. Mixed reality is also sometimes called hybrid reality.

In MR, there is merging of real and virtual worlds in order to produce an environment which is enriched interactively and where physical and digital objects both co-exist [1].

Combining or merging of the real world and the virtual world is defined as MR [4]. This is also one way of defining MR. It can also be defined as merging of the real world and the virtual world so as to produce new visualizations and new environments where physical objects as well as digital objects co-exist and also interact in real time [7].

2.2 History of XR

The history of XR consists of a lot of key events which have been instrumental in its journey. Some of them are discussed below.

Starting from centuries ago, the year 1838 proved to be a great year toward the beginning of XR journey. Charles Wheatstone, in the year 1838, invented the stereoscope. While writing about it in his paper, Charles Wheatstone referred to the stereoscope as an instrument. He himself referred to the stereoscope as an instrument in his paper [44]. A stereoscope lets the users view a pair of separate images for each eye, creating a 3D image with an illusion of depth.

Then, moving to the years after the 1950s, Morton Heilig, a cinematographer, invented Sensorama in the year 1957, which is addressed as one of the first experiences of VR or one of the first machines of VR. This proved to be a great milestone achievement in the XR journey. The Sensorama simulator was patented in the year 1962. It provided an immersive experience of cinema. Here real-world experiences were simulated. A user could view a 3D film with stereo sound, smell, etc., which gave an immersive experience. Sensorama included a chair which was a motional one and a sound system which was stereo sound, along with stereoscopic color display. To ensure that there was complete immersive experience, there was provision to experience aroma and wind via the inclusion of emitters for aroma and fans. Sensorama simulated a motorcycle moving through Brooklyn that provided an experience in which the user is sitting on the motorcycle, the wind is gushing, and there is the presence of different sounds and aromas of the city, together creating an immersive environment.

In the year 1961, engineers from Philco developed a headset called Headsight. It was the first VR motion tracking headset.

Ivan Sutherland, a professor at Harvard, constructed a device called the Sword of Damocles in the year 1968, which was a head-mounted display. The Sword of Damocles supported a stereo view which was updated correctly in accordance with the user's head position and orientation [3].

In the year 1975, Myron Krueger created VIDEOPLACE, an artificial reality, and in this system the silhouettes of the users which were grabbed by the cameras had their projections on a big screen. Also, it provided interaction for the participants [2, 3].

Toward the end of the 1980s, Binocular-Omni-Orientational Monitor (BOOM) was made by Fake Space Labs. BOOM was a complex system. It was composed of a stereoscopic displaying device. A broad virtual and moving environment along with a mechanical arm tracking was provided by it [2].

BOOM mounts displays that are small in front of the eyes, though more like binoculars than goggles, just like the HMD.

The period between the 1980s and the 1990s witnessed a lot of developments—for example, in this period, VPL Research company, founded by Jaron Lanier, made or developed two very famous VR devices, namely:

- DataGlove
- Eyephone

When it comes to VR, these were the first commercially sold VR devices [3], and they were made during the period between the 1980s and the 1990s. During the same period between the 1980s and the 1990s, the term virtual reality was coined. Jaron Lanier, who was the founder of VPL Research as mentioned above, coined the term virtual reality.

At Boeing Corporation, a research was being conducted during the time period of the early 1990s. It was during this period of time that the concept of overlaying computer graphics on top of real world came up, which how AR technology actually got its name. At Boeing, Caudell and Mizell (1992) were working back then in early 1990s, and they worked on making the process of conveying wiring instructions for aircraft assembly simple to construction workers. They referred to this proposed solution of overlaying computer-presented material on top of the real world as augmented reality [48].

CAVE (CAVE Automatic Virtual Environment) was developed at the University of Illinois in Chicago. The first CAVE was developed here. It was demonstrated at the 1992 SIGGRAPH conference. CAVE is a VR and scientific visualization system [3].

Moving forward and talking about the years after 2000, Oculus Rift is then considered a turning point in the journey of XR. Luckey Palmer, the founder of Oculus VR company, created a prototype of Oculus Rift which is a VR headset. In 2014, Oculus VR got acquired by Facebook.

The year 2016 witnessed the launch of MR HMD HoloLens™ by Microsoft.

If someone just looks at HoloLens in a glance, then they will see that it has various things that are similar with AR HMDs [8].

In the year 2017, IKEA Place app was launched, which is an AR app. It lets users view how a furniture will look like in the house. So, prior to purchasing the furniture, the users will be able to view how the furniture which they intend to purchase will actually look like in their house.

There onward in the preceding years until the present time, VR, AR, and MR applications have witnessed a rise. Their usage increased. Now, XR technologies are widely being adopted in various applications, which we will be discussing in the chapter.

2.3 Understanding AR

To understand the XR concept briefly, let us try to understand different aspects of each of the three technologies, i.e., AR, VR, and MR. Beginning with AR, let us first discuss regarding its different aspects.

Till date AR has obtained huge attention for growing number of technological developments [42]. The functioning of AR is such that AR through its functioning has grabbed the attention of researchers and developers in various areas of industry [12]. Be it the healthcare industry, education industry, etc. AR is turning out to be an useful technology. A natural complement to mobile computing is AR [6].

Off lately, Augmented Reality Smart Glasses (ARSG) have been found out as a technology which is powerful, providing support to shop-floor workers [13]. Gradually in the field of surgery, AR is being brought [41]. AR helps in planning of surgery and in patient's treatment [36]. In the education industry, AR is a technology which is obtaining greater influence on the area of teaching everyday [9].

2.3.1 AR Hardware

Displays, input devices, tracking, and processor are the hardware components for AR.

2.3.1.1 Displays

There are different types of displays used in AR like head-mounted displays (HMD), spatial displays, handheld displays, etc. [10].

2.3.1.2 Input Devices

The input devices include gloves, touch screen, gesture devices, etc.

2.3.1.3 Tracking

There are various types of tracking devices such as GPS, digital cameras and other optical sensors, wireless sensors, solid state compasses, accelerometers, etc.

2.3.1.4 Processor

The processor is a very important component as augmented reality requires processing power. The data is interpreted by a processor.

Processing devices: AR smartphones, computers, and special devices use graphics, GPUs, CPUs, flash memory, RAM, Bluetooth, WiFi, GPS, etc., to process the 3D images and sensor signals.

2.3.2 Software

It is one of the essential elements when it comes to AR. There are various software development kits that are used to develop augmented reality applications.

2.3.3 Types of AR

There are different types of AR. They are as follows:

- Marker-based AR
- Markerless AR
- Projection-based AR
- Overlap-based AR [49]

2.3.4 Different AR Interfaces

The different AR interfaces are as follows:

- Tangible AR interfaces
- Hybrid AR interfaces
- Collaborative AR interfaces
- Emerging multimodal interfaces [10]

2.3.5 Example of AR Use

AR can be utilized in various sectors.

To understand the use of AR, discussed below are different examples of its utilization in various areas.

Let us begin with an example of its use in an industrial setup. In [52], the authors have presented how their spatial AR system, ASTOR, which is an autostereoscopic optical see-through spatial AR system, can be utilized to render virtual 3D imagery which visually appears inside the workspace of an industrial CNC (computer numerical control) machine, geometrically registered with the tools, workpiece, and workspace [52].

There are a lot of key technologies of Industry 4.0. AR, out of a lot of key technologies, is one of the most enabling and promising technologies that provide support to workers of factories and engineers at workplaces.

The authors in [53] propose an AR tool which is novel so as to provide assistance to operators for the detection of production errors and assembly errors during inspection activities [53].

2.4 Understanding VR

VR concept is not new [11]. It has been around since a long time now. A computer generated simulation of a realistic experience is VR [45]. VR environment's conventionally held view is the one in which the user is completely immersed in, and is able to interact with, total synthetic world [46].

With VR, there is total control on users visual experience and auditory experience as they interact inside a synthetic environment [23].

In the duration of the last two decades, VR has evolved to a new level of sophistication [17]. Thanks to the VR concepts, the users are allowed the feeling of immersion without having any exposure to any kind of risk, and hence VR concepts are very attractive [39]. In the usual scientific scheme, VR holds a special position by coupling humanities sciences with engineering [43]. Interactivity, immersion, and presence are the terms which are often heard when talking about VR. In actual real time, the degree to which a medium's users can participate in the modification of the content or form of the mediated content is called interactivity [51].

A user's involvement in a virtual environment wherein the user's real world and time awareness generally becomes disconnected is immersion [54].

The individual or personalized experience one gets of being situated in a particular environment or a particular place despite the fact that the user is actually physically situated in another environment or place is called presence [50]. Another way of defining presence is the point or degree up to where a user accepts that a virtual world is real. When a user has to be brought into a virtual space, the one that plays an important part of it is presence [55]. The VR technologies have immersion, interactivity, and presence as their core characteristics [54].

In the area of education, VR is an influential tool in providing support and enabling learning and teaching processes [24]. VR and also along with it AR technologies enable students to carry out experiments in a secure environment [16]. In the area of healthcare, the important techniques in healthcare simulation consists of virtual simulation among others [26]. VR simulator and AR simulator both have been marketed since the time of early 2000 for laparoscopic surgery [29].

2.4.1 VR Hardware

The basic and important hardware components of VR systems consist of input devices and output devices. They are very important for the functioning of the VR systems. Another hardware component which is important for the functioning of VR systems is computer.

2.4.1.1 Input Devices

Input devices are the ones which decide the way or the manner a user will communicate with the computer [3]. The input devices include data gloves, controllers for VR, track pads, device controlling buttons, etc.

2.4.1.2 VR Output Devices

The VR output devices include HMD, for example, which is a graphic display that stimulates the senses to present a VR environment.

Output devices receive feedback which is presented to users via its corresponding output device in order to stimulate the senses [30].

2.4.2 Software in VR

Different virtual software development kits are used to develop a virtual reality experience for various applications.

2.4.3 Types of VR

There are three types or categories of VR systems. They are as follows:

- ➢ Non-immersive
- ➢ Immersive
- ➢ Semi-immersive

2.4.3.1 Non-Immersive

They utilize desktops for the reproduction of world images.

2.4.3.2 Immersive

Immersive systems are the ones which give a completely simulated experience.

An important difference between immersive VR and non-immersive VR is related to level of interaction between VR environment and user [40].

2.4.3.3 Semi-Immersive

For semi-immersive systems, examples include Fish Tank VR. They are between the two types discussed above [2].

For the purpose of appropriate image rendering, the absolute minimal information which immersive VR needs is orientation and the position of the head of the viewer. In addition to this, there can be tracking of other parts of the body like the hands so as to allow interaction, legs or chest so as to allow graphical user representation, etc. 3D objects have six degrees of freedom (DOF) which is the orientation, i.e., pitch, yaw, and roll angles, and position coordinates, i.e., the x, y, and z offsets. Every tracker should support this data or should support a subset of this data.

There are different trackers, such as the following:

- Magnetic trackers
- Acoustic trackers, etc.

2.4.4 Magnetic Trackers

When it comes to immersive applications, magnetic trackers are the most commonly utilized tracking devices in it. Magnetic trackers generally comprise of an emitter which is a static part, and some movable parts, i.e., receivers, which are even called sensors sometimes. These trackers even comprise a control station unit. The receiver and emitter assemblies are quite alike. Both of them comprise three antennae which are mutually perpendicular. When the emitter's antennae is supplied with current, magnetic fields are generated, which the receiver's antennae will pick up. The receiver sends its measurements to the control unit which calculates the orientation and position of the given sensor [3].

2.4.5 Acoustic Trackers

For the purpose of determining the orientation and position of an object in space, ultrasonic waves are utilized by acoustic trackers. Multiple receivers and emitters, whose geometry is known already, are utilized to obtain a set of distances to calculate the orientation and position as the utilization of sound enables finding out the relative distance between two points only [3].

2.4.6 Example of VR Use

The authors in this particular paper [35], for engineering students, work on the development of an immersive VR pedagogical simulator of industrial robotic arms. Utilizing the proposed system, students will know the effects of the trajectories which are designed by themselves. They will be able to see the effects of the trajectories on various robotic arms and cell environments without being required to buy all of them, and they are also safe from damaging the cell components. The student will be alerted when there is collision of the elements in the scene as the simulation will be checking for it and will alert the student when it happens.

Now, this can be gained with a robotic simulator, but to help students better understand robotics, the integration with immersive VR is intended. Here cardboard glasses are used which are not costly, and for the purpose of interacting with the simulation from their computer, these glasses let the students utilize their own smartphone. Through this method, the aim is to avoid the use of huge expenditure and space of educational institutions in purchasing, maintaining, and storing robotic arms and other expensive materials. It was showcased through experimentation that the proposed work is fully able to fulfil the real-time requirements of an immersive VR system to create an enhanced realistic experience for the students, avoiding stumbling and lag in the process [35].

2.5 Understanding MR

The merging of the real world and the virtual world is one of the ways as to how MR can be defined [4]. Another way to define MR is such that it is the fusion of the physical world and the digital world that explores the relation between human, computer, and environmental interactions [31].

2.5.1 MR Hardware

Different displays are available to be utilized in MR environments. Below are some of the most commonly utilized displays in MR environments:

- Head-mounted displays (HMDs)
- Hand-held displays
- Hand-held projectors, etc.

When it comes to MR, it is found that out of the different displays available for MR, HMDs are mostly utilized [37].

Here we will be discussing further regarding the MR device HoloLens which is a hardware device. As discussed earlier in the chapter, HoloLens is one of the first MR devices. HoloLens is basically a completely untethered, stand-alone, holographic computer. Here the terms untethered and standalone suggest that to execute a HoloLens application, an additional connection to an external computer is not required. Holographic indicates virtual 3D objects' generation capability in a user's real environment, which can be inspected from any view angle [37].

2.5.2 Example of MR Use

MR also can be utilized in various sectors. To understand the use of MR, discussed below are some examples of MR use in different areas.

For orthopedic open surgery, the authors in [27] explore the potentialities of MR utilizing HoloLens so as to develop a hybrid training system. In [27], quantitative and qualitative tests were carried out by the authors. The results obtained encourage the usage of HoloLens technology for the implementation of a hybrid simulator for orthopedic open surgery [27]. The authors in [28] developed a mandibular motion tracking system (ManMoS) for orthognathic surgery. One of the key points is of this developed system is that MR surgical simulation was generated here. It was found that this developed surgical simulation system appears to meet clinical demands well. It is also a vital facilitator of communication between surgeons and orthodontists [28].

In this article [33], the authors describe a MR experience for learning Spanish as a foreign language, and it is in a virtual world where it all takes place. The virtual world where it takes place is the one which mirrors a boulevard in Madrid. The authors basically put forward an application for the purpose of learning Spanish as a foreign language built on a virtual world which mirrors the Gran Vía Boulevard in Madrid. Students with the aim of purchasing a ticket for the particular show which they wish to attend put together information on shows available in different theaters. For the students to make a final decision, they receive help from a teacher present in the real world. There are different learning activities for students—for example, those activities include having collaboration among peers, having interaction with the teacher, and exploring a mirror world. For the purpose of exploration and collaboration, multiuser virtual environments abbreviated as MUVEs enable to deploy interactive and immersive environments as per requirement. In this paper, the controlled events were conducted in a mirror world, while activities were enhanced with information from the real world [33].

2.6 Aspects of XR

Having discussed and understood each of the XR technologies, i.e., AR, VR, and MR in brief, we will now discuss some vital aspects of XR. In particular, we will be discussing only two important vital aspects of XR out of the various vital aspects of XR, i.e.:

- XR experience
- XR impact

2.6.1 XR Experience

Firstly, we will discuss regarding the XR experience. So, XR experience has an effect on all the senses—for example, visual sense is affected by using hamlets, HMDs, Oculus Rift, etc. For auditory sense, audio tools like KAI Tech or Oculus leave an effect. Tactile sense is affected by tactile using haptic devices like gloves, backpacks, etc., to send vibrations or electrostatic shock. For the sense of smell system or olfactory system, there are devices which change the smell in a VR environment and even taste, which work more like an autosuggestion that is facilitated by visual senses and auditory senses [16].

Getting access to XR experience is becoming easier. The convergence of AR, VR, and MR is represented by XR [14]. AR-, VR-, and MR-based applications are being worked upon and utilized in many areas, which let people gain access to XR experience—for example, specifically talking about AR and then the availability of AR and ease in its hardware can make it available to common users [22]. AR has found its applications in various areas like learning, sports, advertising, medical application, manufacturing application, etc., and due to it having applications in various diverse areas, it has taken the world by storm [21]. Distributed collaboration processes in different application domains are supported by AR systems [38].

Now, talking about VR, then what may result in a knowledge improvement due to VR is the fact that it represents an involving and alternative reality [15].

Talking about MR, when a training is underway, VR/MR system enables people to visualize and also interact with simulated real artefacts [19]. Most of the experiences of MR are regarding the visual domain, with the main difference being between the types of display [34]. As per the industrial needs and demands, MR device manufacturers are presently developing new devices [18].

2.6.2 XR Impact

Another vital aspect of XR is the impact it creates. Its impact is such that it can transform the way how different things function and the way one works—for example, it lets people get education as well as training in a virtual environment. This is very advantageous. Virtual simulation training could be called an invaluable tool that enables students to put into practice their set of clinical skills in an innovative and new manner of student/tutor interaction during the exceptional time period of pandemic. For teaching and learning, simulation-based training is emerging [5]. Not just students and teachers but also professionals from different sectors such as medical professionals, people from the aviation sector, people working in coal mines, and likewise people from various other sectors can simulate different scenarios without much risk and can learn and observe from them. This will help them deal with different scenarios in the real world. A lot of industries have quite successfully implemented AR/VR [20].

Undoubtedly, XR technologies are here to stay [25].

2.7 Characteristics of XR

Some of the characteristics of XR are as follows:

- Teleportation/presence
- Haptics
- Interactiveness
- Field of view

2.7.1 Teleportation/Presence

This indicates how much immersive the experience is—meaning how much real it feels.

2.7.2 Haptics

The association with tactile experiences is while immersing in XR like, for example, playing some sports, driving a car, etc.

2.7.3 Interactiveness

It indicates the various ways of joining in the simulation or adventure which is facilitated by different types of media content within an XR application.

2.7.4 Field of View

To provide the user with a real experience, the application needs to allow a 360° view [16].

2.8 Advantages of XR

There are various advantages of XR. Some of them are as follows:

- Better or enhanced learning experience
- Efficient training
- Enhanced customer experience

2.8.1 Better or Enhanced Learning Experience

With XR, students can have better or enhanced learning experience—Stanford Virtual Heart Project is a perfect example for this. This project is extended to Stanford medical students and trainees who can interact with the virtual heart as well as inspect the virtual heart, manipulate it, even walk inside it, and understand the different aspects.

2.8.2 Efficient Training

XR-based training can be very useful and efficient—for example, the authors in [32] proposed the use of VR-based pilot training for people working in underground coal mines. They even conducted an experiment in this regard. Their results suggested that, including almost each case of their experiment, high immersive VR which is combined with wide FoV is assessed as the best solution for training [32].

2.8.3 Enhanced Customer Experience

XR provides an enhanced customer experience—for example, the AR-based IKEA Place app lets users see how a furniture will look like in the house. Before actually purchasing the furniture, the users will be able to see how the furniture which they are thinking to purchase will look like in their house.

2.9 Conclusion

Extended reality (XR) technologies are growing greatly and are being included in different sectors. There are so many possibilities with XR. In this chapter, the concept of XR is discussed. A brief insight to XR is provided in this chapter. The history related to XR, along with different characteristics and the benefits it provides, is explained in this chapter.

References

1. Zaldívar-Colado, U., Garbaya, S., Tamayo-Serrano, P., Zaldívar-Colado, X., Blazevic, P., A mixed reality for virtual assembly. *26th IEEE International Symposium on Robot and Human Interactive Communication (RO-MAN)*, pp. 739–744, 2017, doi: 10.1109/ROMAN.2017.8172385.
2. Cipresso, P., Giglioli, I.A.C., Raya, M.A., Riva, G., The Past, Present, and Future of Virtual and Augmented Reality Research: A Network and Cluster Analysis of the Literature. *Front. Psychol.*, 9, 2086, 2018.
3. Mazuryk, T., Virtual Reality History, Applications, Technology and Future, 1999.
4. Gerup, J., Soerensen, C.B., Dieckmann, P., Augmented reality and mixed reality for healthcare education beyond surgery: an integrative review. *Int. J. Med. Educ.*, *11*, 1–18, 2018, doi: https://doi.org/10.5116/ijme.5e01.eb1a.
5. De Ponti, R., Marazzato, J., Maresca, A.M., Rovera, F., Carcano, G., Ferrario, M.M., Pre-graduation medical training including virtual reality during COVID-19 pandemic: A report on students' perception. *BMC Med. Educ.*, 20, 1–7, 2020.
6. Wagner, D. and Schmalstieg, D., First steps towards handheld augmented reality. *7th IEEE Int. Symp. Wearable Comput.*, pp. 127–135, 2003.
7. McMillan, K., Flood, K., Glaeser, R., Virtual reality, augmented reality, mixed reality, and the marine conservation movement. *Aquat. Conserv. Mar. Freshwater Ecosyst.*, 27, S1, 162–168, 2017, doi: https://doi.org/10.1002/aqc.2820.
8. Lang, S., Kota, M.S.S.D., Weigert, D., Behrendt, F., Mixed reality in production and logistics: Discussing the application potentials of Microsoft HoloLensTM. *Procedia Comput. Sci.*, 149, 118–129, 2019.
9. Cabero-Almenara, J., Osuna, J.B., Llorente-Cejudo, C., Martínez, M.D.M.F., Educational Uses of Augmented Reality (AR): Experiences in Educational Science. *Sustainability*, 11, 4990, 2019.
10. Carmigniani, J., Furht, B., Anisetti, M., Ceravolo, P., Damiani, E., Ivkovic, M., Augmented technologies, systems and applications. *Multimed. Tools Appl.*, 51, 341–377, 2011, doi: https://doi.org/10.1007/s11042-010-0660-6.

11. Stylidis, K., Dagman, A., Almius, H., Gong, L., Söderberg, R., Perceived quality evaluation with the use of extended reality. *Proc. Design Soc., Int. Conf. Eng. Design*, vol. 1(1), pp. 1993–2002, 2019.
12. Shin, D.H. and Dunston, P.S., Identification of application areas for augmented reality in industrial construction based on technology suitability. *Autom. Constr.*, 17, 882–894, 2008.
13. Syberfeldt, A., Danielsson, O., Gustavsson, P., Augmented reality smart glasses in the smart factory: Product evaluation guidelines and review of available products. *IEEE Access*, 5, 9118–9130, 2017.
14. Margetis, G., Apostolakis, K.C., Ntoa, S., Papagiannakis, G., Stephanidis, C., X-Reality Museums: Unifying the Virtual and RealWorld Towards Realistic Virtual Museums. *Appl. Sci.*, 11, 338, 2021.
15. Bozzelli, G., Raia, A., Ricciardi, S., De Nino, M., Barile, N., Perrella, M., Tramontano, M., Pagano, A., Palombini, A., An integrated VR/AR framework for user-centric interactive experience of cultural heritage: The ArkaeVision project. *Digit. Appl. Archaeol. Cult. Herit.*, 15, e00124, 2019.
16. Bucea-Manea-Ţoniş, R., Bucea-Manea-Ţoniş, R., Simion, V.E., Ilic, D., Braicu, C., Manea, N., Sustainability in Higher Education: The Relationship between Work-Life Balance and XR E-Learning Facilities. *Sustainability*, 12, 14, 5872, 2020, doi: https://doi.org/10.3390/su12145872.
17. Seth, A., Vance, J.M., Oliver, J.H., Virtual reality for assembly methods prototyping: a review. *Virtual Reality*, 15, 5–20, 2011.
18. Muñoz, A., Mahiques, X., Solanes, J.E., Martí, A., Gracia, L., Tornero, J., Mixed reality-based user interface for quality control inspection of car body surfaces. *J. Manuf. Syst.*, 53, 75–92, Oct. 2019.
19. Borsci, S., Lawson, G., Broome, S., Empirical evidence, evaluation criteria and challenges for the effectiveness of virtual and mixed reality tools for training operators of car service maintenance. *Comput. Ind.*, 67, 17–26, 2015, 2015/02/01/.
20. Noghabaei, M., Heydarian, A., Balali, V., Han, K., Trend Analysis on Adoption of Virtual and Augmented Reality in the Architecture, Engineering, and Construction Industry. *Data*, 5, 26, 2020.
21. Nee, A.Y.C., Ong, S.K., Chryssolouris, G., Mourtzis, D., Augmented reality applications in design and manufacturing. *CIRP Ann.*, 61, 2, 657–679, 2012.
22. Kascak, J., Teliskova, M., Torok, J., Baron, P., Zajac, J., Husar, J., Implementation of augmented reality into the training and educational process in order to support spatial perception in technical documentation, in: *Proc. IEEE 6th Int. Conf. Ind. Eng. Appl. (ICIEA)*, pp. 583–587, Apr. 2019.
23. Silva, J.N.A., Southworth, M., Raptis, C., Silva, J., Emerging Applications of Virtual Reality in Cardiovascular Medicine. *JACC. Basic Transl. Sci.*, 3, 3, 420–430, 2018, https://doi.org/10.1016/j.jacbts.2017.11.009.

24. Kaminska, D., Sapinski, T., Wiak, S., Tikk, T., Haamer, R.E., Avots, E., Helmi, A., Ozcinar, C., Anbarjafari, G., Virtual reality and its applications in education: Survey. *Information*, 10, 318, 2019.
25. Fast-Berglund, Å., Gong, L., Li, D., Testing and validating Extended Reality (xR) technologies in manufacturing. *Procedia Manuf.*, *25*, 31–38, 2018.
26. Viglialoro, R.M., Condino, S., Turini, G., Carbone, M., Ferrari, V., Gesi, M., Augmented Reality, Mixed Reality, and Hybrid Approach in Healthcare Simulation: A Systematic Review. *Appl. Sci.*, *11*, 5, 2338, 2021, https://doi.org/10.3390/app11052338.
27. Condino, S., Turini, G., Parchi, P.D., Viglialoro, R.M., Piolanti, N., Gesi, M., Ferrari, M., Ferrari, V., How to Build a Patient-Specific Hybrid Simulator for Orthopaedic Open Surgery: Benefits and Limits of Mixed-Reality Using the Microsoft HoloLens. *J. Healthcare Eng.*, 2018, 5435097, 2018.
28. Fushima, K. and Kobayashi, M., Mixed-reality simulation for orthognathic surgery. *Maxillofac. Plast. Reconstr. Surg.*, 38, 13, 2016.
29. Nomura, T., Mamada, Y., Nakamura, Y., Matsutani, T., Hagiwara, N., Fujita, I., Mizuguchi, Y., Fujikura, T., Miyashita, M., Uchida, E., Laparoscopic skill improvement after virtual reality simulator training in medical students as assessed by augmented reality simulator. *Asian J. Endosc. Surg.*, 8, 408–412, 2015.
30. Bamodu, O. and Ye, X., Virtual Reality and Virtual Reality System Components. *Advanced Materials Research*, pp. 765–767, 2013, 10.2991/icsem.2013.192.
31. Kuleto, V., Stanescu, M., Ranković, M., Šević, N.P., Paun, D., Teodorescu, S., Extended reality in higher education, a responsible innovation approach for generation y and generation z. *Sustainability*, 13, 11814, 2021.
32. Grabowski, A. and Jankowski, J., Virtual Reality-based pilot training for underground coal miners. *Saf. Sci.*, 72, 310–314, 2015.
33. Kloos, C., Maroto, D., Ibáñez, M., Rueda, J., Leony, D., Learning a Foreign Language in a Mixed-Reality Environment. *IEEE Internet Comput.*, 15, 06, 44–47, 2011, doi: 10.1109/MIC.2011.78 (ibanez2011).
34. Hughes, C.E., Stapleton, C.B., Hughes, D.E., Smith, E.M., Mixed reality in education, entertainment, and training. *IEEE Comput. Graphics Appl.*, 25, 6, 24–30, 2005, https://doi.org/10.1109/ MCG.2005.139.
35. Román-Ibáñez, V., Pujol-López, F.A., Mora-Mora, H., Pertegal-Felices, M.L., Jimeno-Morenilla, A., A Low-Cost Immersive Virtual Reality System for Teaching Robotic Manipulators Programming. *Sustainability*, *10*, 4, 1102, 2018, https://doi.org/10.3390/su10041102.
36. Eckert, M., Volmerg, J.S., Friedrich, C.M., Augmented Reality in Medicine: Systematic and Bibliographic Review. *JMIR Mhealth Uhealth*, 7, 4, 2019, doi: 10.2196/10967.
37. Constanza, E., Kunz, A., Fjeld, M., Mixed Reality: A Survey. *Lect. Notes Comput. Sci.*, 5440, 47, 2009, 10.1007/978-3-642-00437-7_3.

38. Lukosch, S., Lukosch, H., Datcu, D., Cidota, M., Providing Information on the Spot: Using Augmented Reality for Situational Awareness in the Security Domain. *Comput. Support. Coop. Work (CSCW)*, 24, 613–664, 2015, https://doi.org/10.1007/s10606-015-9235-4.
39. Passos, C., Silva, M., Mol, A., Carvalho, P., Design of a collaborative virtual environment for training security agents in big events. *Cognit. Technol. Work*, 19, 2-3, 315–328, 2017, https://doi.org/10.1007/s10111-017-0407-5.
40. Nykänen, M., Puro, V., Tiikkaja, M., Kannisto, H., Lantto, E., Simpura, F., *et al.*, Implementing and evaluating novel safety training methods for construction sector workers: Results of a randomized controlled trial. *J. Saf. Res.*, 75, 205–221, 2020, http://doi:10.1016/j.jsr.2020.09.015.
41. Haavik, T., Keep your coats on: Augmented reality and sensework in surgery and surgical telemedicine. *Cognit. Technol. Work*, 18, 1, 175–191, 2016, https://doi.org/10.1007/s10111-015- 0353-z.
42. Lahanas, V., Loukas, C., Smailis, N., Georgiou, E., A novel augmented reality simulator for skills assessment in minimal invasive surgery. *Surg. Endosc.*, 29, 2224–2234, 2015.
43. Barreau, J., Nouviale, F., Gaugne, R., Bernard, Y., Llinares, S., Gouranton, V., An immersive virtual sailing on the 18th-century ship Le Boullongne. *Presence Teleoperators Virtual Environ.*, 24, 3, 201–219, 2015, https://doi.org/10.1162/pres_a_00231.
44. Wheatstone, C., Contributions to the physiology of vision. —Part the first. On some remarkable, and higher to unobserved, phenomena of binocular vision. *Philos. Trans. R. Soc. London*, 128, 371–394, 1838.
45. Mann, S., Havens, J.C., Iorio, J., Yuan, Y., Furness, T., All reality: values, taxonomy, and continuum, for virtual, augmented, eXtended/MiXed (X), Mediated (X, Y), and multimediated reality/intelligence. *Paper presented at the Presented at the AWE 2018*, 2018.
46. Milgram, P. and Kishino, F., A taxonomy of mixed reality visual displays. *IEICE Trans. Inf. Syst.*, 77, 12, 1321–1329, 1994.
47. Cruz-Neira, C., Sandin, D.J., DeFanti, T.A., Kenyon, R.V., Hart, J.C., The CAVE: audio visual experience automatic virtual environment. *Commun. ACM*, 35, 6, 64–72, 1992, Doi:10.1145/129888.129892.
48. Höllerer, T.H. and Feiner, S.K., Mobile Augmented Reality, in: *Telegeoinformatics: Location-Based Computing and Services*, H. Karimi and A. Hammad (Eds.), Taylor & Francis Books Ltd, Boca Raton, Florida, USA 01/2004.
49. Arena, F., Collotta, M., Pau, G., Termine, F., An Overview of Augmented Reality. *Computers*, 11, 2, 28, 2022, https://doi.org/10.3390/computers11020028.
50. Witmer, B.G. and Singer, M.J., Measuring presence in virtual environments: a presence questionnaire. *Presence Teleoperators Virtual Environ.*, 7, 3, 225–240, 1998.
51. Steuer, J., Defining Virtual Reality: Dimensions Determining Telepresence. *J. Commun.*, 42, 73–93, 1992, https://doi.org/10.1111/j.1460-2466.1992.tb00812.x.

52. Olwal, A., Gustafsson, J., Lindfors, C., Spatial Augmented Reality on Industrial CNC Machines. *SPIE*, 6804, 2008, 10.1117/12.760960.
53. Marino, E., Barbieri, L., Colacino, B., Fleri, A., Bruno, F., An Augmented Reality inspection tool to support workers in Industry 4.0 environments. *Comput. Ind.*, 127, 103412, 2021, 10.1016/j.compind.2021.103412.
54. Radianti, J., Majchrzak, T.A., Fromm, J., Wohlgenannt, I., A systematic review of immersive virtual reality applications for higher education: Design elements, lessons learned, and research agenda. *Comput. Educ.*, 147, 103778, 2020.
55. Scavarelli, A., Arya, A., Teather, R.J., Virtual reality and augmented reality in social learning spaces: a literature review. *Virtual Reality*, 25, 257–277, 2020.

3

Different Uses of Extended Reality

Manisha Vohra

Independent Researcher, India

Abstract

In today's time, in the technological area, extended reality (XR) technologies are highly discussed and brought into use or implementation. XR technologies presently can be utilized in numerous sectors. Owing to the benefits, possibilities, etc., that it provides in different applications or different uses, they are bound to evolve more and reach out further to be used in various sectors. In this chapter, different XR technologies are described briefly. Along with it, this chapter also briefly discusses different uses of XR technologies with examples.

***Keywords*:** Extended reality (XR) technologies, augmented reality (AR), virtual reality (VR), mixed reality (MR), education, healthcare, industry

3.1 Introduction

Technology gives benefits, eases out the work, and has the ability to revolutionize things; hence, technology is very vital. Technology even brings challenges which is a con, but after evaluating its pros and cons and all the other aspects, a particular technology is put into use in different feasible areas and applications. Today's world is very modernized with respect to technology. In today's technologically modernized world, what we are seeing is that technology is playing absolutely great roles in different businesses and different areas. Altogether there are advancements taking place in, say, about almost each and every sector, and these are technological advancements. Each technology will always have its way of working, own set of advantages, limitations, possibilities, etc., which make them unique.

Email: manishavohra94@gmail.com

Manisha Vohra (ed.) Introduction to Extended Reality (XR) Technologies, (37–60) © 2025 Scrivener Publishing LLC

With each technology, there is always a buzz created. However, how feasible and effective it is for use in a particular sector can only be told after a thorough investigation in that direction. Technologies generally evolve with time. Currently, various technologies are present, and among them, many are evolving such as edge computing, cloud computing, big data, Internet of Things (IoT), digital twin, robotics, and the list goes on. However, having said this, in this chapter, we will be talking and discussing about augmented reality (AR), virtual reality (VR), and mixed reality (MR) and their different uses in various applications. These technologies are also evolving. AR, VR, and MR are known as the extended reality (XR) technologies.

Extended reality, also known as XR, i.e., its abbreviation, is a blanket term which includes different immersive technologies like augmented reality (AR), virtual reality (VR), and mixed reality (MR).

Basically, extended reality is a blanket term, and it is inclusive of immersive technologies like virtual reality (VR), augmented reality (AR), and mixed reality (MR) which can extend the reality. By bringing together the real world and virtual world or blending the real world and virtual world, the reality can be extended. There is no limitation of extended reality being limited to these three immersive technologies. In the future, if a new immersive technology that has the ability to create a complete virtual environment or blend the real world and virtual world is created and thus through it extends the reality, then it will also get included in XR. Therefore, extended reality is a blanket term that consists of different immersive technologies.

Augmented reality, abbreviated as AR, is an experience wherein there is overlaying of digital information on the real world. This experience lets the user view the real world with different digital details such as animation, images, etc.

Unlike virtual reality which is a simulated three-dimensional environment generated via the help of a computer, augmented reality is where there is overlaying of digital information on the real world. Basically, the experience of the real world by the user will be enriched, i.e., augmented reality will add to the user's experience of the real world with digital details.

Abbreviated as VR, virtual reality is a simulated three-dimensional environment generated with the help of a computer where the users can interact with the virtual surrounding by using specialized equipment like headset, sensor comprising gloves, etc.

Here, in the case of VR, the users find themselves immersed in an environment having simulated realities or, in other words, in a simulated digital environment wherein the users have to utilize a specific headset to interact with the virtual surrounding.

Mixed reality, abbreviated as MR, blends or merges the real-world environment and the virtual environment. Here, in mixed reality, real-world objects and virtual objects can co-exist and interact with each other in real time, too. Mixed reality is also sometimes called hybrid reality.

3.2 Augmented Reality

3.2.1 A Walk Through the World of Augmented Reality

AR became a distinct field of research by the late 1990s [10]. Great innovation is driven by AR [12]. AR is a real-time technique which enables the user to view virtual objects or to view scenarios superimposed on real-world images interactively [14]. AR does not create a complete artificial environment; instead of this, AR aims to supplement the real world [22]. Immersive experience of the user comes to life with AR [38]. AR completely, unlike VR, makes the present environment better instead of replacing it [40]. The manner in which people have interactions with environments that are unfamiliar can be revolutionized by the utilization of AR techniques [32].

AR basically creates an environment wherein, on a predominant real-world scene, virtual objects are superimposed [46]. Output and input devices are what an AR interface consists of, which concur to better simulate a user's presence in the AR environment [42]. Complicated spatial information can be registered against the real world by tracking the user's position and orientation [32].

The combination of virtual environment and physical environment is what AR systems are based on [53]. AR systems have different features. Real-time interaction in AR environments is one of their main features [28]. To be able to work in teams, experimentation and interaction with superimposed virtual information in a natural way are what collaborative AR enables for participants, too [21]. Long back AR was commercialized, and it has played out a huge role in reshaping the current manners of performing different activities [7]. Magnificent innovation is being driven by AR [12].

For providing support to service technicians in maintenance, mobile augmented reality solutions are a promising technology [24]. In the early development of a product and for knowledge workplace, the use of AR technology can be beneficial [9]. Now, for many years, certain AR platforms and underlying concepts have been around [19]. If the adaptation of technology is done optimally, it could potentially bring in a new phase of destination marketing, couch surfing, etc. [20].

In the early 1990s, the term augmented reality was coined. However, way earlier than this, the very first completely functional AR system was made in the late 1960s when Ivan Sutherland and his colleagues (1968) built a mechanically tracked 3D sign on a laboratory wall.

Research was being conducted during the time period of the early 1990s at the Boeing Corporation. During this time period, AR technology, which is, in other words, the concept of overlaying computer graphics on top of the real world, actually got its name. Caudell and Mizell (1992) worked at Boeing back then, and they were working on simplifying the process of conveying wiring instructions for aircraft assembly to construction workers, and it was them who referred to their proposed solution of overlaying computer-presented material on top of the real world as augmented reality [47].

In 1975, Myron Krueger created VIDEOPLACE. It is artificial reality. In this system called VIDEOPLACE, the silhouettes of the users which were grabbed by the cameras were projected on a big screen. Also, interaction for the participants was provided by it [48, 49].

3.2.2 AR Hardware and Software

The different hardware components for AR include input devices, displays, processor, and tracking.

Input devices: Basically, input devices are the ones which enable the users to have an interaction with AR systems. Between these devices and the AR system, the AR interface acts as a mediator.

Displays: AR consists of various types of displays which are utilized in them such as the spatial displays, head mounted displays (HMD), handheld displays, etc. [50].

When it comes to the software, there are ARKit and ARCore development platforms by Apple and Google, respectively, through which they have done interpretation of AR. Both are the two most vital players in the market. ARKit is basically an iOS app development kit, while ARCore is a development kit for Android apps [51].

3.2.3 AR Types

The different types of AR are as follows:

- Marker-based AR
- Markerless AR

- ➢ Projection-based AR
- ➢ Overlap-based AR [51]

3.2.4 Types of Different AR Interfaces

In the case of AR applications, there are basically four main ways of interaction. They are mentioned below as follows:

- ➢ Tangible AR interfaces
- ➢ Hybrid AR interfaces
- ➢ Collaborative AR interfaces
- ➢ The emerging multimodal interfaces [50]

3.2.5 Methodologies for Combining Real Images and Virtual Objects

As per the method of overlaying virtual components on the real-world environment, any one of the methodologies mentioned below can be utilized to combine real images and virtual objects

- ➢ Video mixing: A camera acquires digital information, and a computer reworks it. On a monitor, the result is then displayed via which the real scene is observed by the user indirectly.
- ➢ Image projection: On the surfaces of physical objects, images are directly projected.
- ➢ Optical combination: While the user just directly observes real scene, in the user's visual field, virtual images are projected [52].

3.2.6 Further Understanding AR Technology

Geolocation- and artefact-based are two major lines along which AR technology has been developed.

To a particular point in space, i.e., a location or place, geolocated AR ties digital data. Nowadays, different information is being built into virtual spaces that are tied to a physical location which includes information regarding a place, what is surrounding you or around you, what was there previously, restaurant menus of the restaurants that are there in front of you, local buses timetables, and also current information regarding them, local trains, or airplanes, and so on. Information can be accessed by a mobile device with a suitable software when it is at the physical location. It is important to understand how geolocated AR works, it works by firstly defining the point of interest (POI) or a physical map reference and then adding virtual assets onto that POI. The POIs can be revealed and content can be examined when the users have an appropriate application installed on their mobile device that explores a location.

Now, let us understand how artefact-based AR works; it works by utilizing a camera and image-recognition software in order to identify physical markers, objects, or patterns and, in response to this, display related data—augments. Now, talking about augments, it can be prebuilt 2D objects or 3D objects, videos, audio, animations, and interactions, or it can be combinations of these and other data which is obtained from around the Internet. Now, no longer just QR codes and bar codes are required to be utilized as markers. Instead, any pattern, object, or image can be utilized as a marker, all thanks to recent developments in image recognition and mobile technology which enable this [38].

Nowadays, it is feasible to utilize AR technology for learning, all thanks to advances in mobile technology which actually make this feasible [33].

AR and VR are already being embraced in training courses and education by major educational institutions. Including technology like AR, which is a cutting-edge technology, in addition to basic computer skills that have been a core addition of the curriculum since many years increases up the total overall experience to a completely new level.

What will become the standard for the next generation computing and also act like a smart tool for learning purposes is the assured emergence of AR applications in the education sector. So, in this direction, in AR, the following popular trends are creating explorative opportunities that are explorative in the sector of global education.

The first trend is that, when it comes to experiencing AR, students get totally immersed in educational content which includes videos, audios, or games, allowing the students to view educational content in the space which is surrounding them or around them. The next trend is that students can have an interaction with educational content utilizing AR technology. By moving about and changing perspectives, students can easily interact with educational content, thanks to AR. There is ease of interaction within AR-based experiences. This makes it one of the main reasons for teachers to get virtual educational experiences in classrooms. With AR technology, teaching and learning will become consequently become more engaging, effective, and interactive [38].

To make the experiences of learning better, AR is a vital technology [8].

3.3 Virtual Reality

3.3.1 A Walk Through the World of Virtual Reality

In new environments which are totally computer-generated, VR runs over them. What the user can touch, take, or have an interaction with is virtual. Just to make better the real world and experience of the user, AR utilizes virtual elements. When it comes to VR, the physical world gets replaced by VR. However, when it comes to AR, it does not do so; 100% is the level of immersion of VR. There is complete detachment of the users from the real world or we call it the physical world. The users are having complete awareness regarding the surroundings. They can touch, perceive, and have an interaction with the real world with the help of all digital information which the application gives [35]. In other words, an environment is created by the VR technology inside, the user of which gets the feeling and also seems to be moving in a virtual world that is computer-generated in the exact same way that people move in a natural environment; the user, while being immersed in the virtual world, cannot perceive the real world which actually still surrounds the user.

AR, on the other side, opposite to this, lets the user view the real world, augmenting the real world with superimposed virtual objects. So, basically, it can be said that VR replaces reality, and AR supplements it, thus creating an environment where real objects and virtual objects co-exist harmonically [54].

Different technologies can be integrated by VR systems that enable users to interact with a virtual scenario in a multi-sensory manner [25]. In experiments which are conducted in a virtual environment, it is possible to share resources of this environment to a greater number of connected users who wish to perform the same experiment, which would not be possible on our computers [36].

Presently, VR is being utilized in various fields especially in engineering, medicine, and computer science. Nowadays, in the engineering field, VR is being effectively utilized in engineering education [6]. For the implementation of novel training and educational approaches, VR lately has become a very efficient tool [5]. Technology can be utilized by students to create interesting and interactive products which not only demonstrate their understanding but also advance their learning [18]. On different medical fields, there is an impact of advances in VR [15]. There are various advantages of VR medical simulation which can make training outcomes better [16]. Under a trained surgeon's supervision, a surgical trainee learns to carry out surgery; this is the standard surgical training which has traditionally been one of apprenticeship. An option to supplement standard training is training utilizing a VR simulator. The technical skills of surgical trainees get improved by VR. However, VR training's clinical impact is not known [41].

Among different people, a simple way of representing and disseminating cultural heritage is through VR environments which are web-based [1]. When it comes to the sector of tourism, VR is especially interesting as a channel to communicate intangible tourism experiences to a larger audience [26].

VR has been utilized in various fields which include, among others, manufacturing, medicine, e-commerce, etc. [37].

3.3.2 VR Hardware and Software

VR Hardware

Input devices and output devices are the vital and basic hardware components of VR systems. They are of importance for the functioning of VR systems. Apart from these, a computer is also another hardware component which is vital for the functioning of VR systems.

- Input devices: The manner in which a user will communicate with the computer is decided by input devices [3]. The input devices comprise of controllers for VR, data gloves, track pads, device control buttons, etc.
- VR output devices: The VR output devices, for example, include HMD. It is a graphic display which stimulates senses to present the VR environment.

Feedback is obtained by output devices and presented to users through its corresponding output devices so as to stimulate the senses. On the basis of the senses which are visual, auditory, haptic, etc., output devices are classified [28].

VR Software

Different virtual software development kits are utilized to develop virtual reality experience for various applications.

3.3.3 Types of VR

There are three types of VR systems. They are as follows:

- Non-immersive
- Immersive
- Semi-immersive
- Non-immersive: For the reproduction of world images, they utilize desktops.
- Immersive: Complete simulated experience is provided by immersive systems.
- Semi-immersive: Semi-immersive systems example includes a fish tank VR. These systems are between the two above [2].

In today's time, there are various VR and AR [17].

3.4 A Walk Through the World of Mixed Reality

In MR experiences, most of the experiences are regarding the visual domain, with the main differentiation being between display types [11].

Onto the real world, MR interfaces can overlay video, graphics, and audio. This enables creating shared workspaces which combine the advantages of virtual environments and also seamless collaboration with real environment.

Information overlay might be utilized by remote collaborators to annotate the view of the user or might make better face-to-face conversation by making the production of shared interactive virtual models. MR techniques in this manner can produce a shared sense of presence and reality. Thus, for multi-user collaborative lab and work applications, MR approaches are ideal [31].

In MR applications, when it comes to them, the traditional ones are built on a number of assumptions or a series of assumptions regarding the environment they will operate in. This quite often needs time-consuming offline measurement and calibration for model construction purposes or instrumentation of environment for tracking. Which particular tracking technology will be utilized in a MR application, i.e., the selection of tracking technology in a MR application, quite largely depends upon the environment [3].

One of the emerging technologies is MR, and it is being driven and included in modern education [29]. Along with many other sectors of application, MR is also finding its way in the education sector as well. The authors in [5] present a MR environment for geometry education [5]. For MR applications, the HoloLens already carries different advanced features [27].

3.4.1 MR Hardware

For wide deployment, Microsoft HoloLens showcases great potential as it is easy to use, it also offers a display quality which is decent, and it also comfortable. This device is a self-contained device. Almost all the hardware like camera, processor, and speaker, which are required to make the physical world better with virtual content, are embedded [43].

After the successful introduction of Microsoft HoloLens, the MR device which is most well-known and commercially available is Microsoft's HoloLens 2. The HoloLens 2 device offers hands-free interaction utilizing natural gestures [30].

3.5 Further Understanding XR Technologies

Different work challenges require innovative technologies—for example, bringing improvement in the efficiency of different phases of a building's or infrastructure's life is a challenge, and this challenge requires considering technologies like VR and AR which are innovative. It is during the last decade that AR/VR systems for construction began to emerge. For the purpose of supporting continuous improvement, these applications aim to virtualize or augment the content of building information modeling (BIM) in real time [2]. Along with smartphone adoption ubiquity, propagation of VR and AR applications which leverage smartphone technology has grown. Cost-effective and portable AR and VR technologies provided by smartphone-based mobile applications provide tremendous potential for education [45]. For the consumer market, there is the availability of powerful and reasonably low-priced AR and VR devices, which is made possible due to technical advancement [13]. Digital health technologies include AR and VR that enable users to engage partially (AR) or either completely (VR) in immersive and interactive digital experiences [4].

There has been a great growth of the market of XR lately due to technological progress and also due to the simultaneous great reduction of cost of essential hardware. Now, this growth of market of XR has led to the creation of new perspectives related to adopting XR technologies in education.

XR experiences can become more accessible and more immersive to local users as well as remote users through advances in wireless and cellular networks [30].

Generally, under the framework of Industry 4.0, new technologies have emerged, such as VR, AR, and MR in an attempt to bridge the physical world with virtual worlds [34].

An excellent technology facilitating teaching processes enabling learners to more actively control their learning strategies and providing support to the connectivity and interactivity which students and faculties experience is XR [55].

Via leveraging XR in lifelong learning, there is transformation of educational system in a manner which is complementary to the rapid adoption of online and hybrid learning, and they are both critical to the future of work [55].

3.6 Different Uses or Applications of XR Technologies

3.6.1 AR and VR in Hand Rehabilitation

The part of the body which is quite often injured in accidents which are work-related, accounting for a third of all accidents at work and often involving surgery and long periods of rehabilitation, is the human hand. Many applications of AR and VR have been utilized to improve the process of rehabilitation. Still no sound evidence is found regarding the effectiveness of such applications nor the main drivers of therapeutic success.

For hand rehabilitation, reviewing the efficacy of AR and VR interventions was the objective of this study carried out by the authors in [56].

In 2019, in the month of October, a systematic search of publications was carried out in the Web of Science, Cochrane library, IEEE Xplore, and PubMed databases. The terms which were searched were (1) hand, (2) video game or videogame, (3) hand, (4) VR or AR, and (5) rehabilitation or therapy.

The articles were included based on certain conditions like they should be written in English language, they should be regarding VR or AR applications, they should be about hand rehabilitation, and so on. To filter and assess the articles, PRISMA protocol guidelines were followed.

A total of eight works was selected. From these works which were selected, there were improvements shown in the intervention group by six works, and two had no statistical differences between groups.

The authors of [56] were able to identify the motivators of patients' adherence, namely, real-time feedback to patients, challenge, and increased individualized difficulty. Tracking which is automated, simple easy integration in the setting of home, and accurate metrics recording might increase the scalability and facilitate the assessments of healthcare professionals.

The advantages and drivers for success of AR/VR application for hand rehabilitation were provided by the systematic review carried out by the authors in [56]. Patients can benefit from the utilization of AR or VR interventions for hand rehabilitation; this is what the available evidence suggests [56].

3.6.2 AR for Industrial Application

The authors in [39], for industrial education and training applications, present an innovative AR prototype. This system utilizes HMD integrating a calibrated camera and a laser pointer to augment an industrial object interactively with virtual sequences which are designed to train the user for specific maintenance tasks. By just pointing on a specific object component, the training leverages user interactions. The prototype architecture includes two main modules which are vision-based: the first one being the camera localization and second one being user-interaction handling. For camera localization, markerless trackers are included in the first module. In the second module, for red laser dot tracking, the authors [39] developed fast image processing methods. The system which is proposed is able to augment interactively in real time an industrial object by combining these processing elements, thereby making the learning process more intuitive and interesting. In integrating AR technology into industrial applications, one of the key factors is to provide assistance in maintenance procedural tasks. In a simple virtual demonstration of assembling/disassembling procedures related to upper-limb exoskeleton components, the authors [39] applied their prototype. The system is robust to viewpoint changes, and it is also able to obtain good accuracy with a textureless and a lightweight object as what the experimental evaluations showcase. Also, for industrial training applications, it enables to assure a precise, fast, and useful interaction [39].

3.6.3 AR-Based Real-Time Remote Maintenance Support

Interesting innovations and new techniques are constantly being introduced in the realm of the present industrial revolution by offering a fertile ground for further investigation and also by offering improvements in the industrial engineering domain. To be more specific, in the field of XR, cutting-edge digital technologies have become mainstream, which include AR. Also, thanks to cloud computing, provision of high-quality services has also been enabled, especially in the field of maintenance.

As modern machines are getting more complicated, well-trained and experienced personnel should carry out maintenance.

Even though AR is a backbone technology which facilitates the development of robust maintenance support tools, they are limited to the provision of predefined scenarios, covering only a limited number of scenarios.

In this work, to support remote maintenance and repair operation on the basis of AR, a framework is designed and developed.

The developed framework's applicability is tested *in vitro* in a lab-based machine shop and in a real-life industrial scenario.

To verify that each and every requirement is met, the developed application was tested in a real-life industrial scenario.

As per the results, they clearly give an indication that the current research work has managed to successfully address the functional requirements. The current research work has been successful in delivering a zero-time content authoring AR tool, which minimizes the mean time to repair MTTR further. Having said that, there is still a fertile ground for improvement in the future [34].

3.6.4 AR Glasses in Smart Factory

In the smart factories of the future, something that has been identified as an important technology providing support to shop-floor operators is augmented reality smart glasses (ARSG). They are quite increasingly popular.

The paper [57] aims to facilitate and also accelerate the adoption of ARSG by the manufacturing industry by improving our knowledge on how to evaluate and select ARSG efficiently for shop-floor context. In the past few years, the market for ARSG has exploded. Also, there is a large variety of available products from which selection needs to be made. Hence, it becomes tough to select, and a lot of time also gets consumed for the identification of optimum alternatives. So, in order to address this problem, the authors in this paper [57], to evaluate ARSG, present an efficient step-by-step process, which includes concrete guidelines, i.e., what parameters to consider and also their recommended minimum values.

By utilizing the evaluation process that is suggested, optimal decisions can be quite quickly made by manufacturing companies regarding what products to implement on their shop floors. The evaluation process in practice is demonstrated by the authors in the paper, thereby presenting a comprehensive review of products which are presently available along with a recommended best buy. Along with this, the paper identifies and even discusses topics which are meriting research attention to make sure that ARSG are successfully implemented on the industrial shop floor [57].

3.6.5 Identifying the Application Areas for AR in Industrial Construction on the Basis of Suitability of Technology

Different research studies on AR in the architecture, engineering, and construction (AEC) industry have suggested its feasibility. Having said that, the realization of the use of AR in AEC not just needs to demonstrate its feasibility but also needs validation of its suitability. On the basis of the suitability of AR technologies, in [46], the application areas of AR in industrial construction are comprehensively identified.

With the purpose of exploring the suitability of AR, the authors in [46], from the viewpoint of human factors, assess work tasks regarding visual information requirements to find the rationale for the benefits of AR in work tasks.

Then, on the basis of the assessment of work tasks, a comprehensive map is presented by the authors [46], which identifies AR application areas in industrial construction. It is revealed by the comprehensive map that out of a total of 17 work tasks which are classified, eight work tasks may potentially gain benefit from the support of AR [46].

3.6.6 VR in Education

A survey was carried out on VR and its applications in education by the authors in [58]. They have provided great information in their paper. The education system has always adapted to whichever technology that has been available and also to the needs of the students.

On another development's threshold, we are present.

The generation which is beginning their education right now has been online for their entire lives.

It is a challenge to educate generation Z. An approach which is quite different to maximize engagement and efficiency is required. There are various advantages of utilizing VR in education that were already proven.

Firstly, spectacular visualization is provided by VR, which a traditional classroom cannot provide.

VR provides virtually unlimited access to books, information, or articles. In the classroom, the use of modern technology brings an increase in engagement and stimulates cooperation as well as involvement. For highly efficient blended learning, VR is utilized; it is also utilized for encouraging self-study and the individual pursuit of knowledge.

Even though it is clearly of benefit to utilize modern technology in the education environment, it is not without dangers or risks. The lack of flexibility is one of the main issues. Besides that, there are various other issues which need to be evaluated.

A human teacher is a moderator. In terms of the information which the students obtain, that information's natural filter is the human teacher. It is essential to evaluate the validity of data which is obtained and also to evaluate its relevance.

If there is a lot of focus on digital education solutions, the balance between teaching hard and soft skills might be deformed. Even though we might have the temptation to replace all old-fashioned solutions with modern digital ones, there needs to be an equilibrium between state-of-the-art solutions and human interaction, mentoring, and teacher–student relationship [58].

3.6.7 MR in Industrial Application

Whenever it comes to industrial applications, MR can be very useful.

In an industry, the number of robots is growing each year, which are used to automate various processes in which they are utilized.

On the basis of MR, a system for interactive programming of industrial robots is represented by this paper [59].

For immersion in MR, Microsoft HoloLens glasses were utilized.

A user who does not have programming skills can easily assign the manipulator with task by using the system that was developed. There are three parts of the system, namely, the time-optimal trajectory planning, MR-based simulator, and intuitive geometry path planning—they are the main system parts. With the help of MR, users get to have an interaction with robots and the spatial environment via highly intuitive interfaces like virtual tools and gestures and obtain instant feedback with the help of optical tracking devices. Instead of interacting with a real robot, having an interaction with virtual robot model makes the job of the operator safer [59].

3.6.8 AR System for Maintenance and Repair

For repair guidance on the basis of AR, the authors in [44] present a solution. The solution is such that it covers not just the software-related issues but also the issues which are related to the hardware.

A markerless CAD-based tracking system was developed by the authors [44] that can deal with different illumination conditions during the tracking stage, partial occlusions, and rapid motion.

Under real industrial conditions, the system underwent various extensive test series and proved to be useful for different maintenance and repair scenarios [44].

3.6.9 Clinical Use of VR Distraction System to Reduce Anxiety and Pain in Dental Procedures

A virtual environment (VE) which is not too expensive and available commercially could have an impact which is significant in the reduction of perceived pain which is involved in a variety of medical procedures. The utilization of VR as a form of distraction for dental patients is examined by this study. Both subjective and objective measures are utilized to determine a patients' reported anxiety level and physiological factors.

This research's physiological results suggest that the use of a VR distraction system might be a beneficial option for patients having mild to moderate fear and anxiety associated with dental treatments.

If summarized, the current study provides initial support for the use of VR as a technique to control fear and anxiety during dental procedures, and this initial support is quite encouraging.

In order to find out that whether VR can become a viable form of anxiety and fear control during dental treatments, added empirical research will be required. For treatment of dental pain, the techniques that prove effective will likely prove effective for other painful procedures as well [45].

3.6.10 AR Role in Anatomical Education

With regard AR implementation in anatomical education, the results or outcomes of this have not yet been reviewed so far.

A narrative review was performed of the literature concerning these outcomes. In databases like Scopus, Cochrane, etc., a search for papers was done, with the aim to explore the results of implementing AR in the study of anatomy.

From every paper, the authors [23] extracted the following data: year of publication, authors, type of study, number of participants, level of outcome as per Kirkpatrick hierarchy, AR acceptability, impact on examination performance, and ability to facilitate the understanding of the spatial organization of structures and to motivate students to learn anatomy.

A total of seven papers was found to be eligible for analysis. It was proved that, in general, AR was enjoyable and also highly accepted as a tool for teaching anatomy.

Randomized controlled studies are required to prove if AR could effectively replace or supplement other anatomy pedagogy methods [23].

3.6.11 VR Method in Aircraft Maintenance Service

Ever since the invention of aircraft, the center of research has been the safety of flight and airline operations because even minute errors in the maintenance of aircraft might cause serious accidents.

Therefore, at all times, the maintenance of aircrafts is critical to the aviation industry.

It is vital to train for aviation maintenance in order to prevent maintenance errors. For this reason, in this study [60], an aircraft maintenance virtual reality (AMVR) system was developed. For a Dornier-228 aircraft, a walk-around visual inspection of its fuel system was designed and also tested in a virtual environment.

To verify the effectiveness of utilizing the AMVR system in training, students tested the developed system. It was acknowledged by the students that the developed system was beneficial to their learning. This proved that the developed system is quite effective in training students on how to improve their aircraft maintenance skills [60].

3.6.12 VR in Healthcare Application

The Stanford Virtual Heart Project is one of the very useful projects in utilization in which a VR headset is required to be worn by the user. This project was developed by cardiologists at Standford and experts of cardio-surgery in collaboration with Lighthaus, Inc. Also, Oculus supported in the realization of this project. This project is very useful because of some reasons. First, it helps families to have a better understanding of their child's cardiac anatomy. It is difficult to explain congenital heart defects. However, thanks to this project which uses VR technology and provides an interactive and immersive visualization experience, a child's heart condition can be explained to their families far better compared with explaining to them using drawings and plastic models, thus making it easier for the families to understand. Also, the Stanford Virtual Heart Project is extended to Stanford medical students and trainees who can interact with as well as inspect the virtual heart and manipulate it, walk inside it, and understand the different aspects [61].

3.6.13 MR in Healthcare Application

At a London teaching hospital, the authors in [62] carried out a proof-of-concept study utilizing MR technology to deliver remote-access teaching ward round.

It was completely agreed by the students that MR technology's use was enjoyable and also provided teaching. On the MR content utilized, there was positive feedback given by most of the students, and the students agreed that they could have an interaction with and have their queries answered by the clinician who led the ward round. It was demonstrated that this method is acceptable, feasible, and effective for the delivery of clinical education by quantitative and free text feedback from students, faculty members, and patients.

To transform medical education delivery and allow a consistent access to teaching which is of high quality, the authors, in their paper [62], have utilized this technology in a novel way.

The acceptability, feasibility, and effectiveness of utilizing MR technology for delivering a remote-access, interactive teaching ward round are supported by the results obtained by the authors in their paper [62]. To allow consistent access as well as equal access to learning opportunities, the authors propose that institutions across the world could implement this technology.

In order to assess additional value that MR technology brings to students' learning compared to traditional teaching methods, further work is needed as per the author in [62].

3.7 Conclusion

In this book chapter, different XR technologies are briefly described. Also, this chapter discusses in detail the different uses of XR technologies with examples.

References

1. Koeva, M., Luleva, M., Maldjanski, P., Integrating Spherical Panoramas and Maps for Visualization of Cultural Heritage Objects Using Virtual Reality Technology. *Sensors*, 17, 4, 829, 2017, https://doi.org/10.3390/s17040829.
2. Assila, A., Beladjine, D., Messaadia, M., Towards AR/VR Maturity Model Adapted to the Building Information Modeling, in: *Product Lifecycle Management Enabling Smart X*. PLM 2020. IFIP Advances in Information and Communication Technology, vol. 594, F. Nyffenegger, J. Ríos, L. Rivest, A. Bouras (Eds.), Springer, Cham, 2020, https://doi.org/10.1007/978-3-030-62807-9_59.
3. DiVerdi, S. and Hollerer, T., GroundCam: A Tracking Modality for Mobile Mixed Reality. *Virtual Reality Conference, 2007. VR '07*, 10–14 March, IEEE, pp. 75–82, 2007.
4. Logan, D.E., Simons, L.E., Caruso, T.J., Gold, J.I., Greenleaf, W., Griffin, A., King, C.D., Menendez, M., Olbrecht, V.A., Rodriguez, S., Silvia, M., Leveraging Virtual Reality and Augmented Reality to Combat Chronic Pain in Youth: Position Paper From the Interdisciplinary Network on Virtual and Augmented Technologies for Pain Management. *J. Med. Internet Res.*, 23, 4, e25916, 2021 Apr 26.
5. Nikolakis, G., Fergadis, G., Tzovaras, D., Strintzis, M.G., A mixed reality learning environment for geometry education, in: *Methods and applications of artificial intelligence*. SETN 2004. Lecture notes in computer science, vol. 3025, G.A. Vouros and T. Panayiotopoulos (Eds.), Springer, Berlin, 2004, https ://doi.org/10.1007/978-3-540-24674 -9_11.
6. Vergara, D., Rubio, M.P., Lorenzo, M., On the Design of Virtual Reality Learning Environments in Engineering. *Multimodal Technol. Interact.*, 1, 2, 11, 2017, https://doi.org/10.3390/mti1020011.
7. Parekh, P., Patel, S., Patel, N., Shah, M., Systematic review and meta-analysis of augmented reality in medicine, retail, and games. *Vis. Comput. Ind. Biomed. Art*, 3, 1, 1–20, 2020 Dec.
8. Garzón, J., Pavón, J., Baldiris, S., Systematic review and meta-analysis of augmented reality in educational settings. *Virtual Real.*, 23, 447–459, 2019, https://doi.org/10.1007/s10055-019-00379-9.
9. Schumann, M., Fuchs, C., Kollatsch, C., Klimant, P., Evaluation of augmented reality supported approaches for product design and production processes. *Procedia CIRP*, 97, 160–165, 2021.
10. Krevelen, D. and Poelman, R., A Survey of Augmented Reality Technologies, Applications and Limitations. *Int. J. Virtual Real.*, 9, 2, 1–20, 2010.
11. Hughes, C.E., Stapleton, C.B., Hughes, D.E., Smith, E.M., Mixed reality in education, entertainment, and training. *IEEE Comput. Graph. Appl.*, 25, 6, 24–30, 2005, https ://doi.org/10.1109/MCG.2005.139.

12. Fombona, J., Pascual-Sevillano, M.A., Gonzalez-Videgaray, M., M-learning and Augmented Reality: A Review of the Scientific Literature on the WoS Repository. *Comunicar*, 52, 63–71, 2017.
13. Eschen, H., Kötter, T., Rodeck, R., Harnisch, M., Schüppstuhl, T., Augmented and Virtual Reality for Inspection and Maintenance Processes in the Aviation Industry. *Procedia Manuf.*, **19**, 156–163, 2018.
14. De Marchi, L., Ceruti, A., Marzani, A., Liverani, A., Augmented reality to support on-field post-impact maintenance operations on thin structures. *J. Sens.*, 2013, 1–10, 2013.
15. Yokoyama, I., Sarai, T., Asai, T., Kitou, N., Nozaki, H., Kondo, Y., Nomura, Y., Morizane, A., Sekikawa, M., Liu, D., Virtual reality and augmented reality applications and simulation in vascular access management with three-dimensional visualization. *J. Vasc. Access*, 20, 1S, 65–70, 2019, https://doi.org/10.1177/1129729818776904.
16. Ruthenbeck, G.S. and Reynolds, K.J., Virtual reality for medical training: The state-of-the-art. *J. Simul.*, 9, 16–26, 2015.
17. Puggioni, M.P., Frontoni, E., Paolanti, M., Pierdicca, R., Malinverni, E.S., Sasso, M., A content creation tool for AR/VR applications in education: The ScoolAR framework, in: *International conference on augmented reality, virtual reality and computer graphics*, pp. 205–219, Springer, Cham, 2020 Sep 7.
18. Del Siegle, Seeing Is Believing: Using Virtual and Augmented Reality to Enhance Student Learning. *Gift. Child Today*, 42, 1, 46–52, 2019, https://doi.org/10.1177/1076217518804854.
19. Bahri, H., Krcmarik, D., Moezzi, R., Kočí, J., Efficient use of mixed reality for bim system using microsoft HoloLens. *IFAC-PapersOnLine*, 52, 235–239, 2019.
20. Yung, R. and Khoo-Lattimore, C., New realities: A systematic literature review on virtual reality and augmented reality in tourism research. *Curr. Issues Tourism*, 22, 2056–2081, 2019.
21. Liarokapis, F. and Anderson, E., Using augmented reality as a medium to assist teaching in higher education, in: *Proceedings of the 31st annual conference of the European association for computer graphics (Eurographics 2010)*, pp. 9–16, Norrköping, 2010.
22. Olsson, T., Lagerstam, E., Kärkkäinen, T., Väänänen-Vainio-Mattila, K., Expected user experience of mobile augmented reality services: a user study in the context of shopping centres. *Pers. Ubiquitous Comput.*, 17, 2, 287–304, 2013.
23. Chytas, D., Johnson, E.O., Piagkou, M., Mazarakis, A., Babis, G.C., Chronopoulos, E., Nikolaou, V.S., Lazaridis, N., Natsis, K., The role of augmented reality in anatomical education: an overview. *Ann. Anat.-Anat. Anz.*, 229, 151463, 2020 May 1.
24. Quandt, M., Beinke, T., Freitag, M., User-Centered Evaluation of an Augmented Reality-based Assistance system for Maintenance. *Procedia CIRP*, 93, 921–926, 2020.

25. Gavish, N., Gutiérrez, T., Webel, S., Rodríguez, J., Peveri, M., Bockholt, U., Tecchia, F., Evaluating virtual reality and augmented reality training for industrial maintenance and assembly tasks. *Interact. Learn. Environ.*, 23, 6, 778–798, 2015.
26. Griffin, T., Giberson, J., Lee, S.H., Guttentag, D., Kandaurova, M., Virtual Reality and Implications for Destination Marketing, in: *Proceedings of the TTRA International Conference*, Quebec City, QC, Canada, 20-22 June 2017.
27. Coolen, B., Beek, P.J., Geerse, D.J., Roerdink, M., Avoiding 3D Obstacles in Mixed Reality: Does It Differ from Negotiating Real Obstacles? *Sensors*, 20, 1095, 2020.
28. Lee, J.-Y., Lee, S.-H., Park, H.-M., Lee, S.-K., Choi, J.-S., Kwon, J.-S., Design and implementation of a wearable AR annotation system using gaze interaction. *Consumer Electronics (ICCE), 2010 Digest of Technical Papers International Conference on*, 9–13 Jan, pp. 185–186, 2010.
29. Krishna, M.V.P., Mehta, S., Verma, S., Rane, S., Mixed Reality in Smart Computing Education System, in: *2018 International Conference on Smart Systems and Inventive Technology (ICSSIT)*, IEEE, pp. 72–75, 2018.
30. Panagiotidis, P., Augmented and Mixed Reality in Language Learning. *Eur. J. Educ.*, 4, 28–44, 2021.
31. Müller, D., Bruns, F.W., Erbe, H., Robben, B., Yoo, Y., Mixed reality learning spaces for collaborative experimentation: A challenge for engineering education and training. *Int. J. Online Eng.*, 3, 4, 15–19, 2007.
32. Julier, S., Baillot, Y., Brown, D., Lanzagorta, M., Information filtering for mobile augmented reality. *IEEE Comput. Graph. Appl.*, 22, 5, 12–15, 2002.
33. Serio, A.D., Ibanez, M.B., Kloos, C.D., Impact of an augmented reality system on students' motivation for a visual art course. *Comput. Educ.*, 68, 586–596, 2013.
34. Mourtzis, D., Siatras, V., Angelopoulos, J., Real-Time Remote Maintenance Support Based on Augmented Reality (AR). *Appl. Sci.*, 10, 1855, 2020.
35. Fernandez, M., Augmented Virtual Reality: How to Improve Education Systems. *High. Learn. Res. Commun.*, 7, 1–15, 2017.
36. Stark, E., Bisták, P., Kucera, E., Haffner, O., Kozák, S., Virtual Laboratory Based on Node.js Technology and Visualized in Mixed Reality Using Microsoft HoloLens, in: *Proceedings of the 2017 Federated Conference on Computer Science and Information Systems*, pp. 315–322, Prague, Czech Republic, 3–6 September 2017.
37. Santana-Fenandez, J., Gomez-Gil, Del-Poso-San-Cirilo, L., Design and Implementation of a GPS guidance system for agricultural tractors using augmented reality technology. *Sensors*, 10, 11, 10435–10447, Nov 2010.
38. Shoikova, E., Nikolov, R., Kovatcheva, E., Smart Digital Education Enhanced by AR and IoT Data, in: *Proceedings of the 12th International Technology, Education and Development Conference (INTED)*, pp. 5861–587, Valencia, Spain, 5–7 March 2018.

39. Besbes, B., Collette, S.N., Tamaazousti, M., Bourgeois, S., Gay-Bellile, V., An interactive augmented reality system: A prototype for industrial maintenance training applications, in: *Proceedings of the 2012 IEEE International Symposium on Mixed and Augmented Reality (ISMAR)*, pp. 269–270, Bari, Italy, 5–8 November 2012.
40. Doil, F., Schreiber, W., Alt, T., Patron, C., Augmented reality for manufacturing planning, in: *Proceedings of the workshop on Virtual environments 2003*, pp. 71–76, ACM Press, New York, 2003.
41. Nagendran, M., Gurusamy, K.S., Aggarwal, R., Loizidou, M., Davidson, B.R., Virtual reality training for surgical trainees in laparoscopic surgery. *Cochrane Database Syst. Rev.*, 2013, CD006575, 2013, doi: 10.1002/14651858.CD006575.pub3.
42. Caruso, G. and Re, G.M., AR-Mote: A wireless device for Augmented Reality environment. *3D User Interfaces (3DUI), 2010 IEEE Symposium on*, pp. 99–102, 20–21 March, 2010.
43. Radkowski, R. and Kanunganti, S., Augmented reality system calibration for assembly support with the microsoft hololens, in: *Proceedings of the International Manufacturing Science and Engineering Conference*, p. V003T02A021, College Station, TX, USA, 18–22 June 2018.
44. Platonov, J., Heibel, H., Meier, P., Grollmann, B., A mobile markerless AR system for maintenance and repair, in: *Proc. 5th IEEE and ACM International Symposium on Mixed and Augmented Reality (ISMAR 06)*, pp. 105–108, 2006.
45. Wiederhold, M.D., Gao, K., Widerhold, B.K., Clinical use of virtual reality distraction system to reduce anxiety and pain in dental procedures. *Cyberpsychol. Behav. Soc. Netw.*, 17, 359–365, 2014.
46. Shin, D.H. and Dunston, P.S., Identification of application areas for augmented reality in industrial construction based on technology suitability. *Autom. Constr.*, 17, 882–894, 2008.
47. Höllerer, T.H. and Feiner, S.K., Mobile Augmented Reality, in: *Telegeoinformatics: Location-Based Computing and Services*, H. Karimi and A. Hammad (Eds.), Taylor & Francis Books Ltd, Boca Raton, Florida, USA, 01/2004.
48. Cipresso, P., Giglioli, I.A.C., Raya, M.A., Riva, G., The Past, Present, and Future of Virtual and Augmented Reality Research: A Network and Cluster Analysis of the Literature. *Front. Psychol.*, 9, 2086, 2018.
49. Mazuryk, T., Virtual Reality History, Applications, Technology and Future, 1999.
50. Carmigniani, J., Furht, B., Anisetti, M., Ceravolo, P., Damiani, E., Ivkovic, M., Augmented reality technologies, systems and applications. *Multimedia Tools Appl.*, *51*, 341–377, 2010.
51. Arena, F., Collotta, M., Pau, G., Termine, F., An Overview of Augmented Reality. *Computers*, *11*, 28, 2022, https://doi.org/10.3390/computers11020028.

52. Dini, G. and Mura, M., Application of Augmented Reality Techniques in Through-life Engineering Services. *Procedia CIRP*, 38, 14–23, 2015, 10.1016/j.procir.2015.07.044.
53. Gerup, J., Soerensen, C.B., Dieckmann, P., Augmented reality and mixed reality for healthcare education beyond surgery: An integrative review. *Int. J. Med. Educ.*, 11, 1, 2020.
54. Hincapié, M., Caponio, A., Rios, H., González Mendívil, E., An introduction to Augmented Reality with applications in aeronautical maintenance. *13th International Conference on Transparent Optical Networks*, pp. 1–4, 2011, doi: 10.1109/ICTON.2011.5970856.
55. Kuleto, V., Stanescu, M., Ranković, M., Šević, N.P., Paun, D., Teodorescu, S., Extended reality in higher education, a responsible innovation approach for generation y and generation z. *Sustainability*, 13, 11814, 2021.
56. Pereira, M.F., Prahm, C., Kolbenschlag, J., Oliveira, E., Rodrigues, N.F., Application of AR and VR in hand rehabilitation: A systematic review. *J. Biomed. Inf.*, 111, 1–10, 2020.
57. Syberfeldt, A., Danielsson, O., Gustavsson, P., Augmented reality smart glasses in the smart factory: Product evaluation guidelines and review of available products. *IEEE Access*, 5, 9118–9130, 2017.
58. Kamińska, D., Sapiński, T., Wiak, S., Tikk, T., Haamer, R.E., Avots, E., Helmi, A., Ozcinar, C., Anbarjafari, G., Virtual Reality and Its Applications in Education: Survey. *Information*, 10, 10, 318, 2019, https://doi.org/10.3390/info10100318.
59. Ostanin, M. and Klimchik, A., Interactive Robot Programing Using Mixed Reality. *IFAC-PapersOnLine*, 51, 50–55, 2018, 10.1016/j.ifacol.2018.11.517.
60. Wu, W.-C. and Vu, V.-H., Application of Virtual Reality Method in Aircraft Maintenance Service—Taking Dornier 228 as an Example. *Appl. Sci.*, 12, 14, 7283, 2022, https://doi.org/10.3390/app12147283.
61. Silva, J.N.A., Southworth, M., Raptis, C., Silva, J., Emerging Applications of Virtual Reality in Cardiovascular Medicine. *JACC. Basic Transl. Sci.*, *3*, 3, 420–430, 2018, https://doi.org/10.1016/j.jacbts.2017.11.009.
62. Bala, L., Kinross, J., Martin, G., Koizia, L.J., Kooner, A.S., Shimshon, G.J., Hurkxkens, T.J., Pratt, P.J., Sam, A.H., A remote access mixed reality teaching ward round. *Clin. Teach.*, *18*, 4, 386–390, 2021, https://doi.org/10.1111/tct.13338.

Section 2
FUNDAMENTALS OF EXTENDED REALITY

4

Introduction to Augmented Reality and Virtual Reality

S.N. Kumar[1]* and S. Suresh[2]

[1]*Department of EEE, Amal Jyothi College of Engineering, Kottayam, Kerala, India*
[2]*Department of CSE, KPR Institute of Engineering and Technology, Coimbatore, Tamil Nadu, India*

Abstract

Advancement in technology paves the way to virtual reality, augmented reality, and mixed reality, which integrates real-world physical objects with virtual objects. Virtual reality (VR) and augmented reality (AR) have immense applications in real-world processes, and it is a boon to mankind for a better understanding of many objects and concepts. Virtual reality is a complete immersion in the artificial environment created using software, while augmented reality maps the virtual phenomena into real-world physical objects. 3D visualization is the key feature of AR/VR technology that gains prominence in different sectors. Positional tracking and visualization are the vital features of AR/VR for 3D visualization and analysis. This chapter focuses on the introduction to AR/VR, highlighting the characteristics, components, and recent research works with applications. The 3D perspective enables AR/VR technology to stand ahead in real-world problems to find the best solutions, and the market for AR/VR technology is also tremendously increasing.

***Keywords*:** Virtual reality, augmented reality, mixed reality, machine learning

4.1 Introduction

Augmented virtual reality has immense applications in our day-to-day life activities [1–3], and some of the applications are depicted in Figure 4.1. The comparative analysis of AR and VR reveals that VR is an expensive

**Corresponding author*: appu123kumar@gmail.com

Manisha Vohra (ed.) Introduction to Extended Reality (XR) Technologies, (63–88) © 2025 Scrivener Publishing LLC

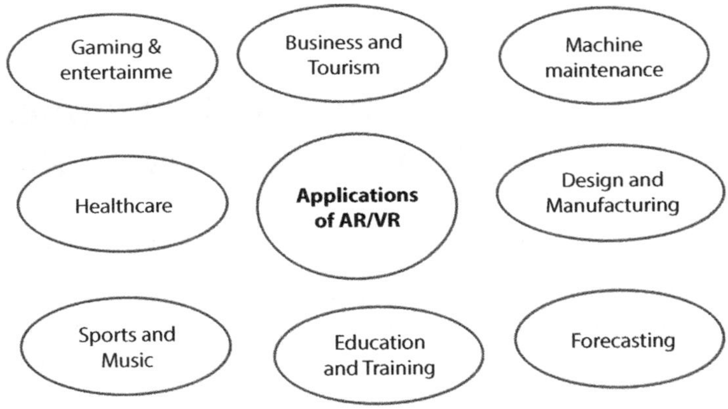

Figure 4.1 Generic applications of AR/VR technology.

one, while the former one, AR, involves the addition of features to the real-world environment. Virtual reality, in fact, simulates a completely real-time environment and flags the audience to a virtual world.

Augmented reality, virtual reality, and mixed reality are illustrated in Figure 4.2. Augmented reality and virtual reality aid the users in visualizing real-world entities in a better manner such that augmented reality

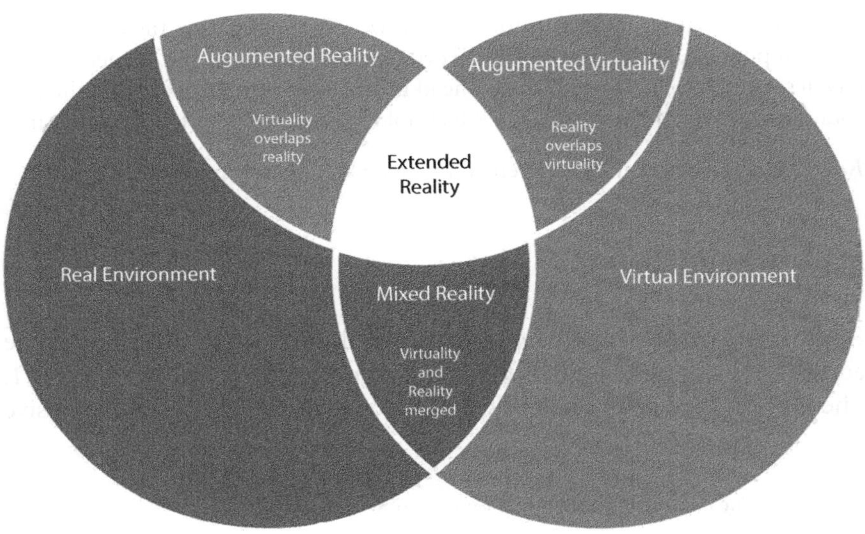

Figure 4.2 Illustration of augmented reality, virtual reality, and mixed reality.

focuses on the key idea "virtual features overlay on the real world" and virtual reality focuses on the key idea "reality is overlaid on the virtual world" [4].

Augmented reality mixes the real-world objects with digital objects. It enhances the surrounding environment by the incorporation of digital elements such as camera and smartphone. Specialized equipment is needed to utilize the benefit of AR—for example, smart glasses are a widely used AR device that relies on smart glasses software for data. The data are collected in real time through the camera and processed for display to viewers. It reflects the digital world components in the real-world scenario. The precise definition of augmented reality and its components are depicted in Figure 4.3. Augmented reality enhances the real-world entities' visualization by the incorporation of graphics (image/audio/video) [5]. The widely used components in augmented reality are handheld devices, specialized monitors, virtual displays, and snap chat lenses.

A typical example of AR technology is depicted in Figure 4.4. The camera captures the real-world objects, and the graphics system generates the

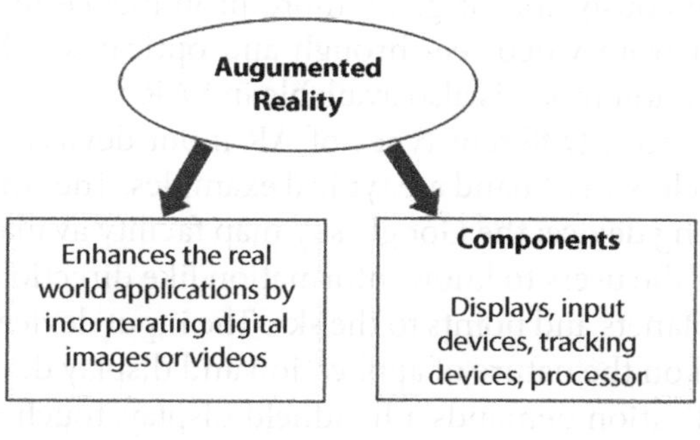

Figure 4.3 Augmented reality and its components.

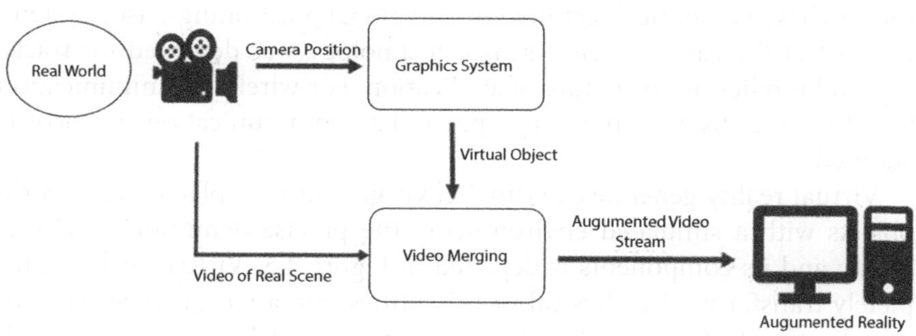

Figure 4.4 Typical example of augmented reality.

virtual entities necessary to be overlapped on the captured video. The video merger block depicted here performs the magic of combining real-world video with graphics and provides proficient visualization to the users.

AR display devices: There are three categories of the display: head-mounted display, handheld display, and spatial augmented reality (SAR). Head-mounted display is placed on the head; it can be video see-through or optical see-through mode. Two cameras are used in video see-through mode that generates the real-world objects of the augmented scene and virtual objects. In optical see-through mode, a single camera is used and provides the user with a graphical representation of the real-world objects. Synchronization was found to be efficient in video see-through mode, while there is a possibility of time delay in scene visualization in optical see-through mode. The video see-through mode is present in handheld display, and in the market, nearly three different types of handheld display are available. A smart phone is a good example of a handheld display. Spatial augmented reality (SAR) utilizes video-projectors, holograms, or other tracking technologies to view the real-world objects in the virtual environment without wearable gadgets. Multiple users can utilize this facility simultaneously, and it gains more prominence in the real-world scenario. Apart from video see-through and optical see-through modes, direct augmentation mode is also available in SAR.

AR input devices: Different types of AR input devices are in practice. Gloves and wireless wrist band are typical examples. The smart phone itself is used a pointing device; the Google sky map facility available in Android phones enables the users to know information like direction and the name of the stars or planets and points to the sky. The input devices are chosen or designed based on the nature of application and display devices employed. When the application demands a handheld display, touch screen as input device can be used.

AR tracking devices: It comprises of digital cameras, accelerometers, sensors based on optical technology, and global positioning-based system. In most of the cases, wireless sensor technology was deployed for tracking, and it relies on the nature of application. For wireless communication based on the distance measure, appropriate communication protocol is adopted.

Virtual reality generates a virtual environment by replacing real-world objects with a simulated environment. The precise definition of virtual reality and its components is depicted in Figure 4.5. Virtual reality completely transforms the physical world entities into a virtual experience or visualization to the users [6]. The components of VR are specialized VR headsets, goggles, controllers, and a Google cardboard.

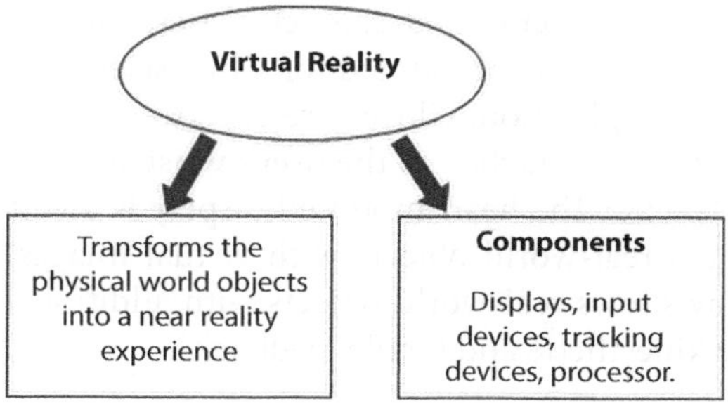

Figure 4.5 Virtual reality and its components.

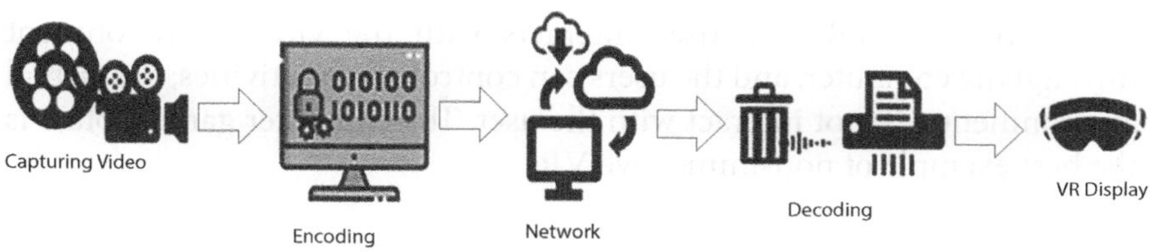

Figure 4.6 Typical example of virtual reality.

An example of virtual reality is depicted in Figure 4.6. The acquisition of video is done by multiple cameras, and the data is preprocessed and then encoded for transmission through the network. On the receiver side, decoding is done, and the display is done using a VR display unit.

VR input devices: Trackers are used to capture the user's movements, and 3D input devices manipulate the objects. Desktop as input devices are simple and are of low cost; however, the effect of immersion is less. The rendering of images requires tracking of user position and orientation. The following are the characteristics involved in the appropriate selection of tracking devices.

Update rate: It represents the count of measurements taken during each second.

Latency: It is the delay between the user interaction and the start of the action.

Accuracy: It is the measure of error in the measured position and orientation with respect to the actual values.

Resolution: It is the finite change in position or orientation that can be measured.

Apart from the above-mentioned characteristics, range, easiness in use, and smaller weight are also accounted for while selecting the input tracking device for VR application. Gloves are used to detect the angles of the fingers, and the tracker attached to the user's wrist aids in measurement.

VR output devices: The head-mounted display is a widely used output device; it replaces real-world objects with virtual images. Opaque head-mounted display shows real-world objects with additional details. Haptic displays ensure kinesthetic and tactile feedback.

The different types of VR are as follows: non-immersive VR, semi-immersive VR, and fully immersive VR.

Non-immersive VR: The user interacts with the virtual environment through the computer, and the users can control some activities; the virtual environment will not interact with the user. The computer game Dota 2 is the best example of non-immersive VR.

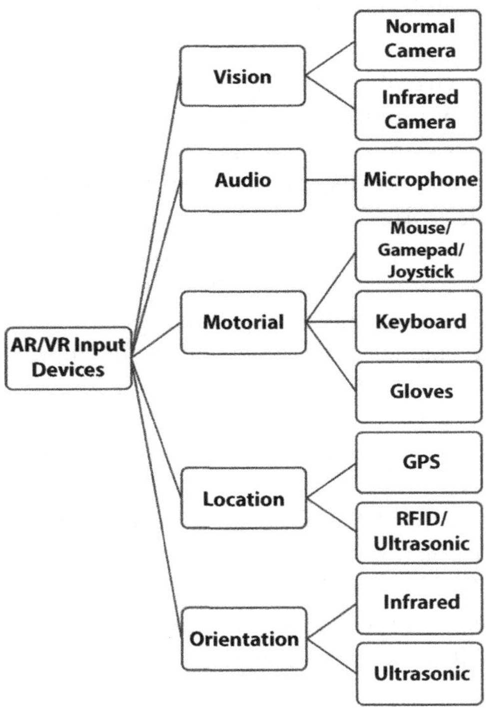

Figure 4.7 AR/VR input devices.

Fully immersive VR: The operation of fully immersive VR is opposite to that of non-immersive virtual reality. The user experiences a virtual environment as if present in that environment. The VR glasses and gloves are needed to provide a virtual environment, and the data acquired from the sensors are processed by the computer to generate the virtual environment. VR gaming zone is the best example, where specialized gears are used by the users for interaction with the virtual environment. Multiple users can interact with the same environment.

Semi-immersive VR: It is a combination of the above two; VR glass or computer screen are used to visualize the virtual environment. The virtual environment experience cannot be enhanced by the user. A virtual tour is the best example of semi-immersive VR, which uses a device-based or web-based system.

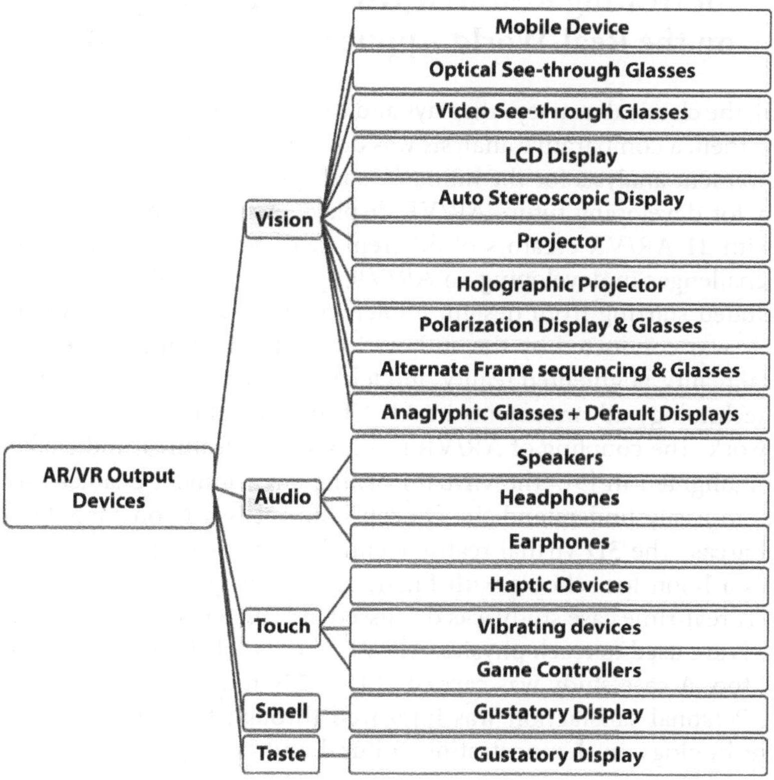

Figure 4.8 AR/VR output devices.

Figure 4.7 depicts the widely used AR/VR input devices. Some of the typical AR/VR input devices are explained above, and the figure below represents the choice of AR/VR input devices based on the application. Five groups of input devices and widely used devices in each group are represented here.

Figure 4.8 depicts the widely used AR/VR output devices. Some of the typical AR/VR output devices are explained above, and the figure below represents the choice of AR/VR input devices based on the application. Five groups of input devices and widely used devices in each group are represented here.

This chapter gives an overview of AR and VR with their applications in the real world. Section 4.2 highlights the motivating research works focusing on the real-world applications of AR/VR. The conclusion is drawn in Section 4.3.

4.2 Motivating Research Works Focusing on the Real-World Applications of AR/VR

In [6], the classical near-eye displays and their challenges are addressed initially; then, a comparative analysis was done with the AR/VR displays. The requirement analysis for the human visual system was done, which paves a way for developing future AR/VR displays. A survey was carried out in [7] with 21 AR/VR creators of different fields to investigate the features and challenges in developing an AR/VR application. Eight obstacles were concluded starting from design, implementation, and testing. A detailed review was conducted by the authors in [8], highlighting the features of virtual reality, augmented reality, and telepresence in the healthcare sector. The technology advancements in AR/VR in clinical care was analyzed in this work. The coupling of AR/VR technology, its features, and challenges are highlighted in [9]. The virtual learning environment enables the students to easily understand the concepts, and it is a boon for schools in rural areas. The 3D virtual reality technology helps in improvising skills and is a boon for schools with financial crisis in purchasing equipment [10]. A real-time case study was discussed in [10], where 3D virtual reality models are used to teach physics. AR/VR find its role in the archaeological field, too. A case study was carried out on 739 museum visitors in Rome [11]. Personal satisfaction was improved through the utilization of AR/VR technology in demonstrating cultural and heritage monuments and objects [11]. The work [12] states the role of AR/VR in the tourism sector.

The citation network analysis and text mining techniques reveal the usage of AR/VR in tourism, highlighting its features and benefits.

In [13], the authors proposed an AR-based tool ScoolAR for imparting active participation-based training to students. With the use of AR/VR tools in education, the understanding capacity of students is improved and the teachers can focus more on outcome-based education since AR/VR technology mimics a real-time scenario, and in many cases, students can interact with the system. A qualitative as well as quantitative analysis of challenges to be faced by the future AR/VR technology is highlighted in [14]. The current cloud-based data storage will not be sufficient, and a novel hybrid cloud platform model named data networking is proposed in this work [15]. The AR/VR technology in the mobile computing application for 5G technology and beyond is described in [16]. The AR coupled with VR and gaze tracking finds its role in industrial maintenance [17]. The SmartMarca Project is a user-centered comparative study to understand the effectiveness of augmented reality and virtual reality in school environments [18]. This aims to measure how immersive technologies influence learning results, engagement, and knowledge retention in students [18]. The characteristics of AR/VR technology, challenges, and future scope are highlighted in [10]. The use of AR/VR technology by musicians and singers during stage performance was highlighted in [19]. The characteristics of the 5G network and the integration of 5G networking with the AR/VR technology were put forward in [20]; the influence of edge computing was also discussed in this work. The evolution of AR technology is depicted in Figure 4.9.

Ivan Sutherland's developed the first head-mounted display system with enhanced sensory perception of the world with computer-generated graphics called "The Sword of Damocles" in 1968. However, the term "augmented reality" was not coined until 1990 by Boeing researcher Tim Caudell. In 1974, Myron Kruger, a computer researcher, dedicated to artificial reality laboratory with projections and cameras for an interactive experience. Boeing researcher Tom Caudell, in 1990, coined the term "augmented reality". The first fully functional AR system was developed in USAF Armstrong's Research Lab by Louis Rosenburg, a researcher, in 1992 for training US Air Force pilots to control and guide machinery. Julie Martin, a writer and producer, in 1994 introduced AR to the theater experience. For the first time, a yellow line marker was overlaid in a live NFL game in 1998 by Sportsvision broadcasts. AR technology was used for better navigation of displayed map data in X-38 spacecraft by NASA in 1999. In ARToolKit, an open-source software library was developed by Hirokazu Kato in 2000. Sportvision developed a Skycam system in 2003 with graphics overlaid in an aerial shot of the field video. Esquire Magazine in 2009

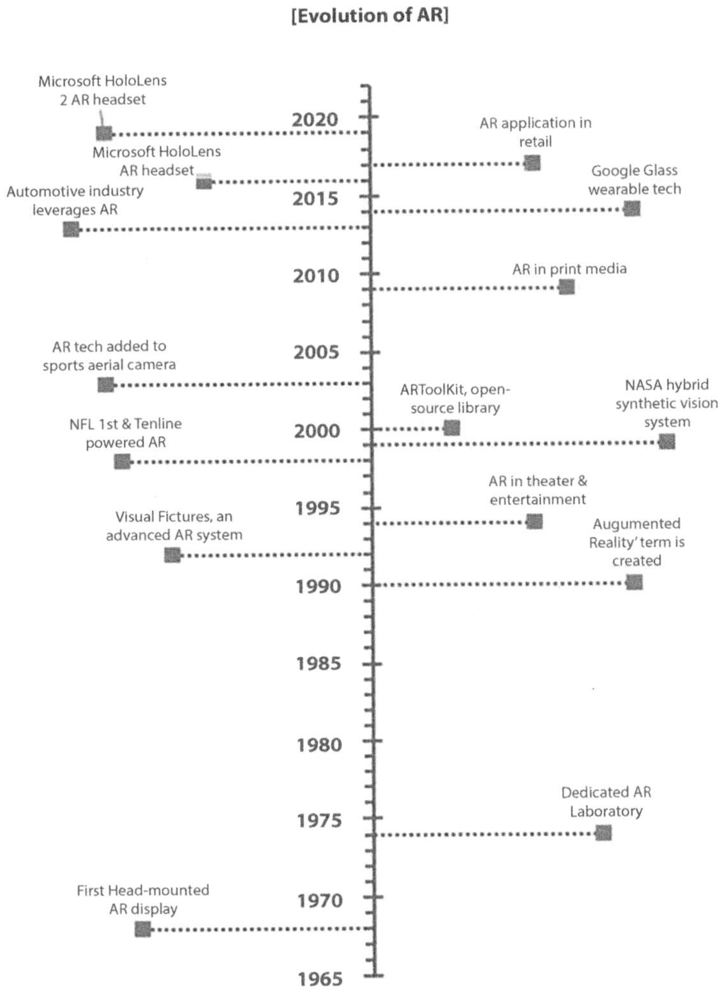

Figure 4.9 Evolution of AR technology.

used AR for print pages to come alive. Volkswagen introduced the Mobile Augmented Reality Technical Assistance in 2013 for repairing vehicles through a step-by-step procedure. Google Glass devices were introduced in 2014, a pair of AR glasses for experiencing augmented reality in applications like Google Maps Search. HoloLens was introduced by Microsoft in 2016 as a wearable AR technology where users scan the environments and create their own AR experiences. IKEA, in 2017, provided an AR app called IKEA Place which virtually previews decors before purchase. In 2019, HoloLens 2 was introduced by Microsoft.

The deep learning neural network model that aids the AR/VR devices for household applications was proposed in [21] and validated on benchmark data sets. The building information modeling based on AR/VR technology that helps the construction companies was outlined in [22]. The coupling of AR/VR technology with the brain–computer interface was described in [23] that aids the physicians for treatment planning and diagnosis. A detailed analysis was carried out on [24] focusing on the applications of AR/VR in healthcare, games, and retail marketing. In [25], the authors discussed the importance of AR/VR in anatomical education. The teaching potential of AR was found to be proficient and improved the learning skills of students. The study [26] speculates how AR is presently being used to improve historical and holocaust teaching and indicates that AR reforms the way that specific subjects are taught, along with being gifted to bring novel practices or rejuvenate ancient ones at heritage sites, museums, and other areas of historical value. The history of VR is depicted in Figure 4.10.

The Sensorama theater was invented by Morton Heilig, a cinematographer, in 1957, which provides interactive experience that stimulated the users with immersive multisensory technology. Philco Corporation engineers Comeau and Bryan invented the motion tracking HMD called the Headsight in 1962. It allows users to experience the surrounding without actually going there. Thomas Furness, a military engineer, invented the first flight simulator in 1966 with VR technology, used for training purposes for the Air Force. Ivan Sutherland had the first VR/AR head-mounted display invented in 1968. The Aspen Movie Map was developed by MIT in 1978 for a "Surrogate Travel" experience from the photographs taken from a car. The movie Tron in 1982 brought the concept of VR to the people. Furness developed Visually Coupled Airborne Systems Simulator (VCASS), a Super Cockpit program that helps pilots to make better decisions with technology in 1986 for Air Force simulation projects.

The "virtual reality" term was coined by the computer scientist John Lanier in 1987 and developed Visual Programming Lab (VPL), VR gear, EyePhone HMD, and the first VR goggles. The Virtuality Group released a series of arcade game machines in VR goggles to the general public in 1991. Sega VR headset was released by Sega in 1991. Nintendo Virtual Boy introduced the first portable console that could display 3D graphics in 1995. Georgia Tech and Emory University researchers created Virtual Vietnam in 1997 to help veterans in therapy sessions for treating post-traumatic stress disorder. In 1999, The Matrix, released in theaters, popularizes virtual reality among people. SAS cube is a PC-based cubic room that was introduced in 2001, which led to Virtools VRPack. Google maps Street View Google was announced in 2007 with immersive media which

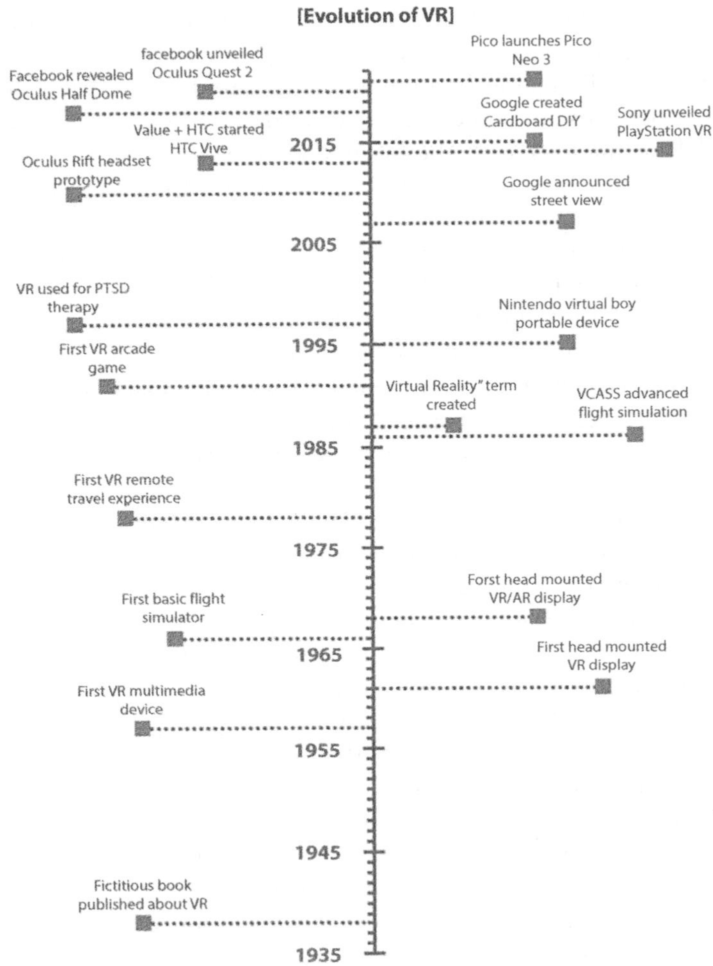

Figure 4.10 Evolution of VR technology.

gives VR experience of streets with panoramic images captured by a camera mounted on a moving car. Palmer Luckey in 2010 designed a prototype, the Oculus Rift virtual reality headset. Valve corporation shared VR content Oculus and other vendors in 2013 to reach all communities. Sony introduced PlayStation VR in 2014, gaming console PlayStation 4. Google developed Cardboard in 2015, designed to be worn on the head with a phone for stereoscopic viewing. Facebook announced Oculus Half Dome for viewing 140° of VR experience in 2018.

Another work [27] examines the effect of AR and VR on the abstract writing of EFL students and gives the results that the integration of real and unreal worlds might be a good asset in teaching. The paper [38] highlights that AR and VR applications enable scholars to explore learning content in a new and exciting way and concludes that mixed reality lets students interact and learn in surroundings beyond their physical reach. This literature [40, 42, 43] review identifies the importance of AR in education, the influence of this technology on education processes, open questions as well as likelihoods and challenges for designers and experts. The consequences specify that the rewards of AR systems in education are "learning gains" and "motivation"; AR has an average result on learning effectiveness that may be reaching maturity. The systematic study [28] reviews the progress of applications in AR with a medicinal use case into 5 years. The paper concludes a growing inclination in the number of literatures on AR in medication and domains using display technologies. The study [31] describes current applications of AR in diverse arenas of dentistry and maxillofacial operation. Another study [41, 44] provides the outline of the works on the application of VR/AR in oral and maxillofacial operation by producing a simulated atmosphere of the clinical process. Virtual arrangement enhanced the correctness of implanting dental transplants using any figure guidance or lively navigation. The article [29, 30] examines the role of AR in industrial manufacturing. The item advocates that VR is extra-immersive and appealing over the machinery of 3D presence and AR seems to be an extra-active medium for assigning auditory evidence. The study [37] investigated the manufacturing industry, automotive sector, and railway sector based upon brainstorming sessions and evaluations as to what are the factors that are limiting AR in the industrial market. This work [32] proposes a 3D olden structure typically used by Samsung Note 5 smartphones as well as VR INSTANCE spectacles to construct a visualized reminiscence rehabilitation (inspires aging persons to recall enjoyable actions) system and delivers not only recollection as entertaining but it may also assist in dementia anticipation for well and sub-healthy (midway phase amid well-being and illness) aging people. The work [33] assesses the therapeutic uses and effectiveness of mixed reality and video games for emotion regulation and stress management. In [36], a circumstantial context and an appraisal context of mixed realism technologies to endorse welfare in elder adults on the physical, emotional, and psychological well-being characteristics are highlighted.

The work [34] presents a holographical 3D head-mounted display appropriate for spectators with diverse pupillary remoteness built on 4K-spatial light modulators (SLMs). The work [35] designs a low-cost clever glove, which can be used for gesture chasing in actual time interaction with a simulated mechanical arm in a PC that enables the scholars to advance their plans on AR and VR. The paper [39] explores the applications of AR/

VR in the business environment, focusing on the management of human resources, virtual business meetings, and presentations.

The study [45] provided a critical review and generic classification comprising of VR/AR knowledge features, application fields, security situations, and assessment approaches to better realize the state-of-the-art of VR/AR claims in building safety (VR/AR-CS). The paper [54] presents an approach named instinctive self-examination methods using AR for building renovation and preservation of energy-effective constructions. The article was about using mixed reality (MR) for electrical construction design communication [63] to study MR's effect on the yield and superiority of electrical channel creation. The systematic literature review [46] steered on 74 AR application-related documents from 2012 to 2017 aimed to identify authoring (A), context awareness (CA), and interaction analysis (IA) relationships over an examination of advanced methods in the background of maintenance applications. It revealed the potential of AR to categorize AR conservation claims by technical willingness stages.

The paper [47] discussed a study of an innovative drill means for Le Fort I osteotomy built on immersive virtual reality (iVR) to test the validity and usefulness of VR operation for clinical exercise. Several mentor verbal and maxillofacial doctors who assessed the claim for face and contented soundness commented on the established training device, its practicality, serviceability, and the pertinence of VR operation for orthognathic clinical exercise. The proposed work [50] established a ground-breaking medicinal exercise simulator on the Oculus Gear-VR platform and scrutinized for the sign of soundness within this proof-of-concept VR claim while obtaining expressive criticism relating to the technology among the medicinal occupation. The study [60] analyzed the abilities of VR and AR environments for claustrophobia (nervousness illness) treatments using heart rate variability (HRV) and anxiety questionnaires.

The work [48] employs AR in searching physical boundary collections of a library so that consumers are provided with a new means to involve resources and the library staff. The AR-based outreach would serve as comfortable progress both for library technology and marketing. The quantifiable investigational study [49] uses applied fairness theory to inspect how AR value and workers' control of admittance to their private data influence user gratification in online shopping, entertaining facilities, and elementary facility upkeep settings. The research [51] developed an AR-based mobile application to investigate the application of AR to advance alertness on green ingesting of electronic strategies being used at households and workplaces. The paper examined key study enquiries relating to technology reception, knowledge improvements, and related blocks to acceptance.

The research [52] is to test a proof of concept for computer-aided design (CAD) in VR and to identify the best set of features for VR modeling and practices in this new domain.

The paper [53] planned and established a context-based AR system named ARGeo which is a supplementing device for the geologist's information gathering to be used in isolated locations. It offers the conception of a fully 3D-simulated topography that can be used to integrate geotagged simulated elements. ARGeo logically mixes mobile strategies and AR to the geologists' research and its potential to other Earth Science-related fields. The work [55] developed an innovative mobile augmented reality (MAR) application to match current flood hazard management (FRM) tools, intended to evaluate the potential usefulness of it through conducting a small user study in preparation, plan, and ecological management. The paper [56] proposes a self-powered VR-based triboelectric 3D-control sensor, a novel self-powered system by the connection of interaction electrification and electrostatic initiation which displays excessive latency for battery-less AR interface, automation, and energy-redeemable claims.

The paper [57] puts forward AR-based filmic direction for facility organization tasks and examined the usability of AR as a tool to provision aligning tasks in the architecture, engineering, construction, and facility management (AEC/FM) manufacturing. The research paper [58] aimed to study an appropriate application of AR in agriculture. It presents a novel approach, how to use a drone for soil map color image gaining, involuntary segmentation, and sampling point choice. The wearable AR technology guides the user/planter to gather the trials representing organization regions for precision farming purposes. The present study [59] meant to discover whether the interpretation recital on VR and AR is diverse from that on old LCD/desktop display, and the alteration is 10% more time in reading than using the classical displays for answering multiple choice questions. VR's role in tourism was investigated in [61], and responses were collected from tourists with respect to the usage of VR in thematic analysis. The work [62] aims to investigate which methods and user valuation approaches are most commonly used in motor rehabilitation studies that use AR applications. The work [64] examined what consumer–brand relationships can be facilitated through AR for the mobile shopping experience.

A detailed discussion on AR and VR in construction problems in industry was carried out in the paper [65]. AR is used for problem-solving in scheduling and project progress tracking, communication for networking, data attainment and fault supervision, and time and cost management. Subsequently, VR is used in employee training, structure safety management, defect and quality management, and visualization. The paper concludes that AR and VR are beneficial, and an automatic system for faults administration in building construction project development was highlighted. The paper [68] presents an AR/VR-based IoT model scheme that can be used for the accomplishment of upkeep tasks in a compound atmosphere to recover protection, preserve readiness, and lessen mistakes, reducing the time desirable for scheduled or unplanned involvements. The paper [72] presents an outline of earlier and current research and application aspects of using AR knowledge in the tourism domain while recognizing and classifying key issues having the most important influence on the positive use of such applications.

The paper [75] gives an overview of VRGIS (applications of virtual reality GIS) and ARGIS (applications of augmented reality GIS) solutions for tackling urban and environmental planning, smart cities, physical activity, emergency training, and civic health difficulties. The work [73] proposes an AR-aided smart window for cyber-physical machine tool (CPMT), inspired by cyber-physical systems (CPS) integrating physical mechanism tool and machining procedures with computation and computer networking capabilities. The proposed system is a cutting-edge human–machine interface (HMI) that offers users instinctive connections with CPMT. The literature evaluating the Microsoft HoloLens over an AR assembly application [74] argues that it is a feasible stage to bring an application that gives assembly instructions, providing an opportunity to explore a hands-free head-mounted display's (HMD's) ability and what a user interface looks like for such an application. The work [78] performed a detailed investigation and analysis of studies in the field of visualization using a combination of high determination spherical landscapes, a variety of charts, video, sound, GNSS, and text data for Bulgarian country social tradition. The paper [81] recommends a sensor fusion based on the fly motion tracking for mobile AR/VR utilizing high-frequency and passive systems and yields from the inertial sensor proficient of providing a smooth and vigorous 6-DoF gesture tracking.

The work [66] proposes a portable hand haptic system (Arduino-based sensor architecture) with Leap Motion as a haptic interface that is used in numerous VR requests for testing the immersion and features of the planned system. The planned system offers an advanced presence and greater involvement that anyone can use to easily deliver a variety of tangible reactions at a low cost. The literature [67] deliberate on the design and execution of an AR-based motion-sensing teaching software that explains magnetic fields in secondary physics education. This study delivers an instance for the application of AR technology that discovers the properties of using natural interaction on students' physics education and the profound understanding associated with old-style learning tools. The study [71] analyzes the main profits and barriers to teachers' acceptance of using AR applications in an e-learning environment in primary schools. The results indicated that there is a readiness to use and a high receiving rate toward AR from primary school teachers' provision of a suitable ICT infrastructure. Another work [76] that explores a 3D geospatial urban environment with VR characterizes an influential location-based tool for teaching in the field of 3D knowledge which advances the inspiration of students in activities related to navigation and wayfinding. In [79], the skills of diverse computational software for scheming VR utilities in engineering teaching was highlighted. The work [80] explores the reality convert software device developed in Python and associated websites, which permit users to easily convert chemical structures/biomolecular objects (pdb and sdf files) to high-quality 3D representations directly that is well-suited for AR/VR applications. The paper [83] studies an evaluation between the effect of the VR-based knowledge environment and AR-based learning environment in a review-based astronomy course; the results reveal that adaption of 2D image-based VR and AR could decrease the psychological load of the students.

The authors in [69] explore present and forthcoming medical applications of AR for the evaluation of breast cancer. It discusses advances in inspecting methods with surface interpretation, volume interpretation, and depth-3-dimensional (D3D) imaging leveraging for both AR and VR imaging competencies. The paper concludes that adapting AR technology may augment diagnosis, save cost, and advance patient care. The authors in [70] propose an AR-based new telepresence application implemented using Microsoft HoloLens to ease and improve remote medical training, which allows distant learners to perform complex medical procedures such as point of care ultrasound (PoCUS) without pictorial interference. The study [77] highlights home-based VR-augmented neuro-rehabilitation drill, joining action remark, execution and providing rigorous, repetitive, and inspiring training situations that led to enhancements in lower limb muscle strength and motor function following chronic incomplete spinal cord injury. The authors in achieved a systematic assessment that inspects the current research on simulated, varied, or enlarged reality-based simulators in spinal surgery procedures. The results revealed that virtual reality-based simulator training has outdone other approaches regarding various outcomes. The work [82] explores the new connection of VR technology and aging with importance on both its use for physical health purposes as well as for societal engagement.

4.3 Conclusion

This chapter is an introduction part of AR/VR and its applications. Artificial intelligence has immense applications in many sectors, the incorporation of artificial intelligence improves the AR/VR technology experience, and especially the replacement of traditional computer vision approaches by deep learning techniques maximizes efficiency. The concept of AR and VR is first highlighted in this chapter with its components and characteristics. The potential benefits of AR/VR technology in recent years are also highlighted in this work. The subsequent chapters in this book focus on domain-specific applications of AR/VR. Automation is gaining prominence in all sectors, and the AR/VR technologies enable the users to easily understand the concepts and plan, monitor the activities, and detect fault and clearance. The AR/VR technology is a boon for children and disabled and elderly people in improving their living standards.

Acknowledgment

The author SN Kumar would like to acknowledge the support from the Schmitt Centre for Biomedical Instrumentation for supporting this research work.

References

1. Sahu, C.K., Young, C., Rai, R., Artificial intelligence (AI) in augmented reality (AR)-assisted manufacturing applications: a review. *Int. J. Prod. Res.*, 59, 16, 4903–59, 2021 Aug 18.
2. Özgen, D.S., Afacan, Y., Sürer, E., Usability of virtual reality for basic design education: a comparative study with paper-based design. *Int. J. Technol. Des. Educ.*, 31, 2, 357–77, 2021 Apr.
3. Yahya, M.A. and Dahanayake, A., A Needs-Based Augmented Reality System. *Appl. Sci.*, 11, 17, 7978, 2021 Jan.
4. Logan, D.E., Simons, L.E., Caruso, T.J., Gold, J.I., Greenleaf, W., Griffin, A., King, C.D., Menendez, M., Olbrecht, V.A., Rodriguez, S., Silvia, M., Leveraging Virtual Reality and Augmented Reality to Combat Chronic Pain in Youth: Position Paper From the Interdisciplinary Network on Virtual and Augmented Technologies for Pain Management. *J. Med. Internet Res.*, 23, 4, e25916, 2021 Apr 26.
5. Siriwardhana, Y., Porambage, P., Liyanage, M., Ylianttila, M., A Survey on Mobile Augmented Reality With 5G Mobile Edge Computing: Architectures,

Applications, and Technical Aspects. *IEEE Commun. Surv. Tutor.*, 23, 2, 1160–92, 2021 Feb 25.

6. Kourtesis, P., Collina, S., Doumas, L.A., MacPherson, S.E., Validation of the Virtual Reality Everyday Assessment Lab (VR-EAL): an immersive virtual reality neuropsychological battery with enhanced ecological validity. *J. Int. Neuropsychol. Soc.*, 27, 2, 181–96, 2021 Feb.
7. Zhan, T., Yin, K., Xiong, J., He, Z., Wu, S.T., Augmented reality and virtual reality displays: Perspectives and challenges. *Iscience*, 22, 101397, 2020 Jul.
8. Ashtari, N., Bunt, A., McGrenere, J., Nebeling, M., Chilana, P.K., Creating augmented and virtual reality applications: Current practices, challenges, and opportunities, in: *Proceedings of the 2020 CHI Conference on Human Factors in Computing Systems*, 2020 Apr 21, pp. 1–13.
9. Hilty, D.M., Randhawa, K., Maheu, M.M., McKean, A.J., Pantera, R., Mishkind, M.C., Rizzo, A., A review of telepresence, virtual reality, and augmented reality applied to clinical care. *J. Technol. Behav. Sci.*, 5, 2, 178–205, 2020 Jun.
10. Pidel, C. and Ackermann, P., Collaboration in virtual and augmented reality: a systematic overview, in: *International Conference on Augmented Reality, Virtual Reality and Computer Graphics*, 2020 Sep 7, Springer, Cham, pp. 141–156.
11. Bogusevschi, D., Muntean, C., Muntean, G.M., Teaching and learning physics using 3D virtual learning environment: A case study of combined virtual reality and virtual laboratory in secondary school. *J. Comput. Math. Sci. Teach.*, 39, 1, 5–18, 2020 Jan.
12. Trunfio, M., Lucia, M.D., Campana, S., Magnelli, A., Innovating the cultural heritage museum service model through virtual reality and augmented reality: the effects on the overall visitor experience and satisfaction. *J. Herit. Tour.*, 19, 1–9, 2020 Dec.
13. Loureiro, S.M., Guerreiro, J., Ali, F., 20 years of research on virtual reality and augmented reality in tourism context: A text-mining approach. *Tour. Manag.*, 77, 104028, 2020 Apr 1.
14. Puggioni, M.P., Frontoni, E., Paolanti, M., Pierdicca, R., Malinverni, E.S., Sasso, M., A content creation tool for AR/VR applications in education: The ScoolAR framework, in: *International conference on augmented reality, virtual reality and computer graphics*, 2020 Sep 7, Springer, Cham, pp. 205–219.
15. Shannigrahi, S., Mastorakis, S., Ortega, F.R., Next-generation networking and edge computing for mixed reality real-time interactive systems, in: *2020 IEEE International Conference on Communications Workshops (ICC Workshops)*, 2020 Jun 7, IEEE, pp. 1–6.
16. Erol-Kantarci, M. and Sukhmani, S., Caching and computing at the edge for mobile augmented reality and virtual reality (AR/VR) in 5G, in: *Ad Hoc Netw.*, pp. 169–77, 2018.
17. Burova, A., Mäkelä, J., Hakulinen, J., Keskinen, T., Heinonen, H., Siltanen, S., Turunen, M., Utilizing VR and gaze tracking to develop AR solutions

for industrial maintenance, in: *Proceedings of the 2020 CHI Conference on Human Factors in Computing Systems*, pp. 1–13, 2020 Apr 21.

18. Pierdicca, R., Frontoni, E., Puggioni, M.P., Malinverni, E.S., Paolanti, M., Evaluating augmented and virtual reality in education through a user-centered comparative study: SmartMarca project, in: *Virtual and Augmented Reality in Education, Art, and Museums*, pp. 229–261, IGI Global, Hershey, PA, USA, 2020.
19. Petrović, N., Augmented and Virtual Reality Web Applications for Music Stage Performance, in: *2020 55th International Scientific Conference on Information, Communication and Energy Systems and Technologies (ICEST)*, IEEE, pp. 33–36, 2020 Sep 10.
20. Krogfoss, B., Duran, J., Perez, P., Bouwen, J., Quantifying the Value of 5G and Edge Cloud on QoE for AR/VR, in: *2020 Twelfth International Conference on Quality of Multimedia Experience (QoMEX)*, IEEE, pp. 1–4, 2020 May 26.
21. Zehtabian, S., Razghandi, M., Bölöni, L., Turgut, D., Predictive caching for AR/VR experiences in a household scenario, in: *2020 International Conference on Computing, Networking and Communications (ICNC)*, IEEE, pp. 591–595.
22. Assila, A., Beladjine, D., Messaadia, M., Towards AR/VR Maturity Model Adapted to the Building Information Modeling, in: *IFIP International Conference on Product Lifecycle Management*, pp. 753–765, Springer, Cham, 2020 Jul 5.
23. Putze, F., Vourvopoulos, A., Lécuyer, A., Krusienski, D., Bermúdez i Badia, S., Mullen, T., Herff, C., Brain-computer interfaces and augmented/virtual reality. *Front. Hum. Neurosci.*, 14, 144, 2020 May 12.
24. Parekh, P., Patel, S., Patel, N., Shah, M., Systematic review and meta-analysis of augmented reality in medicine, retail, and games. *Vis. Comput. Ind. Biomed. Art*, 3, 1, 1–20, 2020 Dec.
25. Chytas, D., Johnson, E.O., Piagkou, M., Mazarakis, A., Babis, G.C., Chronopoulos, E., Nikolaou, V.S., Lazaridis, N., Natsis, K., The role of augmented reality in anatomical education: an overview. *Ann. Anat.-Anat. Anz.*, 229, 151463, 2020 May 1.
26. Challenor, J. and Ma, M., A Review of Augmented Reality Applications for History Education and Heritage Visualisation. *Multimodal Technol. Interact.*, 3, 39, 2019, https://doi.org/10.3390/mti3020039.
27. Soleimani, H., *et al.*, Augmented Reality and Virtual Reality Scaffoldings in Improving the Abstract Genre Structure in a Collaborative Learning Environment: A CALL Study. *J. Engl. Lang. Teach. Learn.*, 11, 327–356, 2019.
28. Eckert, M., Volmerg, J.S., Friedrich, C.M., Augmented Reality in Medicine: Systematic and Bibliographic Review. *JMIR Mhealth Uhealth*, 7, 4, 1–17, 2019, doi: 10.2196/10967.
29. Bottani, E. and Vignali, G., Augmented reality technology in the manufacturing industry: A review of the last decade. *IISE Trans.*, 51, 3, 284–310, 2019, Taylor & Francis, doi:10.1080/24725854.2018.1493244.

30. Huang, K.-T., Ball, C., Francis, J., Ratan, R., Boumis, J., Fordham, J., Augmented Versus Virtual Reality in Education:An Exploratory Study Examining Science Knowledge Retention When Using Augmented Reality/ Virtual Reality Mobile Applications. *Cyberpsychol. Behav. Soc. Netw.*, 22, 2, 105–110, Feb 2019, http://doi.org/10.1089/cyber.2018.0150.
31. Farronato, M., Maspero, C., Lanteri, V., *et al.*, Current state of the art in the use of augmented reality in dentistry: a systematic review of the literature. *BMC Oral Health*, 19, 135, 2019, https://doi.org/10.1186/s12903-019-0808-3.
32. Tsao, Y.-C., Shu, C.-C., Lan, T.-S., Development of a Reminiscence Therapy System for the Elderly Using the Integration of Virtual Reality and Augmented Reality. *Sustainability*, 11, 4792, 2019, https://doi.org/10.3390/su11174792.
33. Pallavicini, F. and Bouchard, S., Editorial: Assessing the Therapeutic Uses and Effectiveness of Virtual Reality, Augmented Reality and Video Games for Emotion Regulation and Stress Management. *Front. Psychol.*, 10, 2763, 2019, DOI:10.3389/fpsyg.2019.02763.
34. Gao, H., Xu, F., Liu, J., Dai, Z., Zhou, W., Li, S., Yu, Y., Zheng, H., Holographic Three-Dimensional Virtual Reality and Augmented Reality Display Based on 4K-Spatial Light Modulators. *Appl. Sci.*, 9, 1182, 2019, https://doi.org/10.3390/app9061182.
35. Minh, V., Katushin, N., Pumwa, J., Motion tracking glove for augmented reality and virtual reality. *Paladyn J. Behav. Rob.*, 10, 160–166, 2019, 10.1515/pjbr-2019-0012.
36. Lee, L.N., Kim, M.J., Hwang, W.J., Potential of Augmented Reality and Virtual Reality Technologies to Promote Wellbeing in Older Adults. *Appl. Sci.*, 9, 3556, 2019, https://doi.org/10.3390/app9173556.
37. Martinetti, A., Marques, H.C., Singh, S., van Dongen, L., Reflections on the Limited Pervasiveness of Augmented Reality in Industrial Sectors. *Appl. Sci.*, 9, 3382, 2019, https://doi.org/10.3390/app9163382.
38. Siegle, D., Seeing Is Believing: Using Virtual and Augmented Reality to Enhance Student Learning. *Gift. Child Today*, 42, 1, 46–52, 2018, https://doi.org/10.1177/1076217518804854.
39. Zhao, H., Zhao, Q.H., Ślusarczyk, B., Sustainability and Digitalization of Corporate Management Based on Augmented/Virtual Reality Tools Usage: China and Other World IT Companies' Experience. *Sustainability*, 11, 4717, 2019, https://doi.org/10.3390/su11174717.
40. Garzón, J., Pavón, J., Baldiris, S., Systematic review and meta-analysis of augmented reality in educational settings. *Virtual Reality*, 23, 447–459, 2019, https://doi.org/10.1007/s10055-019-00379-9.
41. Ayoub, A. and Pulijala, Y., The application of virtual reality and augmented reality in Oral & Maxillofacial Surgery. *BMC Oral Health*, 19, 238, 2019, https://doi.org/10.1186/s12903-019-0937-8.
42. Khan, T., Johnston, K., Ophoff, J., The Impact of an Augmented Reality Application on Learning Motivation of Students. *Adv. Hum. Comput. Interact.*, 2019, 1–14, 2019, 10.1155/2019/7208494.

43. Elmqaddem, N., Augmented Reality and Virtual Reality in Education. Myth or Reality? *Int. J. Emerg. Technol. Learn. (iJET)*, 14, 234, 2019, 10.3991/ijet.v14i03.9289.
44. Yokoyama, I., Sarai, T., Asai, T., Kitou, N., Nozaki, H., Kondo, Y., Nomura, Y., Morizane, A., Sekikawa, M., Liu, D., Virtual reality and augmented reality applications and simulation in vascular access management with three-dimensional visualization. *J. Vasc. Access*, 20, 1S, 65–70, 2019, https://doi.org/10.1177/1129729818776904.
45. Li, X., Yi, W., Chia, H.-L., Wang, X., Chan, A.P.C., A critical review of virtual and augmented reality (VR/AR) applications in construction safety. *Autom. Constr.*, 86, 150–162, February 2018, https://doi.org/10.1016/j.autcon.2017.11.003.
46. del Amo, I.F., Erkoyuncu, J.A., Roy, R., Palmarini, R., Onoufriou, D., A systematic review of Augmented Reality content-related techniques for knowledge transfer in maintenance applications. *Comput. Ind.*, 103, 47–71, 2018, ORCID: 0000-0001-5491-7437, doi: 10.1016/j.compind.2018.08.007.
47. Pulijala, Y., Ma, M., Pears, M., Peebles, D., Ayoub, A., An innovative virtual reality training tool for orthognathic surgery. *Int. J. Oral Maxillofac. Surg.*, 47, 9, 1199–1205, 2018, https://doi.org/10.1016/j.ijom.2018.01.005.
48. Lund, B.D. and Agbaji, D.A., Augmented Reality for Browsing Physical Collections in Academic Libraries. *Public Serv. Q.*, 14, 3, 275–282, 2018, DOI :10.1080/15228959.2018.1487812.
49. Poushneh, A., Augmented reality in retail: A trade-off between user's control of access to personal information and augmentation quality. *J. Retail. Consum. Serv.*, 41, 169–176, 2018, https://doi.org/10.1016/j.jretconser.2017.12.010.
50. Harrington, C.M., Kavanagh, D.O., Quinlan, J.F., O'Keeffe, D., Traynor, O., Tierney, S., Development and evaluation of a trauma decision-making simulator in Oculus virtual reality. *Am. J. Surg.*, 215, 1, 42–47, JANUARY 01, 2018, DOI: https://doi.org/10.1016/j.amjsurg.2017.02.011.
51. Bekaroo, G., Sungkur, R., Ramsamy, P., Okolo, A., Moedeen, W., Enhancing awareness on green consumption of electronic devices: the application of Augmented Reality. *Sustain. Energy Technol. Assess.*, 30, 279–291, 2018, ISSN 2213-1388, doi:10.1016/j.seta.2018.10.016.
52. Feeman, S.M., Wright, L.B., Salmon, J.L., Exploration and evaluation of CAD modeling in virtual reality. *Comput.-Aided Des. Appl.*, 15, 6, 892–904, 2018, https://doi.org/10.1080/16864360.2018.1462570.
53. Gazcón, N.F., Trippel Nagel, J.M., Bjerg, E.A., Castro, S.M., Fieldwork in Geosciences assisted by ARGeo: A mobile Augmented Reality system. *Comput. Geosci.*, 121, 30–38, 2018. https://doi.org/10.1016/j.cageo.2018.09.004.10.
54. Riexingera, G., Klutha, A., Olbrichb, M., Braunc, J.-D., Bauernhansla, T., Mixed Reality for On-Site Self-Instruction and Self-Inspection with Building Information Models. *51st CIRP Conference on Manufacturing Systems*, Procedia CIRP, vol. 72, pp. 1124–1129, 2018.

55. Haynes, P., Hehl-Lange, S., Lange, E., Mobile Augmented Reality for Flood Visualisation. *Environ. Modell. Softw.*, 109, 380–389, 2018, https://doi.org/10.1016/j.envsoft.2018.05.012.
56. Chen, T., Zhao, M., Shi, Q., Yang, Z., Liu, H., Sun, L., Ouyang, J., Lee, C., Novel augmented reality interface using a self-powered triboelectric based virtual reality 3D-control sensor. *Nano Energy*, 51, 162–172, 2018, https://doi.org/10.1016/j.nanoen.2018.06.022.
57. Liu, F. and Seipel, S., Precision study on augmented reality-based visual guidance for facility management tasks. *Autom. Constr.*, 90, 79–90, 2018, https://doi.org/10.1016/j.autcon.2018.02.020.
58. Huuskonen, J. and Oksanen, T., Soil sampling with drones and augmented reality in precision agriculture. *Comput. Electron. Agric.*, 154, 25–35, 2018, https://doi.org/10.1016/j.compag.2018.08.039.
59. Patrick Rau, P.-L., Zheng, J., Guo, Z., Li, J., Speed reading on virtual reality and augmented reality. *Comput. Educ.*, 125, 240–245, 2018, https://doi.org/10.1016/j.compedu.2018.06.016.
60. Tsai, C.-F., Yeh, S.-C., Huang, Y., Wu, Z., Cui, J., Zheng, L., The Effect of Augmented Reality and Virtual Reality on Inducing Anxiety for Exposure Therapy: A Comparison Using Heart Rate Variability. *Hindawi-J. Healthcare Eng.*, 1–8, 2018. https://doi.org/10.1155/2018/6357351.
61. Tom Dieck, D., Dieck, M.C., Moorhouse, N., Jung, T., Tourists' Virtual Reality Adoption: An Exploratory Study from Lake District National Park. *Leis. Stud.*, 37, 4, 317–383, 2018. DOI: https://doi.org/10.1080/02614367.2018.1466905.
62. Cavalcanti, V.C., de Santana, M.I., Da Gama, A.E.F., Correia, W.F.M., Usability Assessments for Augmented Reality Motor Rehabilitation Solutions: A Systematic Review. *Int. J. Comput. Games Technol.*, 2018, Article ID 5387896, 18, 2018, https://doi.org/10.1155/2018/5387896.
63. Chalhoub, J. and Ayer, S.K., Using Mixed Reality for electrical construction design communication. *Autom. Constr.*, 86, 1–10, 2018, https://doi.org/10.1016/j.autcon.2017.10.028.
64. Scholz, J. and Duffy, K., We ARe at home: how augmented reality reshapes mobile marketing and consumer-brand relationships. *J. Retail. Consum. Serv.*, 44, 11–23, 2018, doi:10.1016/j.jretconser.2018.05.004.
65. Ahmed, S., Mehrab Hossain, Md., Ikramul Hoque, Md., A Brief Discussion on Augmented Reality and Virtual Reality in Construction Industry. *J. Syst. Manag. Sci.*, 7, 3, 1–33, 2017.
66. Kim, M., Jeon, C., Kim, J., A Study on Immersion and Presence of a Portable Hand Haptic System for Immersive Virtual Reality. *Sensors*, 17, 1141, 2017, doi: 10.3390/s17051141.
67. Cai, S., Chiang, F.-K., Sun, Y., Lin, C., Lee, J.J., Applications of augmented reality-based natural interactive learning in magnetic field instruction. *Interact. Learn. Environ.*, 25, 6, 778–791, 2017, DOI: 10.1080/10494820.2016.1181094.

68. Fasiul Alama, M., Katsikasb, S., Beltramelloc, O., Hadjiefthymiadesa, S., Augmented and virtual reality based monitoring and safety system: A prototype IoT platform. *J. Network Comput. Appl.*, 89, 109–119, 2017, http://dx.doi.org/10.1016/j.jnca.2017.03.022.
69. Douglas, D.B., Wilke, C.A., David Gibson, J., Boone, J.M., Wintermark, M., Augmented Reality: Advances in Diagnostic Imaging. *Multimodal Technol. Interact.*, 1, 29, 2017, doi: 10.3390/mti1040029.
70. Wang, S., Parsons, M., Stone-McLean, J., Rogers, P., Boyd, S., Hoover, K., Meruvia-Pastor, O., Gong, M., Smith, A., Augmented Reality as a Telemedicine Platform for Remote Procedural Training. *Sensors*, 17, 2294, 2017, doi: 10.3390/s17102294.
71. Alkhattabi, M., Augmented Reality as E-learning Tool in Primary Schools' Education: Barriers to Teachers' Adoption. *Int. J. Emerg. Technol. Learn. (iJET)*, 12, 2, 91–100, 2017, https://doi.org/10.3991/ijet.v12i02.6158.
72. Kečkeš, A.L. and Tomičić, I., Augmented Reality in Tourism–Research and Applications Overview. *Interdiscip. Descr. Complex Syst.*, 15, 2, 157–167, 2017, DOI: 10.7906/indecs.15.2.5.
73. Liu, C., Cao, S., Tse, W., Xu, X., Augmented Reality-assisted Intelligent Window for Cyber-Physical Machine Tools,45th SME North American Manufacturing Research Conference, NAMRC 45, LA, USA. *J. Manuf. Syst.*, 44, 280–286, 2017.
74. Evans, G., Miller, J., Iglesias Pena, M., MacAllister, A., Winer, E., Evaluating the Microsoft HoloLens through an augmented reality assembly application. *Proc. SPIE 10197, Degraded Environments: Sensing, Processing, and Display 2017*, vol. 101970V, 5 May 2017, https://doi.org/10.1117/12.2262626.
75. Kamel Boulos, M.N., Lu, Z., Guerrero, P., *et al.*, From urban planning and emergency training to Pokémon Go: applications of virtual reality GIS (VRGIS) and augmented reality GIS (ARGIS) in personal, public and environmental health. *Int. J. Health Geogr.*, 16, 7, 2017, https://doi.org/10.1186/s12942-017-0081-0.
76. Carbonell-Carrera, C. and Saorín, J.L., Geospatial Google Street View with Virtual Reality: A Motivational Approach for Spatial Training Education. *ISPRS Int. J. Geo-Inf.*, 6, 9, 261, 2017, https://doi.org/10.3390/ijgi6090261.
77. Villiger, M., Liviero, J., Awai, L., Stoop, R., Pyk, P., Clijsen, R., Curt, A., Eng, K., Bolliger, M., Home-Based Virtual Reality-Augmented Training Improves Lower Limb Muscle Strength, Balance, and Functional Mobility following Chronic Incomplete Spinal Cord Injury. *Front. Neurol.*, 8, 635, 2017, doi: 10.3389/fneur.2017.00635.
78. Koeva, M., Luleva, M., Maldjanski, P., Integrating Spherical Panoramas and Maps for Visualization of Cultural Heritage Objects Using Virtual Reality Technology. *Sensors*, 17, 4, 829, 2017, https://doi.org/10.3390/s17040829.
79. Vergara, D., Rubio, M.P., Lorenzo, M., On the Design of Virtual Reality Learning Environments in Engineering. *Multimodal Technol. Interact.*, 1, 2, 11, 2017, https://doi.org/10.3390/mti1020011.

80. Borrel, A. and Fourches, D., RealityConvert: a tool for preparing 3D models of biochemical structures for augmented and virtual reality. *Bioinformatics*, 33, 23, 3816–3818, 01 December 2017, https://doi.org/10.1093/bioinformatics/btx485.
81. Fang, W., Zheng, L., Deng, H., Zhang, H., Real-Time Motion Tracking for Mobile Augmented/Virtual Reality Using Adaptive Visual-Inertial Fusion. *Sensors*, 17, 5, 1037, 2017, https://doi.org/10.3390/s17051037.
82. Hughes, S., Warren-Norton, K., Spadafora, P., Tsotsos, L.E., Supporting Optimal Aging through the Innovative Use of Virtual Reality Technology. *Multimodal Technol. Interact.*, 1, 4, 23, 2017, https://doi.org/10.3390/mti1040023.
83. Liou, H.-H., Yang, S.J.H., Chen, S.Y., Tarng, W., The Influences of the 2D Image-Based Augmented Reality and Virtual Reality on Student Learning. *Educ. Technol. Soc.*, 20, 3, 110–121, 2017.

5

Augmented Reality, Virtual Reality, Mixed Reality: A Comprehensive Description

J. Prakash

Department of Computer Science and Engineering, PSG College of Technology, Tamil Nadu, India

Abstract

Augmented reality (AR) is a widely known technology. Similarly, virtual reality (VR) and mixed reality (MR) are also widely known technologies. There are various possibilities with them. AR, VR, and MR are the XR technologies which are filled with extraordinary capabilities. They are growing at a rapid speed. These XR technologies can efficiently be put into use in different sectors. They can create a positive impact in different sectors with their presence. In fact, they can revolutionize a sector when applied for different applications within a sector. In this chapter, AR, VR, and MR technologies are briefly discussed and described. Along with it, their history, advantages, etc., are also discussed in the chapter.

Keywords: Augmented reality (AR), virtual reality (VR), mixed reality (MR), real environment, virtual objects, extended reality (XR)

5.1 Augmented Reality

5.1.1 Introduction to Augmented Reality

Among the different technologies present, AR is a powerful and growing area of technology [19]. AR is an arising technology [13]. Humans have various types of senses. AR is the technology which has the potential to be applied to various senses such as hearing, smelling, and so on [1]. AR has been introduced to the world many years ago. AR brings various possibilities. It is an

Email: prakashera36@gmail.com

Manisha Vohra (ed.) Introduction to Extended Reality (XR) Technologies, (89–112) © 2025 Scrivener Publishing LLC

emerging technology [6]. AR technology has become very popular, and now it is no longer so difficult to avail of this technology. In fact, it has become a typical part of everyday life [21]. On the basis of the combination of the physical environment and the virtual environment, AR systems are made [28].

AR is known to create an enriched experience for the users. AR capabilities are extraordinary. Its use is not limited to a specific field or industry. It has the ability to be used in numerous fields. For example, consider the entertainment industry, the immersive experiences it can provide the users with helps in increasing the engagement of the users. Another reason for increased engagement is the interactive experience that users get with AR. Similarly, not just the entertainment industry but also other industries can benefit from AR, and in fact, many industries are currently using AR in different ways.

5.1.2 Definition of Augmented Reality

A lot of definitions for AR are already existing. Most of those definitions are defined according to specific use cases. However, all of those definitions agree that any enhancement of real environment done by computer-generated content is what AR refers to.

The authors in [1] define AR systems as having different properties as follows: The first property is that it blends virtual and real in a real environment. The next property is that they are registered in 3D, and the last one is real-time interactiveness.

The correct alignment of real objects and virtual objects is what registration refers to. The delusion that in a real environment virtual objects exist is greatly affected without accurate registration. Registration is one problem which is difficult. The topic of registration is one which is a continuous and ongoing research topic [1].

All these three things can be described in another way, and these properties of AR can also be regarded as its key features. Another way of stating them is as follows: The first is a combination of real objects and virtual objects in a real environment. Next is the alignment of virtual to real objects geometrically in the real world. Last is the interaction with system in real time, the ability to react to inputs from the user.

In AR environment, user presence can be simulated in a nicer manner. Input and output devices concur to do so, which an AR interface consists of [33]. AR, along with having the ability to add objects to a real environment, also has the potential to remove them. Graphic overlays may also be utilized to remove or hide parts of a real environment from a user [55].

AR is having different strengths which are as follows:

- Immersive system: In a real world, the information is directly integrated.
- Information is interpreted on an immediate basis: Messages provided can be easily understood by the user.
- Being able to give a huge amount of knowledge that is also paperless
- Having the scope of system integration with other devices which are computer-aided
- The procedures are faster: While consulting procedural instruction, the operator does not diminish attention from the environment that is real [50].

Mentioned above are some of the different strengths of AR technology. Next, we will discuss the AR components below.

5.1.3 Augmented Reality Components

The important hardware components which are needed for carrying out AR applications and their functions are as follows:

- Computer
- Display device
- Tracking system
- Interaction tools
- Input devices
- Sensors

Computer: The computer has to create virtual content and also manage all devices, and along with all this, the observer's position and virtual content has to be collimated by a computer, and it has to be with respect to the scene, as per the information being received from the tracking system.

Display device: For display device, on the basis of the occupied position with respect to the user and observed object, three different categories exist. These categories are head-mounted display (HMD), which the user wears on the head, the next is hand-held display (HHD), which is like a cell phone or it is like tablet, and the third is spatial displays (SD).

Tracking system: A tracking system is needed to get the position of the user and orientation in space and record it.

Interaction tools: Different interaction tools like wireless devices and touchpads are to be utilized as additional input devices [50].

Input devices: In the case of AR systems, various types of input devices are there [8]. Input devices let users interact with AR systems [51].

Sensors: In tracking mechanisms, they are useful [51].

For combining virtual objects and real images, as per the method of overlaying virtual components on real-world environment, any of the following methodologies can be utilized:

- Video mixing
- Optical combination
- Image projection

Video mixing: A camera obtains digital information, and a computer reworks it. After this, on a monitor, the result is displayed via which a user notices a real scene indirectly.

Optical combination: In the users' visual field, virtual images are projected while the user directly notices the real scene.

Image projection: There is a direct projection of images on the physical objects' surfaces [50].

AR improves the experience of the user: For the software part, Google and Apple are well known and are the two very important players in the market. Via their development platforms, they have interpreted AR for the software part. Their development platforms are ARKit and ARCore. An iOS app development kit is ARKit. A development kit which is for Android apps is ARCore [51].

5.1.4 Getting to Know Augmented Reality

Let us discuss and try to understand and get to know AR briefly. AR technology is very versatile as it can support us in different fields [30]. AR can be well applied in different applications in a way such that its use will bring many benefits [6]. In fields like maintenance, education, design and reconnaissance, etc., AR can be supportive [30]. For applying AR, some of the interesting domains as well as opportunity-filled problem domains are maintenance and repair operations. A lot of interest has been there in using AR for maintenance tasks [43]. Its influence is increasing in applications where it is been applied. For example, in each day of teaching [6], technology like AR can be a game changer in different sectors, specially the sector like education [11]. Learning becomes better with AR. When interactive learning sessions can be held with the help of AR, learning becomes interesting for students. So, basically, when AR is utilized for learning, it makes things easier to understand.

It was found that, lately, there has been a growing interest in creating special kinds of settings in the education sector by utilizing AR [9]. To make the present models of teaching better, various universities are longing for exploiting new methods of visualization, and in this case, AR is a great promising technology [37]. AR will help a user get a better view, i.e., enhanced view of the environment. AR can enhance the view of reality of the user with additional virtual 3D information [41]. By using AR techniques, how a user's interaction takes place with environments that are new to them can be revolutionized [42]. AR can be potentially utilized in different industries. However, prior to its utilization or implementation, it needs to be demonstrated that it is feasible to be utilized and along with it, its suitability should also be validated especially when it comes to the architecture, engineering, and construction (AEC) industries [14]. AR can benefit as a supporting technology in the industrial work. For example, lately, augmented reality smart glasses (ARSG) are the ones which have been found out as an important technology which provides support to shop-floor operators who are performing different tasks. ARSG are eye-level information presenting hands-free devices. They are providing information at the level of the eye exactly where it is required; hence, they become a user interface which is ideal for an industrial operator [16].

In the production area since a long time, AR has been the focus for research having an aim of improvement [32]. An already existing production environment utilizing AR techniques can be superimposed with virtual planning objects [47].

The authors in [49] have described an innovative manual assembly workstation for assisting operators. The described workstation has the ability of assisting and can assist an operator in previously planned assembly operations by a system which brings together a torque/force sensor and an AR environment [49].

In [34], the authors think that there is a possibility of treating various kinds of psychological disorders utilizing AR. For treating a phobia of cockroach, the authors within the treatment of treating this phobia utilized the exposure of AR. Encouraging results were received. According to the authors in [34], the experience they gained in utilizing AR in the treatment of phobias is vital. It shows that AR can be used for the treatment of psychological disorders [34].

AR is very convenient to be utilized. Any person can access this technology. Any person can gain an experience of AR in simple ways even without having any specialized gadgets, which is a great aspect of AR and is advantageous for all its users. For example, with a smartphone, a person can access AR and get to experience the technology. By improving algorithms, AR systems are implemented on smartphones and are not limited to particular wearable devices [51].

Different types of AR applications (apps) are built for users. One of the most famous AR-based apps is a game called Pokemon Go. Users can easily play this game. Until today, a very large number of users have played and enjoyed this AR-based game on their smartphone. There are even specialized AR-based gadgets available for different applications. For specific work purposes, different gadgets are designed. A perfect example for this is AR-based glasses which are designed for industrial applications. People working in the industrial domain as shop floor operators can utilize it during their work, which will be helpful for them as it is designed specially to help them. AR is useful even for training the working staff. Overall, in different ways, AR is very helpful.

5.1.5 History of Augmented Reality

Discussed and explained below is the history of AR.

During the time period of the early 1990s, the term AR got coined. However, it was in the late 1960s that the very first AR system which was completely functional was built. Ivan Sutherland had built it along with his colleagues (1968). They built a 3D see-through head-worn display which was mechanically tracked, via which the person wearing it could view computer-generated information mixed with physical objects, like the signs on a laboratory wall [26].

Myron Krueger had made VideoPlace in the mid-1970s. It was an AR laboratory which was interactive [51].

During the time period of the early 1990s, there was research being carried out at the Boeing Corporation. At that time period, AR technology, i.e., the concept of overlaying computer graphics on top of the real world, got its name. Caudell and Mizell (1992), both of whom have worked at Boeing back then in the early 1990s, made the process of conveying the wiring instructions for aircraft assembly to construction workers simple—that was what they worked on, and it was them both who called their particular proposed solution of overlaying computer-presented material on the top of real world as augmented reality [26].

In 1993, Knowledge-based Augmented Reality for Maintenance Assistance (KARMA) was created by S. Feiner, D. Seligmann, and B.

MacIntyre. AR and markers that are positioned on a printer are utilized by the KARMA system [51].

5.1.6 Types of Augmented Reality

Different types of AR are mentioned and discussed as follows:

- ➢ Marker-based AR
- ➢ Markerless AR
- ➢ Projection-based AR
- ➢ Overlap-based AR

Marker-based AR: A camera that is coupled to a device marker like a real-world visual object is generally utilized by AR which is marker-based. So, due to this, for the marker utilized, a specific and unique result will be displayed. Different applications which use marker-based AR utilize distinctive and simple models as markers like QR codes because QR codes can be easily recognized. Marker-based AR is many times called image recognition.

Markerless AR: Tools like digital compass, GPS, etc., in these cases integrated in an electronic device, are utilized to give data on the basis of its position. Geolocation or by location is what this application is also called. It is commonly utilized for finding a particular address and mapping an address.

Projection-based AR: Real objects are taken for use where these real objects' artificial light projections from the real world are taken into consideration. Applications which are based on this AR type enable human interaction. It is enabled by sending of light onto a surface in the real world and then, with this projected light, feeling the human contact. When a difference between the actual projection and expected projection is there, then an interaction with the user occurs [51].

Overlap-based AR: Either partial or total replacement of the real-world view takes place here, superimposing an object with an enlarged view of the same object. Recognition of an object is very important in overlap-based AR [51].

5.1.7 Augmented Reality Interfaces

Written below are AR interfaces.

- ➢ Tangible AR interfaces
- ➢ Collaborative AR interfaces

- ➢ Hybrid AR interfaces
- ➢ Emerging multimodal interfaces

Tangible AR interfaces: By exploiting the use of real, physical objects and tools, tangible interfaces support direct interactions with the real world.

Collaborative AR interfaces: The use of multiple displays is included in collaborative AR interfaces for supporting remote activities and co-located activities.

Hybrid AR interfaces: An assortment of interfaces which are different but complementary are combined by hybrid interfaces as well as the possibility to interact through a wide range of interaction devices.

Multimodal AR interfaces: Real objects' input are combined with naturally occurring forms of language and behaviors such as speech, natural hand gestures, touch, or gaze by multimodal AR interfaces [8].

5.1.8 Augmented Reality-Related Discussion with Examples

AR systems have different features, with real-time interaction in AR environments being one of its main features. In order to have an interaction method which is more efficient, considerable research efforts have been put in [35].

Let us further discuss AR with the help of some examples. In the first example, the authors in [54] carry out a study. The study explores AR characteristics and applications and, along with it finds out the success factors for continuous use behavior with an extended view. Some characteristics might influence the user satisfaction degree, and it may be connected to the continuous intention about user acceptance of AR smart phone applications. The authors got the results of their study from which it was stated that information quality and relative vividness influence, but in a positive way, the perceived usefulness, and perceived usefulness positively influences continuous intention [54].

For the second example, with respect to discussing AR, consider the area of tourism. AR can be useful in this area. AR can be a boon for travelers. Many people face the issue of not being able to interact with others during traveling due to language barrier. This is one of the most common issues faced during traveling by travelers. AR can potentially solve this issue quite easily. AR can help in translation. It can make translation simple which increases the understanding and experience of the travelers.

For booking rooms, even before the perspective guests book rooms, they can survey them utilizing AR technology. This is helpful for the perspective guests.

Whenever any guest selects a hotel to stay in, one of the most attractive features that the guest considers during the selection of a hotel is its location. Locational advantage is very important for any hotel. AR may enable the guest to have a glance of the hotel location and also provide a view of nearby destinations' cultural experiences [56].

5.1.9 Augmented Reality Advantages

Written below are some of the advantages of AR.

- AR can provide an increase in engagement.
- Learning becomes better with AR.
- AR can be utilized with ease. Just with the help of a smartphone, through an application, it can be used.

5.2 Virtual Reality

5.2.1 Introduction to Virtual Reality

VR concept is not new. Its first attempt traces back to 1960s [18]. Now VR has become famous and is being utilized in many different kinds of applications. Its utilization can be beneficial [12].

5.2.2 Definition of Virtual Reality

VR can be defined in different ways. In very simple words, a form of environment simulated by a computer is VR [59]. This is one way of defining it. The aim of VR is getting users immersed within an environment that's totally artificial with different forms of technology for the purpose of addressing one or more senses [58].

5.2.3 Virtual Reality Components

VR consists of different components. The basic ones are input devices, output devices, etc. Generally, input devices look after interaction, and output devices look after immersive feelings, while software takes care of control and synchronization of the entire environment. How a user will communicate with a computer is decided by input devices. Users are presented with a virtual environment and the phenomena of the virtual environment with the help of output devices. The output devices are the ones which help in generating a feeling of immersion. These include auditory, visual, or haptic displays [3].

5.2.4 Getting to Know Virtual Reality

Tool aspect and content aspect are two general categories which influence VR application. Creation and also understanding of stories, presence, etc. is what content aspect consists of, while tool aspect consists of the creation of situations, planning, evaluation, etc. The different qualities of tools and media is combined by VR in a unique way.

When considering the content aspect, emphasis is given on the perception and experience of 3D environments such that the user gets the feeling of continuously being present at locations which are augmented or at locations that are generated by the computer.

This implies that the appearance and behavior of these virtual worlds are believable. If there is linking to our experience or intuition, the content aspect leads to the provision of real-time physics provision and also provision of realistic rendering that is accurate.

Compared to a conventional desktop, VR environments differ as what they do is, in a computer-generated data environment, they embed the user. Famous examples are the CAVE systems which are 3D stereoscopic multi-wall environments [57].

Previously, VR was considered to be of concern with respect to the only gaming area, but during the past years, VR has this changed, and now it is considered to be of concern with respect to professional development as well [20]. For work related to designing of a product, VR technologies have been attempted to be applied in different stages of development of a product [18]. To have the what-if scenario, the high level of presence and the complete immersion of VR provide complete flexibility [25]. The question that what exactly is present is a vital question in the case of the design of VR [2]. This needs to be known. A lot of changes in the way a person views and has interaction with information, friends, and the world are promised by the VR's fundamental technology [7]. Through its interaction and overall working performance, each application of VR should be effective [3]. In the design industry and construction industry, HMD-VR utilization is increasing. In fact, it helps the clients to get to know space by being a useful visualization tool and it has proved to be a useful visualization tool [27]. For the implementation of novel training and education-related approaches, VR has become a useful tool lately [39].

VR will change the environment for the users. Replacement of an environment takes place in VR. If AR is compared here, then in the case of AR, it just makes the environment better; it enhances it, but VR replaces it [40]. A learning environment which is virtual has its use in instruction and is making its mark as cooperation is built by a virtual learning environment; also, correspondence opens among instructors and understudies are built [44].

5.2.5 History of Virtual Reality

Discussed and explained below is the history of VR.

In the year 1965, Ivan Sutherland proposed the Ultimate Display, which is the ultimate solution of VR. It is a concept of artificial world construction that included force-feedback, smell, interactive graphics, sound, and taste.

The first VR, which was realized in hardware and not in concept, was the Sword of Damocles. It is a device that was considered as the first head-mounted display (HMD) along with appropriate head tracking that was constructed by Ivan Sutherland. This device supported a stereo view, and this view was updated correctly according to the user's head position and orientation.

At the University of North Carolina (UNC) in 1971, the first prototype of a force-feedback system called Grope was realized.

Myron Krueger, in 1975, created artificial reality which was a conceptual environment, having no existence. It was called Videoplace. In this system, silhouettes of the users grabbed by the cameras were projected on a big screen. Due to image processing techniques which determined the participants' positions in 2D screen's space, the participants were able to interact with one another.

At NASA Ames in 1984, VIVED, i.e., VIrtual Visual Environment Display, was constructed with off-the-shelf technology, a stereoscopic monochrome HMD.

The Eyephone HMD in 1988 and the DataGlove in 1985 were manufactured by the VPL company, and they were the first VR devices that were commercially available.

In VPL Research company, Jaron Lanier, who was the founder of VPL Research as mentioned above, coined the term virtual reality.

BOOM was commercialized in 1989. It was commercialized by the Fake Space Labs. BOOM is a small box. It consists of two CRT monitors which can be seen through the eye holes. The box can be grabbed by the user; the user can keep it by the eyes and move through the virtual world, as the mechanical arm measures the position and orientation of the box.

In the year 1992, CAVE (CAVE Automatic Virtual Environment) was presented. It is a VR and scientific visualization system [3].

5.2.6 Virtual Reality System Types

There are three VR system types, which are as follows:

- Non-immersive systems
- Immersive systems
- Semi-immersive systems

Let us discuss them all one by one.

Non-immersive systems: Basic and inexpensive type of VR applications which use desktops to recreate images of the world are non-immersive systems.

Immersive systems: A fully simulated experience is provided by immersive systems as they have the support of different sensor-based output devices like HMDs for the purpose of making the environment's stereoscopic view better with the help of the user's head movement as well as haptic devices and audio devices.

Semi-immersive systems: Systems between the both systems mentioned above are semi-immersive systems like Fish Tank VR. A three-dimensional scene (3D) scene which is seen on a monitor, these systems give a stereo image of it utilizing a perspective projection which is coupled to the observer's head position [16].

5.2.7 Virtual Reality-Related Discussion with Examples

Virtual reality (VR) inclusion can be a turning point for healthcare, education, industrial sector, and many other sectors. For the purpose of training, VR is used as a tool many times [4]. In the teaching field, one of the important areas where VR technology is applied is medicine. Medical students and even doctors can learn and even test different medical-based procedures and treatments by planning spatial visualization as well as providing opportunities for specific interactions with objects in the VR environment. By providing education in this form, there are doors open to various possibilities which are beneficial. For example, different scenarios of action are introduced, and along with it, for improving efficiency, their many repetitions are introduced. Also, it helps to find out from the point of view of the patient what the best option is. Therefore, with the help of VR, in particular, novice doctors have the opportunity of practicing their skill [59].

In the recent past, for video game creation, VR has been largely used. Not just for gaming purposes, VR applications can reach much farther. VR is such a kind of a platform which puts the user in a virtual world along with an interface which enables for interactions that are realistic. With VR, in a simulated environment, a user can get completely engaged as if the user is really existing in it, giving a unique medium of immersion [60].

5.2.8 Virtual Reality Advantages

Written below are some of the advantages of VR.

- VR can be helpful in training purposes. In the industrial sector, it can help train workers for different situations. Similarly, in the medical sector, it can help doctors and students to learn, train, and prepare themselves for complex situations.
- VR can help in increasing efficiency.
- VR can give the user a feeling of being immersed in a virtual environment as if it was real.

5.3 Mixed Reality

5.3.1 Introduction to Mixed Reality

MR is a technology which is emerging. Compared to other similar technologies, MR deals with a maximum amount of user interaction in the real world. In the area of manufacturing training, MR has been hugely successful [5]. Microsoft Corporation (Redmond, WA, USA) has developed the HoloLens2™. It is a head-mounted MR device which is commercially available [29]. For developing user-ready interactive systems, there is a decisive criterion which is the optimal interaction between humans and technology [31]. MR experiences mostly are about the visual domain [38].

The physical environment which is around the users as well as the digital elements presented through are both perceived by the users in MR systems.

An example to understand this would be the use of semitransparent displays. MR systems are actually designed to provide their users with a given illusion that physical objects and digital objects are both present in the same space. For the purpose of achieving this coexistence illusion, inside the real environment, the digital objects are required to be positioned with precision, and along with it, in real time, they need to be aligned with real objects. The systems in which the physical reality is having dominance as well as the systems in which the virtual aspects are having dominance are the ones included by MR. To different and a wide range of areas, MR concepts are applicable, such as in office environments, automotive industry, etc. [61]. Microsoft, in the year 2016, developed a device called HoloLens, which is a MR-based HMD—that means a device which can be worn, i.e., a wearable device enabling the users to interact with the environment utilizing holograms while stimulating the senses as a whole [64].

In other and simple words, a pair of perspective holographic glasses is what HoloLens is. A the graphics processing unit, a holograph processing unit for handling real-time spatial mapping and processing and a central processing unit are what HoloLens includes. The functions of HoloLens, compared to conventional AR equipment, are more advanced like gaze design, spatial sound design, stereoscopic 3D display, etc. [64].

5.3.2 Definition of Mixed Reality

The combination of the real world and the digital world is called or referred to as MR. In MR, physical and digital objects co-exist and interact in real time. Thus, it encompasses AR as well as augmented virtuality via immersive technology.

5.3.3 Displays in Mixed Reality Environments

Some of the commonly utilized displays in MR environments are as follows:

- Head-mounted displays
- Hand-held displays
- Hand-held projectors

Head-mounted displays: These are likely the most commonly utilized type of displays in the case of MR. These displays comprise of either one visual display unit or two together with systems that are optically compensated, which form a correct virtual image perspectively despite the display being too close to the eyes of the user.

Hand-held displays: By utilizing metaphor of a magic lens via which a reality can be viewed that is enriched by virtual elements, the hand-held displays are used for MR.

Hand-held projectors: Lately, video projector miniaturization suggested their utilization as hand-held MR displays. These projectors could be utilized by users to directly point at objects which are of interest, which will enable a direct projection of information which is computer generated onto the object or next to the object [61].

5.3.4 Getting to Know Mixed Reality

The viewing audience can be provided with experiences that are immersive and have real content and virtual content with the help of MR applications. MR-based applications can be specially developed for this purpose, thus helping the creators by relaxation of the requirement of modeling [45]. Innovative interfaces for the user can be designed where digital as well as physical artifacts exist together in the same computer-based environment using MR as it consists of technologies and concepts which help in this [46]. The first untethered MR system, taking forward the way toward providing the ultimate experience of MR for consumer and for enterprise as well, is HoloLens [61].

In the field of wearable applications, there is a development which is quite promising, which is the Microsoft HoloLens MR headset (Microsoft Corporation, Redmond, WA, USA). As a developer's kit, it was released in March 2016.

The combination of the real world and the digital world is called or referred to as MR as mentioned in its definition earlier. It is a development of importance, enabling for a more natural interaction progressively. This interaction is with both real content as well as digital content. In applications like gaming, education, training, etc., VR headsets have proved to be useful, but in having natural interaction with the real world they preclude.

When utilizing VR headsets during walking, there is no kind of direct connection between the virtual world and the physical world; this is the main challenge when utilizing VR headsets. This is a drawback with VR. Now, this particular drawback, with the help of MR, has found a resolution. Thanks to MR, this drawback has been overcome as, in the real world, physical movements and visual perception of the real world are unconstrained [62].

5.3.5 Mixed Reality-Related Discussion with the Help of Examples

For the users who are accustomed to traditional AR headset systems, MR systems give a considerable leap in visual and interactive experience for them [61].

Based on MR, this paper [63] is representing a system for interactive programming of robots which are utilized for industrial purposes, i.e., industrial robots, and for immersion purposes in MR, Microsoft's HoloLens glasses were utilized.

Reviewing academic papers on HoloLens applications in medical education and simulation, medical and surgical aids and systems, architecture, civil engineering, industrial sector, and other fields of engineering was the purpose of this particular study carried out by the authors in [64]. During the time period of over 5 years, i.e., from the year 2016 to 2020, with 44 different academic research articles which were published, its analysis was done for fulfilling the purpose of the study by the authors in [64].

An investigation was done regarding the trends and current status in research which is based on HoloLens. The investigation was done by field and year, and also visualization technology and functions given to the users were discussed.

It was determined by this study that in medical education and simulation, architecture, civil engineering, industrial engineering, medical and surgical aids and systems, and other fields of engineering, HoloLens is employed. The findings of this study contribute toward the classification of present HoloLens uses in different industries and in the identification of types of visualization techniques and functions [64].

The efficient use of MR techniques in order to manage items of furniture of rooms utilizing Microsoft HoloLens so as to create a BIM system is proposed in [65].

In [66], a novel approach is proposed to utilize maps as interaction interfaces in a mixed reality (MxR) environment which could be applied to a specific virtual heritage setting with a predefined cultural and historical context. The primary focus of the proposed interaction method is named as "Walkable MxR Map", and its primary focus is to utilize immersive, interactive, and walkable maps to enable the users to interact with 3D models, cultural content, and different multimedia content at museums and heritage sites [66].

5.3.6 Mixed Reality Advantages

Written below are some of the advantages of MR.

- Immersive experience
- MR technology provides a largely immersive experience to the viewers or users.
- Using MR, the users can interact with digital as well as physical objects at the same time.

5.4 Further Discussion on Extended Reality (XR) Technologies

During the previous three decades, extended reality (XR) which is here jointly referring to AR, VR, and MR, has become more common in working life. As user-friendliness and also availability of these technologies grow, companies are making more and more investments in different XR applications. The investments made in these technologies are often expected to make better the efficiency and productivity of work [52].

In the recent time, XR systems use is on the growing side [5]. They have become very famous. In which way AR/VR tools can make the information communication among users better has been found out by various researchers in different fields [24]. There are some useful technologies which are taking the shape to be game changers globally. AR and VR are among them [12]. AR devices have become quite mature lately, and so have VR devices [36]. AR systems and VR systems provide various advantages [48]. In communication media also, virtuality and augmentation have an important role. Increasing diversification and sophistication and diversification of communication media are what lead to the urge to measure their effect on users because, at the end, its characteristics are having associations with management decisions and consumer behavior. Media characteristic (MC) framework include the variables like hypertextuality, interactivity, modality, virtuality, augmentation, etc. [53].

During the period of the last 20 years, VR has grown and become highly sophisticated [22].

For the purpose of providing training to operators and professionals, virtual and mixed reality (VR/MR) tools' effectiveness is being debated since a long time [23].

5.5 Conclusion

In today's world, technology has great importance. Sudden changes are difficult to be introduced in our society. Technology brings many changes. It has been introduced slowly in the society [10]. It has made a prominent place in almost every sector in the society. From the automotive sector to the construction sector to education and healthcare sector and so on, technology has a prominent place in all of these sectors, and is it utilized in these sectors quite evidently. Different technologies are put into use as per requirement. Out of many technologies present, AR, VR, and MR have gained a lot of attention in the recent times, and still these technologies are highly gaining a lot of limelight due to the advantages they provide.

Many new tools, concepts, and technologies of AR, VR, and MR have emerged. This makes way for different industrial processes toward economic as well as ergonomic improvement [15]. AR, VR, and MR are actually the XR technologies, and XR is currently creating a lot of buzz and is enjoying its growth across different sectors. The advantages that these technologies provide are phenomenal. AR, VR, and MR technologies, in this chapter, are briefly discussed and described. Also, their history, advantages, etc., are discussed in the chapter. AR, VR, and MR, which are the XR technologies are growing at a rapid speed and their growth is impeccable. These technologies are quite popular now, and if they continue growing, then they might gain even more popularity in the future.

References

1. Azuma, R., Baillot, Y., Behringer, R., Feiner, S., Julier, S., MacIntyre, B., Recent advances in augmented reality. *IEEE Comput. Graphics Appl.*, 21, 34–47, 2001, doi: 10.1109/38.963459.
2. Biocca, F., The cyborg's dilemma: progressive embodiment in virtual environments. *J. Comput.-Mediated Commun.*, 3, 1997, doi: 10.1111/j.1083-6101.1997.
3. Mazuryk, T., Virtual Reality History, Applications, Technology and Future, 1999.
4. Baus, O. and Bouchard, S., Moving from virtual reality exposure-based therapy to augmented reality exposure-based therapy: a review. *Front. Hum. Neurosci.*, 8, 112, 2014, doi: 10.3389/fnhum.2014.00112.
5. Doolani, S., Wessels, C., Kanal, V., Sevastopoulos, C., Jaiswal, A., Nambiappan, H., Makedon, F., A Review of Extended Reality (XR) Technologies for Manufacturing Training. *Technologies*, 8, 4, 1–20, 77, 2020.

6. Cabero-Almenara, J., Barroso-Osuna, J., Llorente-Cejudo, C., del Mar Fernández Martínez, M., Educational Uses of Augmented Reality (AR): Experiences in Educational Science. *Sustainability*, 11, 4990, 2019.
7. Kuleto, V., Stanescu, M., Ranković, M., Šević, N.P., Paun, D., Teodorescu, S., Extended reality in higher education, a responsible innovation approach for generation y and generation z. *Sustainability*, 13, 11814, 2021.
8. Carmigniani, J., Furht, B., Anisetti, M., Ceravolo, P., Damiani, E., Ivkovic, M., Augmented reality technologies, systems and applications. *Multimed. Tools Appl.*, 51, 341–377, 2010.
9. Bacca, J., Baldiris, S., Fabregat, R., Graf, S., Augmented reality trends in education: a systematic review of research and applications. *J. Educ. Technol. Soc.*, 17, 133, 2014.
10. Calabuig-Moreno, F., González-Serrano, M.H., Fombona, J., García-Tascón, M., The Emergence of Technology in Physical Education: A General Bibliometric Analysis with a Focus on Virtual and Augmented Reality. *Sustainability*, 12, 2728, 2020.
11. Bucea-Manea-Oni, R., Bucea-Manea-Oni, R., Simion, V.E., Ilic, D., Braicu, C., Manea, N., Sustainability in higher education: The relationship between work-life balance and xr e-learning facilities. *Sustainability*, 12, 5872, 2020.
12. Mcmillan, K., Flood, K., Glaeser, R., Virtual reality, augmented reality, mixed reality, and the marine conservation movement. *Aquat. Conserv. Mar. Freshwater Ecosyst.*, 27, 162–168, 2017.
13. Margetis, G., Apostolakis, K.C., Ntoa, S., Papagiannakis, G., Stephanidis, C., X-Reality Museums: Unifying the Virtual and Real World Towards Realistic Virtual Museums. *Appl. Sci.*, 11, 338, 2021.
14. Shin, D.H. and Dunston, P.S., Identification of application areas for augmented reality in industrial construction based on technology suitability. *Autom. Constr.*, 17, 882–894, 2008.
15. Muñoz, A., Mahiques, X., Solanes, J.E., Martí, A., Gracia, L., Tornero, J., Mixed reality-based user interface for quality control inspection of car body surfaces. *J. Manuf. Syst.*, 53, 75–92, Oct. 2019.
16. Syberfeldt, A., Danielsson, O., Gustavsson, P., Augmented reality smart glasses in the smart factory: Product evaluation guidelines and review of available products. *IEEE Access*, 5, 9118–9130, 2017.
17. Cipresso, P., Giglioli, I.A.C., Raya, M.A., Riva, G., The past, present, and future of virtual and augmented reality research: A network and cluster analysis of the literature. *Front. Psychol.*, 9, Article 2086, 2018, https://doi.org/10.3389/fpsyg.2018.02086.
18. Stylidis, K., Dagman, A., Almius, H., Gong, L., Söderberg, R., Perceived quality evaluation with the use of extended reality, in: *Proc. Design Soc., Int. Conf. Eng. Design*, vol. 1, no. 1, pp. 1993–2002, 2019.
19. Nee, A.Y.C., Ong, S.K., Chryssolouris, G., Mourtzis, D., Augmented reality applications in design and manufacturing. *CIRP Ann.*, 61, 2, 657–679, 2012.

20. Kaminska, D., Sapinski, T., Wiak, S., Tikk, T., Haamer, R.E., Avots, E., Helmi, A., Ozcinar, C., Anbarjafari, G., Virtual reality and its applications in education: Survey. *Information*, 10, 318, 2019.
21. Kascak, J., Teliskova, M., Torok, J., Baron, P., Zajac, J., Husar, J., Implementation of augmented reality into the training and educational process in order to support spatial perception in technical documentation, in: *Proc. IEEE 6th Int. Conf. Ind. Eng. Appl. (ICIEA)*, pp. 583–587, Apr. 2019.
22. Seth, A., Vance, J.M., Oliver, J.H., Virtual reality for assembly methods prototyping: a review. *Virtual Real.*, 15, 5–20, March 01 2011.
23. Borsci, S., Lawson, G., Broome, S., Empirical evidence, evaluation criteria and challenges for the effectiveness of virtual and mixed reality tools for training operators of car service maintenance. *Comput. Ind.*, 67, 17–26, 2015. 2015/02/01/.
24. Noghabaei, M., Heydarian, A., Balali, V., Han, K., Trend Analysis on Adoption of Virtual and Augmented Reality in the Architecture, Engineering, and Construction Industry. *Data*, 5, 26, 2020.
25. Gong, L., Fast-Berglund, A., Johansson, B., A Framework for Extended Reality System Development in Manufacturing. *IEEE Access*, 9, 24796–24813, 2021, doi: 10.1109/ACCESS.2021.3056752.
26. Höllerer, T.H. and Feiner, S.K., Mobile Augmented Reality, in: *Telegeoinformatics: Location-Based Computing and Services*, H. Karimi and A. Hammad (Eds.), Taylor & Francis Books Ltd., Boca Raton, Florida, USA, 01/2004.
27. Lucas, J.D., Immersive VR in the construction classroom to increase student understanding of sequence, assembly, and space of wood frame construction. *J. Inf. Technol. Construct.*, 23, 179–194, 2018.
28. Gerup, J., Soerensen, C.B., Dieckmann, P., Augmented reality and mixed reality for healthcare education beyond surgery: An integrative review. *Int. J. Med. Educ.*, 11, 1, 2020.
29. Bala, L., Kinross, J., Martin, G., Koizia, L.J., Kooner, A.S., Shimshon, G.J., Hurkxkens, T.J., Pratt, P.J., Sam, A.H., A remote access mixed reality teaching ward round. *Clin. Teach.*, 18, 4, 386–390, 2021, https://doi.org/10.1111/tct.13338.
30. Van Krevelen, D. and Poelman, R., A survey of augmented reality technologies, applications and limitations. *Int. J. Virtual Real.*, 9, 2, 1, 2010.
31. Quandt, M., Beinke, T., Freitag, M., User-Centered Evaluation of an Augmented Reality-based Assistance system for Maintenance. *Procedia CIRP*, 93, 921–926, 2020.
32. Schumann, M., Fuchs, C., Kollatsch, C., Klimant, P., Evaluation of augmented reality supported approaches for product design and production processes. *Procedia CIRP*, 97, 160–165, 2021.
33. Caruso, G. and Re, G.M., AR-Mote: A wireless device for Augmented Reality environment. *2010 IEEE Symposium on 3D User Interfaces (3DUI)*, pp. 99–102, 20–21 March, 2010.

34. Juan, M.C., Botella, C., Alcaniz, M., Banos, R., Carrion, C., Melero, M., Lozano, J.A., An augmented reality system for treating psychological disorders: application to phobia to cockroaches. *ISMAR 2004. Third IEEE and ACM International Symposium on Mixed and Augmented Reality*, pp. 256–257, 2–5 Nov, 2004.
35. Lee, J.-Y., Lee, S.-H., Park, H.-M., Lee, S.-K., Choi, J.-S., Kwon, J.-S., Design and implementation of a wearable AR annotation system using gaze interaction. *2010 Digest of Technical Papers International Conference on Consumer Electronics (ICCE)*, pp. 185–186, 9–13 Jan, 2010.
36. Eschen, H., Kötter, T., Rodeck, R., Harnisch, M., Schüppstuhl, T., Augmented and Virtual Reality for Inspection and Maintenance Processes in the Aviation Industry. *Procedia Manuf.*, **19**, 156–163, 2018.
37. Liarokapis, F. and Anderson, E., Using augmented reality as a medium to assist teaching in higher education, in: *Proceedings of the 31st annual conference of the European association for computer graphics (Eurographics 2010)*, Norrköping, pp. 9–16, 2010.
38. Hughes, C.E., Stapleton, C.B., Hughes, D.E., Smith, E.M., Mixed reality in education, entertainment, and training. *IEEE Comput. Graphics Appl.*, 25, 6, 24–30, 2005, https ://doi.org/10.1109/MCG.2005.139.
39. Nikolakis, G., Fergadis, G., Tzovaras, D., Strintzis, M.G., A mixed reality learning environment for geometry education, in: *Methods and applications of artificial intelligence.* SETN 2004. Lecture notes in computer science, vol. 3025, G.A. Vouros and T. Panayiotopoulos (Eds.), Springer, Berlin, 2004, https ://doi.org/10.1007/978-3-540-24674 -9_11.
40. Santana-Fenandez, J., Gomez-Gil, J., Del-Poso-San-Cirilo, L., Design and Implementation of a GPS guidance system for agricultural tractors using augmented reality technology. *Sensors*, 10, 11, 10435–10447, Nov 2010.
41. Platonov, J., Heibel, H., Meier, P., Grollmann, B., A mobile markerless AR system for maintenance and repair, in: *Proc. 5th IEEE and ACM International Symposium on Mixed and Augmented Reality (ISMAR'06)*, pp. 105–108, 2006.
42. Julier, S., Baillot, Y., Brown, D., Lanzagorta, M., Information filtering for mobile augmented reality. *IEEE Comput. Graphics Appl.*, 22, 5, 12–15, 2002.
43. Henderson, S. and Feiner, S., Exploring the benefits of augmented reality documentation for maintenance and repair. *IEEE Trans. Visual Comput. Graphics*, 17, 10, 1355–1368, 2011.
44. Pridhvi Krishna, M.V., Mehta, S., Verma, S., Rane, S., Mixed Reality in Smart Computing Education System, in: *2018 International Conference on Smart Systems and Inventive Technology (ICSSIT)*, IEEE, pp. 72–75, 2018.
45. Sankaran, N.K., Nisar, H.J., Zhang, J., Formella, K., Amos, J., Barker, L.T., Vozenilek, J.A., LaValle, S.M., Kesavadas, T., Efficacy Study on Interactive Mixed Reality (IMR) Software with Sepsis Prevention Medical Education, in: *2019 IEEE Conference on Virtual Reality and 3D User Interfaces (VR)*, IEEE, pp. 664–670, 2019.

46. Müller, D., Bruns, F.W., Erbe, H., Robben, B., Yoo, Y., Mixed reality learning spaces for collaborative experimentation: A challenge for engineering education and training. *Int. J. Online Eng.*, 3, 4, 15–19, 2007.
47. Doil, F., Schreiber, W., Alt, T., Patron, C., Augmented reality for manufacturing planning, in: *Proceedings of the workshop on Virtual environments 2003*, pp. 71–76, ACM Press, New York, 2003.
48. Gavish, N., Gutiérrez, T., Webel, S., Rodríguez, J., Peveri, M., Bockholt, U., Tecchia, F., Evaluating virtual reality and augmented reality training for industrial maintenance and assembly tasks. *Interact. Learn. Environ.*, 4820, November 2014, 1–21, 2013.
49. Dalle Mura, M., Dini, G., Failli, F., An integrated environment based on augmented reality and sensing device for manual assembly workstations. *Procedia CIRP*, 41, 340–345, 2016.
50. Dini, G. and Mura, M., Application of Augmented Reality Techniques in Through-life Engineering Services. *Procedia CIRP*, 38, 14–23, 2015, 10.1016/j.procir.2015.07.044.
51. Arena, F., Collotta, M., Pau, G., Termine, F., An Overview of Augmented Reality. *Computers*, 11, 28, 2022, https://doi.org/10.3390/computers11020028.
52. Minna, V., Sami, P., Vetoshkina, L., A Systematic Literature Review on Extended Reality: Virtual, Augmented and Mixed Reality in Working Life. *Int. J. Virtual Real.*, 21, 2, 1–28, 2021, 10.20870/IJVR.2021.21.2.4620.
53. Roxo, T., Mafalda, Brito, P., Augmented Reality Trends to the Field of Business and Economics: A Review of 20 years of Research. *Asian J. Bus. Res.*, 8, 94–117, 2018, 10.14707/ajbr.180051.
54. Kim, K., Lee, H., Hwang, J., Zo, H., Understanding augmented reality applications continuance. *2013 International Conference on ICT Convergence (ICTC)*, Jeju, pp. 189–190, 2013, doi: 10.1109/ICTC.2013.6675336.
55. Azuma, R.T., A Survey of Augmented Reality. *Presence: Teleoperators Virtual Environ.*, 6, 4, 355–385, 1997, doi: https://doi.org/10.1162/pres.1997.6.4.355.
56. Nayyar, A., Mahapatra, B., Nhuong Le, D., Suseendran, G., Virtual Reality (VR) & Augmented Reality (AR) technologies for tourism and hospitality industry. *Int. J. Eng. Technol.*, 7, 2.21, 156–160, 2018, https://doi.org/10.14419/ijet.v7i2.21.11858.
57. Blach, R., Virtual Reality Technology - An Overview, in: *Product Engineering: Tools and Methods Based on Virtual Reality*, 2008, 10.1007/978-1-4020-8200-9_2.
58. Scavarelli, A., Arya, A., Teather, R.J., Virtual Reality and Augmented Reality in Social Learning Spaces: A Literature Review. *Virtual Real.*, 25, 2021, 10.1007/s10055-020-00444-8.
59. Paszkiewicz, A., Salach, M., Strzałka, D., Budzik, G., Nikodem, A., Wójcik, H., Witek, M., VR Education Support System—A Case Study of Digital Circuits Design. *Energies*, 15, 277, 2022, https://doi.org/10.3390/en15010277.
60. Chin, N., Gupte, A., Nguyen, J., Sukhin, S., Wang, G., Mirizio, J., Using virtual reality for an immersive experience in the water cycle. *2017 IEEE MIT*

Undergraduate Research Technology Conference (URTC), Cambridge, MA, USA, pp. 1–4, 2017, doi: 10.1109/URTC.2017.8284185.
61. Constanza, E., Kunz, A., Fjeld, M., Mixed Reality: A Survey. *Lect. Notes Comput. Sci.*, 5440, 47, 2009, 10.1007/978-3-642-00437-7_3.
62. Coolen, B., Beek, P.J., Geerse, D.J., Roerdink, M., Avoiding 3D Obstacles in Mixed Reality: Does It Differ from Negotiating Real Obstacles? *Sensors*, 20, 1095, 2020, https://doi.org/10.3390/s20041095.
63. Ostanin, M. and Klimchik, A., Interactive Robot Programing Using Mixed Reality. *IFAC-PapersOnLine*, 51, 50–55, 2018, 10.1016/j.ifacol.2018.11.517.
64. Park, S., Bokijonov, S., Choi, Y., Review of Microsoft HoloLens Applications over the Past Five Years. *Appl. Sci.*, 11, 7259, 2021, https://doi.org/10.3390/app11167259.
65. Bahri, H., Krcmarik, D., Moezzi, R., Kočí, J., Efficient use of mixed reality for bim system using microsoft HoloLens. *IFACPapersOnLine*, 52, 235–239, 2019.
66. Bekele, M.K., Walkable mixed reality map as interaction interface for virtual heritage. *Digit. Appl. Archaeol. Cult. Herit.*, 15, e00127, 2019.

6

Possibilities with Augmented Reality and Virtual Reality

Anant Kumar Patel

Department of Pharmacology, Swami Vivekanand College of Pharmacy, Indore, Madhya Pradesh, India

Abstract

Augmented reality (AR) and virtual reality (VR) technologies are extended reality technologies which are rising largely. They are making their place in many areas due to a lot of possibilities with them. In this book chapter, there is a discussion regarding the possibilities with AR and VR. Using examples, different possibilities in various sectors are discussed.

Keywords: Augmented reality (AR), virtual reality (VR), extended reality (XR), education, medical, industry, pharmacy

6.1 What is Augmented Reality?

Extended Reality (XR) consists of different technologies like mixed reality (MR), VR and AR [70]. Talking specifically about AR then AR is one of the mainstream technology of XR [3]. AR means overlay of digital information on real-world scenarios. Quite spectacular innovation is driven by AR [9]. One of the main process steps in AR is of acquisition of image [6]. AR instead of fully replacing the reality, supplements it [29]. AR makes better users perception of and interaction with the actual world [64]. Various conferences began on AR as it became a distant field of research by the late 1990s [1]. Augmented reality—this technology got its this name around the early 1990s. AR technology is available for users even with the help of a smartphone. Of course, there are different devices

Email: anantpatel08@gmail.com

Manisha Vohra (ed.) Introduction to Extended Reality (XR) Technologies, (113–126) © 2025 Scrivener Publishing LLC

available to access and experience this technology, but AR technology can also be accessed and utilized with just a smartphone. There are various AR-based apps available for users. The very famous game Pokemon Go is an AR-based gaming app, and users can easily play this game on their smartphones. Until now, a large number of people have enjoyed this AR-based game on their smartphones.

There are different types of AR like markerless AR, marker-based AR, overlap-based AR, and projection-based AR.

6.2 What is Virtual Reality?

An environment generated by the computer which is a simulated 3D environment where there is interaction possible for the users with the virtual surroundings is what VR refers to.

VR places a user inside an environment which is computer generated [15]. An environment is created by VR where objects and virtual spaces replace actual world scene completely [65]. In a synthetic environment generated by a computer system, VR tries to instil users with a sense of presence [52].

Lanier coined the word virtual reality. This technology is around since many years ago. The first time this technology was introduced was around the 1960s.

VR creates a completely isolated synthetic environment which is unlike AR technology [2]. In new environments which are totally computer-generated, VR runs over them. Everything which the user can touch, take, or interact with is virtual. Only virtual-world elements are utilized by AR to make the real world and the experience of the user better.

The physical world is replaced by VR. However, AR does not do so [17].

The actual main difference between AR and VR is that real and virtual worlds get integrated by AR while VR is completely digitized and offers total immersion into a simulated environment [20].

There are different types of VR systems such as immersive VR, non-immersive VR, and semi-immersive VR.

6.3 Possibilities with AR and VR

There are a lot of possibilities with AR [40]. The use of AR can be done in areas like education, manufacturing, and medicine among others [22].

For industrial maintenance, AR presents a variety of possibilities [42]. The use of AR technology can be highly beneficial in early product development and also for knowledge workplaces [46].

In different practical day-to-day use cases, mobile AR can potentially be applied [4]. The user experience of applications can be improved by AR applications as they have a high potential of doing so; they can improve the user experience of applications wherein users have to access and interact with information which has a direct spatial relation to their immediate environment [28].

There is development and increase of AR applications in tourism. Recent advancements in mobile computing have led to it [14].

Inside the serious games ecosystem, educational games constitute a major field, trying to educate the players while entertaining them [5].

The authors [18] in this paper, described an interactive AR application prototype for industrial education and training applications. In response to user's interactions, the system provides dynamic registered overlay instructions on an Optical See-through Head-mounted Display (OST-HMD). To present a simple virtual demonstration of assembling/disassembling procedures concerning upper-limb exoskeleton components, the prototype was applied by the authors in paper [18].

The robustness of the system to viewpoint changes, and also its ability to obtain good accuracy with a lightweight and textureless object is showcased by the experimental evaluations. For industrial training applications, it enables to assure a precise, fast, and useful interaction [18].

A physically already existing production environment can be superimposed with virtual planning objects by utilizing AR techniques [27].

Paint-cAR, a marker-based AR application, was introduced by authors in paper [32]. It was introduced for the purpose of providing support to the process of learning to repair paint which is there on a car. It was a vocational education and training (VET) program of the maintenance of cars [32].

For industrial maintenance and repair purposes, a prototypical AR system was developed by authors in paper [38]. In a real industrial context, the AR system which has been developed was evaluated in various tests, and it demonstrated stable and robust behavior [38]. AR is useful in aeronautical maintenance applications as well [71].

AR has been utilized in various fields, but it has not been utilized for treating psychological disorders. In [25], the authors present the first AR system for the treatment of phobia to cockroaches. The system has been tested with one patient. The patient, at the first exposure session, was not able to approach a real cockroach, and after the exposure session utilizing the AR system, the patient was able to approach a real cockroach; the patient was also able to interact with it and kill it herself [25].

To build AR interfaces, AR is a promising technology [49]. AR interface consists of input and output devices [43]. To mobile computing a natural complement exists which is AR [60]. Mobile augmented reality solutions are great for providing support to service technicians in maintenance [45]. The area of AR is strong as well as a rising area [66]. Augmented reality smart glasses are very popular and a supportive technology in smart factories [67]. Thus in industrial applications also AR is useful.

The most common teaching method until the emergence of new technological innovations has been the direct communication between teachers and students usually taking place in the classroom [26].

In order to support and make learning better, there have been considerable efforts in the recent years in the use of technology [8].

To make the experiences of learning better, AR is an important technology.

To establish tendencies, challenges, and affordances of AR technology in educational settings, many studies have been conducted [33]. There has been quite a growing interest in the past years to apply AR to create unique educational settings [34]. AR is considered in areas of teaching. The authors in paper [7] have conducted an overview of role of AR in anatomical education [7]. AR technology has got a following in education market due to its capability to aid or support and bring a more concrete approach to learning [53]. It is possible to create immersive learning experiences via AR [51].

To make student learning better, AR holds great promise [39]. In the field of language learning and teaching, AR offers various opportunities [54]. Also, to deploy Problem Based Learning activities which immerse students into learning activities that are meaningful, AR technology can be utilized [55]. Multiple possibilities are offered by AR technology. Thanks to this, quite quickly AR technology has been assimilate in the education sector [62].

Overall in the field of education, AR technology is very useful and is growing. So, in the educational area also, AR can be very helpful.

However, within the educational domain, not just AR but also VR can be of great help [21].

VR and VE which means virtual environments are getting growingly prevalent in the area of education [47]. In the field of education, another technology which is growing is VR. It is getting more and more utilized in this field [56]. It has a lot of benefits to offer to the students as well as the teachers in the educational field.

VR technology is very attractive technology due to the many opportunities it offers to the users [73]. There are many advantages users can obtain with the help of VR technology in different sectors. Over the last twenty years, VR has evolved to a new level of sophistication [68]. VR is largely utilized in industry and it is getting quite affordable for the end users [11]. Due to this, VR will be able to reach to more and more users. In the area of manufacturing and robotics, VR technologies enable various innovations [50]. VR has been widely utilized off lately in different applications like environmental planning, architecture, education, etc. [12].

To manufacturing planning functions, immersive VR technologies have been introduced lately. This has brought improvements in the quality of planning results as well as led to a reduction in planning times. The complete integration of all planning tasks is being targeted by the introduction of different virtual planning tools [27].

VR in healthcare sector is also gaining popularity. It can provide a lot of benefits in the healthcare sector as well along with other sectors like education, tourism, etc. An important component of a lot VR applications is interacting with a virtual environment [30]. Virtual patient simulation platforms over the time period of past ten years have been developed quite a lot. They have proved to be of help to more grow the ability of medical students to gather information during medical history collection and also to make better their diagnostic problem-solving skills [61]. VR enables different possibilities in healthcare which are beneficial.

To manage pain in clinical populations, VR has been utilized by clinical populations. The use of VR as a form of distraction for dental patients is examined by this study. Both objective and subjective measures have been utilized to find out how a VR system affects the reported level of anxiety of a patient, the physiological factors, and the pain level. The results of the self-evaluation questionnaires were as per prediction. They showcased that patients experienced less pain and anxiety after going through VR treatment. Similar trends in decreased anxiety were reported by physiological data [23].

VR medical simulation has many advantages which can improve the outcomes of training [44].

For education of pharmacy, VR can be useful. The kind of experience and the kind of environment VR can provide is what makes this technology very useful for education of pharmacy. Both the students and the teachers can benefit from VR as it can make learning an interactive-based learning. Students can learn in an interactive environment. As VR technology will further develop, it can potentially be an important part of education of pharmacy [57].

The role of pharmacists has evolved to include more service-based models focusing on disease prevention and management. VR technology can aid pharmacists in providing effective patient counseling and behavior modification support. As VR technologies advance, they can enhance health promotion and disease prevention efforts, addressing the challenges of chronic disease management. VR centers in pharmacies could use algorithms to predict the long-term health impacts of patients' behavioral changes, motivating them to adopt and maintain healthier lifestyles. Virtual reality has previously been used to help people lose weight and get more exercise, which helps fight obesity, diabetes, and disorders of food intake.

Generally, to learn the skills of performing a surgery, trainee surgeons learn under the training, guidance, and supervision of their trained surgeon. This requires a lot of time. This process is even costly and has varied effectiveness. A VR simulator can supplement standard training. This can help the trainee surgeons [36].

In critical care settings, VR simulations can improve decision-making skills by the simulation of different scenarios like low cardiac output syndrome.

In the treatment of pediatric chronic pain conditions, AR and VR interventions are emerging as promising tools [24].

Another sector where the use of VR can be of help is tourism. The use of VR within the tourism area is a growing topic of interest among academics and practitioners [16].

A literature review was done for a particular research [58]. This paper [58] wanted to show how VR could be included in tourism and services of hospitality to better satisfy the demands of travelers. It suggests that VR has the potential to profoundly alter how tourists' experiences and needs are managed. Tourists can use VR to experience a trip ahead of time. Tourists, with the help of VR, can get a preview of different local places of attractions. Tourists benefit from VR navigations when organizing their trips and activities as they are interactive, quite realistic, etc. VR technologies will undoubtedly advance, expanding the prospects in the tourism industry considerably. Regardless which direction these breakthroughs and developments follow, immediately applicable uses and trends have already been found and implemented in the tourism business. While there are many limits, the technology will become a lot more understandable in the future [58].

At present, VR use is being largely applied in different fields, especially in engineering, computer science, and medicine [35]. It has become more feasible to utilize VR at the consumer level and also in education as VR systems have become more affordable. These VR technologies enable opportunities for educators to offer students easy as well as intuitive ways to have an interaction with multimedia lessons [41].

Along with the ubiquity of smartphone adoption, the propagation of VR and AR applications which leverage smartphone technology has grown [31].

To resolve the problems of older adults who encounter different challenges in the latter part of life, technologies like VR and AR have been highlighted as a solution. The authors paper [19] proposed a framework, keeping their focus on specific categories like wellbeing psychologically, socially, etc. They made identification of barriers and challenges which older adults experience in utilizing VR and AR applications. The framework which the authors [19] proposed can be utilized as design principles for consideration in VR and AR designs to promote wellness for older adults. The design in which these design principles have been considered properly can (1) provide a comfortable experience in the use of VR and AR technologies, (2) promote social connectedness or social interaction, and (3) also induce experiences which are pleasant and positive [19].

Overall if we see AR and VR then they are becoming widespread technologies [10]. VR and AR through the help of 3D graphics quite often have a focus on the extension of human-computer interface [13]. Over the time period of last ten years, various researchers in different areas or fields have tried to find out how AR/VR tools can make better communication of information among users [59]. In the recent time, the maturity of VR devices and AR devices have increased considerably [48]. Due to this, both VR and AR devices are growing in popularity. In an important field like education for example, as discussed earlier, these technologies are very useful. VR and AR enable students to have interaction and also learn in environments which in reality are far away from their physical reach [37]. So these VR and AR technologies which are the Extended Reality Technologies are useful in higher education [72] and not just higher education but overall in general these VR and AR technologies are useful in education sector applications. Similarly in various other applications there are different possibilities with AR and VR as discussed above briefly. AR and VR have drawn interest of investors as well as common people in the past five years [63]. These technologies are rapidly growing and coming across to be helpful in various applications.

6.4 Discussion

AR and VR technologies are extended reality (XR) technologies. AR and VR are both very promising technologies. They both have great capabilities. They are making their mark quite well. From the industrial sector to the medical sector, AR and VR technologies are making their mark in various sectors as there are so many possibilities with them. These technologies can help in the course of working and can provide great and fruitful results. Owing to the different possibilities with AR and VR, not just great results can be received but also new heights can be achieved.

6.5 Conclusion

Augmented reality (AR) and virtual reality are extended reality (XR) technologies. They are both well-known XR technologies. In this book chapter, possibilities with AR and VR in various sectors with the help of examples were discussed. With so many possibilities with AR and VR technologies, it can be said that they both can introduce innovation in sectors where they are applied.

References

1. Krevelen, D. and Poelman, R., A Survey of Augmented Reality Technologies, Applications and Limitations. *Int. J. Virtual Real.*, 9, 2, 1–20, 2010.
2. Panagiotidis, P., Augmented and Mixed Reality in Language Learning. *Eur. J. Educ.*, 4, 28–44, 2021.
3. Mourtzis, D., Siatras, V., Angelopoulos, J., Real-Time Remote Maintenance Support Based on Augmented Reality (AR). *Appl. Sci.*, 10, 1855, 2020.
4. Olsson, T., Lagerstam, E., Kärkkäinen, T., Väänänen-Vainio-Mattila, K., Expected user experience of mobile augmented reality services: a user study in the context of shopping centres. *Pers. Ubiquitous Comput.*, 17, 2, 287–304, 2013.
5. Boletsis, C. and McCallum, S., The table mystery: An augmented reality collaborative game for chemistry education, in: Lecture Notes in Computer Science: Vol. 8101. *Serious Games Development and Applications*, M. Ma, M.F. Oliveira, S. Petersen, J.B. Hauge (Eds.), pp. 86–95, 2013, https://doi.org/10.1007/978-3-642-40790-1_9.
6. De Marchi, L., Ceruti, A., Marzani, A., Liverani, A., Augmented reality to support on-field post-impact maintenance operations on thin structures. *J. Sens.*, 1–10, 2013.

7. Chytas, D., Johnson, E.O., Piagkou, M., Mazarakis, A., Babis, G.C., Chronopoulos, E., Nikolaou, V.S., Lazaridis, N., Natsis, K., The role of augmented reality in anatomical education: an overview. *Ann. Anat.-Anat. Anz.*, 229, 151463, 2020 May 1.
8. Serio, A.D., Ibanez, M.B., Kloos, C.D., Impact of an augmented reality system on students' motivation for a visual art course. *Comput. Educ.*, 68, 586–596, 2013.
9. Fombona, J., Pascual-Sevillano, M.A., Gonzalez-Videgaray, M., M-learning and Augmented Reality: A Review of the Scientific Literature on the WoS Repository. *Comunicar*, 52, 63–71, 2017.
10. Davila Delgado, J.M., Oyedele, L., Beach, T., Demian, P., Augmented and virtual reality in construction: drivers and limitations for industry adoption. *J. Constr. Eng. Manage.*, 146, 7, 04020079, 2020.
11. Häfner, P., Häfner, V., Ovtcharova, J., Teaching Methodology for Virtual Reality Practical Course in Engineering Education. *Procedia Comput. Sci.*, 25, 251–260, 2013.
12. Koeva, M., Luleva, M., Maldjanski, P., Integrating Spherical Panoramas and Maps for Visualization of Cultural Heritage Objects Using Virtual Reality Technology. *Sensors*, 17, 4, 829, 2017, https://doi.org/10.3390/s17040829.
13. Starner, T., Mann, S., Rhodes, B., Levine, J., Healey, J., Kirsch, D., Picard, R.W., Pentland, A., Augmented reality through wearable computing. *Presence Teleoperators Virtual Environ.*, 6, 4, 386–398, 1997.
14. Yung, R. and Khoo-Lattimore, C., New realities: A systematic literature review on virtual reality and augmented reality in tourism research. *Curr. Issues Tourism*, 22, 2056–2081, 2019.
15. Yokoyama, I., Sarai, T., Asai, T., Kitou, N., Nozaki, H., Kondo, Y., Nomura, Y., Morizane, A., Sekikawa, M., Liu, D., Virtual reality and augmented reality applications and simulation in vascular access management with three-dimensional visualization. *J. Vasc. Access*, 20, 1S, 65–70, 2019, https://doi.org/10.1177/1129729818776904.
16. Griffin, T., Giberson, J., Lee, S.H., Guttentag, D., Kandaurova, M., Virtual Reality and Implications for Destination Marketing, in: *Proceedings of the TTRA International Conference*, Quebec City, QC, Canada, 20-22 June 2017.
17. Fernandez, M., Augmented Virtual Reality: How to Improve Education Systems. *High. Learn. Res. Commun.*, 7, 1–15, 2017.
18. Besbes, B., Collette, S.N., Tamaazousti, M., Bourgeois, S., Gay-Bellile, V., An interactive augmented reality system: A prototype for industrial maintenance training applications, in: *Proceedings of the 2012 IEEE International Symposium on Mixed and Augmented Reality (ISMAR)*, pp. 269–270, Bari, Italy, 5–8 November 2012.
19. Lee, L.N., Kim, M.J., Hwang, W.J., Potential of Augmented Reality and Virtual Reality Technologies to Promote Wellbeing in Older Adults. *Appl. Sci.*, 9, 3556, 2019, https://doi.org/10.3390/app9173556.

20. Minh, V., Katushin, N., Pumwa, J., Motion tracking glove for augmented reality and virtual reality. *Paladyn J. Behav. Rob.*, 10, 160–166, 2019, 10.1515/pjbr-2019-0012.
21. Puggioni, M.P., Frontoni, E., Paolanti, M., Pierdicca, R., Malinverni, E.S., Sasso, M., A content creation tool for AR/VR applications in education: The ScoolAR framework, in: *International conference on augmented reality, virtual reality and computer graphics*, 2020 Sep 7, Springer, Cham, pp. 205–219.
22. Santana-Fenandez, J., Gomez-Gil, J., Del-Poso-San-Cirilo, L., Design and Implementation of a GPS guidance system for agricultural tractors using augmented reality technology. *Sensors*, 10, 11, 10435–10447, Nov 2010.
23. Wiederhold, M.D., Gao, K., Widerhold, B.K., Clinical use of virtual reality distraction system to reduce anxiety and pain in dental procedures. *Cyberpsychol. Behav. Soc. Netw.*, 17, 359–365, 2014.
24. Logan, D.E., Simons, L.E., Caruso, T.J., Gold, J.I., Greenleaf, W., Griffin, A., King, C.D., Menendez, M., Olbrecht, V.A., Rodriguez, S., Silvia, M., Leveraging Virtual Reality and Augmented Reality to Combat Chronic Pain in Youth: Position Paper From the Interdisciplinary Network on Virtual and Augmented Technologies for Pain Management. *J. Med. Internet Res.*, 23, 4, e25916, 2021 Apr 26.
25. Juan, M.C., Botella, C., Alcaniz, M., Banos, R., Carrion, C., Melero, M., Lozano, J.A., An augmented reality system for treating psychological disorders: application to phobia to cockroaches. *ISMAR 2004. Third IEEE and ACM International Symposium on Mixed and Augmented Reality*, 2–5 Nov, pp. 256–257, 2004.
26. Liarokapis, F. and Anderson, E., Using augmented reality as a medium to assist teaching in higher education, in: *Proceedings of the 31st annual conference of the European association for computer graphics (Eurographics 2010)*, Norrköping, pp. 9–16, 2010.
27. Doil, F., Schreiber, W., Alt, T., Patron, C., Augmented reality for manufacturing planning, in: *Proceedings of the workshop on Virtual environments*, ACM Press, New York, pp. 71–76, 2003.
28. Paelke, V., Augmented reality in the smart factory: Supporting workers in an industry 4.0 environment, in: *Proc. of the 2014 IEEE Emerging Technology and Factory Automation*, pp. 1–4, 2014.
29. Kaufmann, H., Collaborative augmented reality in education, in: *Proceeding of Imagina 2003 Conference*, Monte Carlo, Monaco, pp. 1–4, 2003.
30. Berg, L.P. and Vance, J.M., Industry use of virtual reality in product design and manufacturing: a survey. *Virtual Real.*, 21, 1, 1–17, 2017, https:// doi. org/ 10. 1007/ s10055- 016- 0293-9.
31. Huang, K.-T., Ball, C., Francis, J., Ratan, R., Boumis, J., Fordham, J., Augmented Versus Virtual Reality in Education: An Exploratory Study Examining Science Knowledge Retention When Using Augmented Reality/Virtual Reality Mobile Applications. *Cyberpsychol. Behav. Soc. Netw.*, 22, 2, 105–110, Feb 2019, http://doi.org/10.1089/cyber.2018.0150.

32. Bacca, Baldiris, S., Fabregat, R., Kinshuk, Graf, S., Mobile Augmented Reality in Vocational Education and Training. *Procedia Comput. Sci.*, 75, Vare, 49–58, 2015, doi: 10.1016/j.procs.2015.12.203.
33. Garzón, J., Pavón, J., Baldiris, S., Systematic review and meta-analysis of augmented reality in educational settings. *Virtual Real.*, 23, 447–459, 2019, https://doi.org/10.1007/s10055-019-00379-9.
34. Bacca, J., Baldiris, S., Fabregat, R., Graf, S., Kinshuk, G., Augmented reality trends in education: A systematic review of research and applications. *Educ. Technol. Soc.*, 17, 133–149, 2014.
35. Vergara, D., Rubio, M.P., Lorenzo, M., On the Design of Virtual Reality Learning Environments in Engineering. *Multimodal Technol. Interact.*, 1, 2, 11, 2017, https://doi.org/10.3390/mti1020011.
36. Nagendran, M., Gurusamy, K.S., Aggarwal, R., Loizidou, M., Davidson, B.R., Virtual reality training for surgical trainees in laparoscopic surgery. *Cochrane Database Syst. Rev.*, 2013, CD006575, 2013, doi: 10.1002/14651858.CD006575.pub3.
37. Siegle, D., Seeing Is Believing: Using Virtual and Augmented Reality to Enhance Student Learning. *Gift. Child Today*, 42, 1, 46–52, 2019, https://doi.org/10.1177/1076217518804854.
38. Platonov, J., Heibel, H., Meier, P., Grollmann, B., A mobile markerless AR system for maintenance and repair, in: *Proc. 5th IEEE and ACM International Symposium on Mixed and Augmented Reality (ISMAR'06)*, pp. 105–108, 2006.
39. Dunleavy, M., Dede, C., Mitchell, R., Affordances and limitations of immersive participatory augmented reality simulations for teaching and learning. *J. Sci. Educ. Technol.*, 18, 1, 7–22, 2009.
40. Martinetti, A., Marques, H.C., Singh, S., van Dongen, L., Reflections on the Limited Pervasiveness of Augmented Reality in Industrial Sectors. *Appl. Sci.*, 9, 3382, 2019, https://doi.org/10.3390/app9163382.
41. Parong, J. and Mayer, R.E., Learning science in immersive virtual reality. *J. Educ. Psychol.*, 110, 785–797, 2018.
42. Burova, A., Mäkelä, J., Hakulinen, J., Keskinen, T., Heinonen, H., Siltanen, S., Turunen, M., Utilizing VR and gaze tracking to develop AR solutions for industrial maintenance, in: *Proceedings of the 2020 CHI Conference on Human Factors in Computing Systems*, pp. 1–13, 2020 Apr 21.
43. Caruso, G. and Re, G.M., AR-Mote: A wireless device for Augmented Reality environment. *2010 IEEE Symposium on 3D User Interfaces (3DUI)*, 20–21 March, pp. 99–102, 2010.
44. Ruthenbeck, G.S. and Reynolds, K.J., Virtual reality for medical training: The state-of-the-art. *J. Simul.*, 9, 16–26, 2015.
45. Quandt, M., Beinke, T., Freitag, M., User-Centered Evaluation of an Augmented Reality-based Assistance system for Maintenance. *Procedia CIRP*, 93, 921–926, 2020.
46. Schumann, M., Fuchs, C., Kollatsch, C., Klimant, P., Evaluation of augmented reality supported approaches for product design and production processes. *Procedia CIRP*, 97, 160–165, 2021.

47. Mintz, R., Litvak, S., Yair, Y., 3D-virtual reality in science education: An implication for astronomy teaching. *J. Comput. Math. Sci. Teach.*, 20, 293–305, 2001.
48. Eschen, H., Kötter, T., Rodeck, R., Harnisch, M., Schüppstuhl, T., Augmented and Virtual Reality for Inspection and Maintenance Processes in the Aviation Industry. *Procedia Manuf.*, 19, 156–163, 2018.
49. De Crescenzio, F., Fantini, M., Persiani, F., Di Stefano, L., Azzari, P., Salti, S., Augmented Reality for Aircraft Maintenance Training and Operations Support. *IEEE Comput. Graphics Appl.*, 31, 1, 96–101, 2011.
50. Streusand, D.B., Steuben, J., Turner, C.J., Robotic Interfaces Through Virtual Reality Technology. *Volume 3: Design and Manufacturing, Parts A and B*, pp. 419–428, 2010, doi: 10.1115/IMECE2010-38308.
51. Salinas, P. and González-Mendívil, E., Augmented reality and solids of revolution. *Int. J. Interact. Des. Manuf.*, 11, 4, 829–837, 2017, doi: 10.1007/s12008-017-0390-3.
52. Turner, C.J., Hutabarat, W., Oyekan, J., Tiwari, A., Discrete Event Simulation and Virtual Reality Use in Industry: New Opportunities and Future Trends. *IEEE Trans. Hum.-Mach. Syst.*, 46, 6, 882–894, 2016, doi: 10.1109/THMS.2016.2596099.
53. Antonioli, M., Blake, C., Sparks, K., Augmented reality applications in education. *J. Technol. Stud.*, 40, 2, 96–107, 2014.
54. Cakir, R. and Solak, E., Exploring the effect of materials designed with augmented reality on language learners' vocabulary learning. *J. Educ. Online*, 13, 2, 50–72, 2015, doi: 10.1016/0196-9781(88)90009-5.
55. Villarán, D.I., Ibañez, M.B., Delgado Kloos, C., Augmented reality-based simulations embedded in problem based learning courses, in: Lecture Notes in Computer Science: Vol. 9307. *Design for Teaching and Learning in a Networked World*, G. Conole, T. Klobučar, C. Rensing, J. Konert, E. Lavoué (Eds.), pp. 540–543, 2015, https://doi.org/10.1007/978-3-319-24258-3_.
56. Kovalcík, V., Chmelík, J., Bezdeka, M., Sochor, J., Virtual Reality System as a Tool for Education. *20th International Conference on Computer Graphics, Visualization and Computer Vision*, pp. 15–18, 2012.
57. Coyne, L., Merritt, T.A., Parmentier, B.L., Sharpton, R.A., Takemoto, J.K., The Past, Present, and Future of Virtual Reality in Pharmacy Education. *Am. J. Pharm. Educ.*, *83*, 3, 7456, 2019, https://doi.org/10.5688/ajpe7456.
58. Pestek, A. and Sarvan, M., Virtual reality and modern tourism. *J. Tour. Futures*, 7, 2, 245–250, 2020, 10.1108/JTF-01-2020-0004.
59. Noghabaei, M., Heydarian, A., Balali, V., Han, K., Trend Analysis on Adoption of Virtual and Augmented Reality in the Architecture, Engineering, and Construction Industry. *Data*, 5, 26, 2020.
60. Wagner, D. and Schmalstieg, D., First steps towards handheld augmented reality. *7th IEEE Int. Symp. Wearable Comput.*, pp. 127–135, 2003.
61. De Ponti, R., Marazzato, J., Maresca, A.M., Rovera, F., Carcano, G., Ferrario, M.M., Pre-graduation medical training including virtual reality during

COVID-19 pandemic: A report on students' perception. *BMC Med. Educ.*, 20, 1–7, 2020.
62. Cabero-Almenara, J., Osuna, J.B., Llorente-Cejudo, C., Martínez, M.D.M.F., Educational Uses of Augmented Reality (AR): Experiences in Educational Science. *Sustainability*, 11, 4990, 2019.
63. Cipresso, P., Giglioli, I.A.C., Raya, M.A., Riva, G., The Past, Present, and Future of Virtual and Augmented Reality Research: A Network and Cluster Analysis of the Literature. *Front. Psychol.*, 9, 2086, 2018.
64. Carmigniani, J., Furht, B., Anisetti, M., Ceravolo, P., Damiani, E., Ivkovic, M., Augmented technologies, systems and applications. *Multimed. Tools Appl.*, **51**, 341–377, 2011, https://doi.org/10.1007/s11042-010-0660-6.
65. Shin, D.H. and Dunston, P.S., Identification of application areas for augmented reality in industrial construction based on technology suitability. *Autom. Constr.*, 17, 882–894, 2008.
66. Nee, A.Y.C., Ong, S.K., Chryssolouris, G., Mourtzis, D., Augmented reality applications in design and manufacturing. *CIRP Ann.*, 61, 2, 657–679, 2012.
67. Syberfeldt, A., Danielsson, O., Gustavsson, P., Augmented reality smart glasses in the smart factory: Product evaluation guidelines and review of available products. *IEEE Access*, 5, 9118–9130, 2017.
68. Seth, A., Vance, J.M., Oliver, J.H., Virtual reality for assembly methods prototyping: a review. *Virtual Real.*, 15, 5–20, March 01 2011.
69. 43. Lahanas, V., Loukas, C., Smailis, N., Georgiou, E., A novel augmented reality simulator for skills assessment in minimal invasive surgery. *Surg. Endosc.*, 29, 8, 2224–2234, 2015.
70. Doolani, S., Wessels, C., Kanal, V., Sevastopoulos, C., Jaiswal, A., Nambiappan, H., Makedon, F., A Review of Extended Reality (XR) Technologies for Manufacturing Training. *Technologies*, 8, 4, 77, 1–20, 2020.
71. Hincapié, M., Caponio, A., Rios, H., González Mendívil, E., An introduction to Augmented Reality with applications in aeronautical maintenance. *13th International Conference on Transparent Optical Networks*, pp. 1–4, 2011, doi: 10.1109/ICTON.2011.5970856.
72. Kuleto, V., Stanescu, M., Ranković, M., Šević, N.P., Paun, D., Teodorescu, S., Extended reality in higher education, a responsible innovation approach for generation y and generation z. *Sustainability*, 13, 11814, 2021.
73. Baños, R., Botella, C., García-Palacios, A., Villa, H., Perpiñá, C., Gallardo, M., Psychological variables and reality judgment in virtual environments: the roles of absorption and dissociation. *Cyberpsychol. Behav.*, 2, 143–148, 2009, doi: 10.1089/cpb.1999.2.143.

Section 3

APPLICATIONS OF EXTENDED REALITY

7

Applications of Extended Reality Technologies in Aviation Sector

N. Rajamurugu[1]*, J. Anbarasi[2] and S. Yaknesh[3]

[1]*Department of Aerospace Engineering, KCG College of Technology, Chennai, India*
[2]*Department of Aerospace Engineering, Vel Tech Rangarajan Dr. Sagunthala R&D Institute of Science and Technology, Chennai, India*
[3]*Department of Aerospace Engineering, Chandigarh University, Punjab, India*

Abstract
The aviation sector is one of sectors which are very important as well as very beneficial. It is a huge sector. In this sector, there is a need to always make sure that all the work processes related to the aircraft are taking place smoothly. For this purpose, XR technologies can help. These technologies can be applied in the aviation sector for different applications. In this chapter, different XR technologies are discussed. Along with it, in this chapter, applications of XR technologies in the aviation sector are discussed with the help of different examples from literature review. From the discussion in the chapter, it can be seen that XR technologies application can actually be very beneficial and of great use for the aviation sector.

***Keywords*:** Extended reality (XR), augmented reality (AR), virtual reality (VR), mixed reality (MR), aviation sector, aircraft, aeronautical

7.1 Introduction

The aviation sector is one important sector which requires upgrading with time to ensure the smooth functioning of aircraft-related processes. For traveling from one place to another in a quick span of time, be it from one continent to another or be it from one city to another city present in the

**Corresponding author*: n.rajamurugu@gmail.com

Manisha Vohra (ed.) Introduction to Extended Reality (XR) Technologies, (129–142) © 2025 Scrivener Publishing LLC

same country, an aircraft is one of the most widely used traveling option. It not only helps people in reaching one place and another but it also helps in the transportation of different goods. From food items to handicrafts, a huge variety of goods are transported from one place to another throughout the entire world on a daily basis.

Any error in an aircraft, a maintenance-related error for example, can be very harmful and can cause loss and should be always avoided. The main thing that matters more than monetary loss is the security of the people in the aircraft. There are many technologies which can help the aviation sector. The use of various technologies is included in the aviation industry for its betterment. In the more recent time, among various technologies available for application in the aviation sector, XR technologies are the ones which are gaining popularity. They seem to have a lot of potential and advantages. The application of XR technologies in the aviation industry can be useful.

In the aviation sector, safety-related practices like carrying out time-to-time maintenance-related work, training the employees for the same, etc., the application of XR technologies can be very useful. These technologies can be applied in the different work processes of the aviation sector and can be very helpful.

7.2 What is XR?

All real environments combined with all virtual environments along with human–machine interactions which are generated by computer technology and wearables are referred to as extended reality (XR). There are different types of XR technologies such as mixed reality (MR), virtual reality (VR), and augmented reality (AR) [10]. The convergence of VR, AR, and MR is represented by XR in which each aspect's best elements are utilized and optimized for a given use case scenario and application [42]. In order to handle different areas like education, safety, training, etc., the use of XR systems has been on the increased side lately [11]. Due to the latest advancement of technology that makes XR ever matured, XR systems are getting more and more attention in the industry as well as academia over the period of the last 20 years [32].

AR is one of the emerging technologies [2]. The real world is supplemented by an AR system with virtual objects which appear to coexist in the same space as the real world. Instead of the creation of a completely artificial environment, AR aims toward supplementing the real world [24]. The physical environment is linked by AR with a device-generated environment like video, sound, graphics, or other useful information essentially overlaying digital information on top of the physical world. For many years, some platforms of AR and the underlying concepts have been around [43].

The following properties are what an AR system will have:

- ➢ Combining of virtual objects and real objects in real environment
- ➢ Running interactively and in real time
- ➢ Aligning of real objects and virtual objects with each other [8]

Input devices, displays, tracking, and computers are the main devices for AR [36]. If AR is seen, then it can be noticed that AR is a modern media which is quite advanced and, at present, engaged in a growing number of industries. AR's availability and ease associated with its hardware can make AR available to common users, which is what provides opportunities for us to utilize AR in different scenarios [23]. Since eye-level display makes it easier for the direct perception of the combined AR scene, head-mounted display (HMD) devices have been utilized largely in applications of AR [28]. AR is an emerging technology in its own respect. The paper [15], on the basis of an actual experiment setup made along with logistics engineers from the automotive industry, has given insight into how AR can be used to support kit preparation in the context of material supply to assembly [15]. It is one example of how AR can be utilized for different industrial applications. In future smart factories, augmented reality smart glasses (ARSG) have been recognized as an important technology supporting shop-floor operators. Presently also, ARSG are very popular and their popularity is growing [30].

During the time period of the previous two decades, VR has grown to a new level of sophistication [26]. VR can be defined as a 3D image or an environment's computer-generated simulation which can be interacted within a seemingly real or physical way by a person utilizing special electronic equipment, like a helmet with a screen inside or gloves fitted with sensors [29]. Stepping into a three-dimensional (3D) world through a computer screen is what VR allows. The user can not just step into the 3D world but can look at, even move around, and also have interaction with these worlds as if they were real. Behind VR, the main concept is of illusion. VR has its focus clear on the manifestation of the fantasy world of the mind in computer graphics [9]. All computer technologies which promote virtual environment generation enabling user interaction with them are what VR refers to [34]. An environment is created by VR where virtual spaces and objects do the work of replacing the scene of the real-world scene completely [25]. It was at the beginning of the 1990s that the development of the VR field became quite stormy. In fact, the term virtual reality itself became very famous. There has been an advancement of software as well as hardware which has enabled the computer-generated reality utilizing concept to support daily practice to become more mature over time in the last 10 years [20]. Exploration of advantages and applications of VR in different situations have been done by researchers [19]. The most commonly utilized component of VR is head-mounted display (HMD) [21]. With the introduction of economic devices of high-quality which offer quality user experience, the use of HMD for viewing VR environments has increased in the recent years. Thanks to immersive VR, a user gets placed in a scenario and it provides the user with the presence of being in a particular place where the user is not actually physically present in that place or location [40]. Ever since VR appeared, it has been utilized in various sectors such as education, gaming, etc. [14]. In various prestigious universities nowadays, is there a trend of utilizing interactive 3D applications and VR [27]. In clinical populations, clinicians have utilized VR to manage pain [13].

AR and VR devices' maturity has seen a considerable growth lately [44]. Even though AR and VR are two different terms, both of them are having their basis on the experience of living through the utilization of technology. Thanks to AR and VR, they enable experiments to be performed inside a safe environment [16]. In areas like manufacturing and healthcare, especially for simulating surgeries, mining, retail, etc., AR/VR has its applications [39].

Milgram and Kishino (1994) in a paper originally introduced the term mixed reality [7]. Milgram and Kishino had authored a paper [45] in which they introduced the term mixed reality. MR is a system which is hybrid. Both virtual elements as well as physical elements have their presence in MR [12]. Merging of the virtual worlds and real worlds is how MR is defined [38].

MR can be called as a fusion of the digital world and the physical world, which explores the relationship between human, computer, and environmental interactions [12]. Applications where real-world objects and virtual-world objects are both presented together within a one display can be defined as MR [33]. In the year 2016, Microsoft HoloLens mixed-reality headset (Microsoft Corporation, Redmond, WA, USA) was released in the month of March. It was released as a developers' kit. In wearable applications area, this is one promising development. The HoloLens headset is a headset which is untethered and an optical see-through. It has a holographic display unit via which 3D holograms are overlaid and also anchored to and interacted with the wearer's environment [41]. In MR environments, real objects and digital objects co-exist in real time and are also able to interact with each other [18]. The HoloLens can be utilized with ease and is comfortable [22]. Users are allowed to have interactions with spatially registered virtual holograms that are placed in real environments. This is made possible thanks to MR [17]. A considerable leap is provided by MR systems in visual and interactive experience for users accustomed to traditional AR headset systems [37]. In different fields like education, manufacturing, etc., to provide support for the work of professionals and also as a part of programs for training the skills of employees, managers, and specialists, various different VR/MR systems that vary in terms of hardware, software, functioning, and modes of interaction are utilized nowadays [35].

The present emergence of new concepts, tools, and technologies of AR, MR, and VR makes way for a new scenario for the ergonomic improvement and economic improvement of various present industrial processes [31].

The history of XR technologies is very interesting. In the case of VR, the very first machine of VR was named Sensorama. It was built by Morton Heilig who was a cinematographer. It was built in the year 1956. To surprise the audience of the film, this film booth had integrated various things like 3D, a vibrating chair, colored video along with sounds, and fragrances. Sensorama was built in 1956, but it got patented in the year 1962 by Morton Heilig.

Headsight headset was invented by Philco engineers. The year 1961 was the year of its invention. It featured motion tracking technology, and it was the first VR headgear to feature motion tracking technology.

In the case of AR, the first AR headset was invented in the year 1968. The Sword of Damocles was its name. Ivan Sutherland had invented it. Ivan Sutherland was a Harvard professor. His invented headset projected computer-generated images that made the user's vision of the world better.

In the case of history of MR, the first MR headset was introduced in 2016 by Microsoft. So, Microsoft, in the year 2016, had introduced a headset which was Microsoft's HoloLens headset that became quite popular.

From the time that AR, VR, and MR technologies' first headset was introduced or brought into existence up till now, there has been a lot of progress. These XR technologies are evolving greatly.

7.3 Examples of Different Applications of XR Technologies in the Industry of Aviation

Discussed below are real examples from literature review consisting of different applications of XR technologies in the sector of aviation.

7.3.1 Example 1: Application of AR for Training of Aircraft Maintenance and Operations Support

To date, there have been many incidents of accidents in the aviation sector worldwide. Maintenance work here is of much importance. Maintenance employees of airplane or aircraft face various issues every day. One of the areas of concern in this case is maintenance errors, and in fact it is a great threat. In order to provide help in this area, there are some simulation and computer-based tools present.

For the errors which occur due to violations of procedure, misinterpreting facts, or having insufficient training, to look after all these, computer-based systems can be useful as they can be used to train or support technicians, which can help to reduce these errors. In this direction, AR is a promising technology to build advanced interfaces utilizing visualization systems that are interactive and wearable to implement new methods to display documentation as graphical databases and digital data.

There are different factors which seem to be stopping the efficient implementation of AR. In order to overcome the different obstacles, the authors in [6] have created a system prototype and carried out experiments by asking people to participate in it. The results obtained were encouraging. It seemed that the ones who participated in the experiments understood how to utilize the prototype, and they expressed that they would appreciate its implementation. This particular example points out toward the potential use of AR for aircraft applications [6].

7.3.2 Example 2: Application of AR in Aircraft Maintenance

There can be different types of AR systems present for different applications. Each AR system, irrespective of its application, will have certain requirements which are the same for all types of AR systems—for example, camera, tool for tracking purposes, etc., are among the same requirements all AR systems have. In the case of VR, each thing's creation is done artificially. It is done to define the positions of the objects. In the case of AR, whatever change is occurring in the real world needs to be followed so as to adjust the virtual world as per the reality, and due to these, various types of trackers are utilized. Every tracker type has some particular conditions of operation, and they are utilized for various types of tasks. Trackers are important and required. They provide robustness, great accuracy, etc. After all of these, whatever information cameras and trackers have gathered is analyzed. Data is processed and what would be the objects' position in reality is tried to be figured out. It is at this particular time, on images of real world, that objects that are virtual are superimposed by the AR system, and the users are provided with instructions which are of great use. The authors in [3] have presented an example of AR system which is representing a maintenance process over a training kit. The training kit is used to train operators to perform maintenance on aircraft body RV-10. It is shown in the example's image that correct identification of objects that are real is done, and there is superimposition of virtual objects with reference frame of the real world which is estimated, and the instructions are shown on the screen to the users. AR is having a lot of flexibility. Especially in the area of maintenance, AR implementation in different processes is very easy. AR helps in making less errors during ongoing maintenance tasks due to the added knowledge it gives. Information which is not simple to avail or information which is difficult to retrieve is provided by AR. Operating cost of processes can be reduced by industries using AR. Training of workers involves a high cost. In the aviation industry, a maintenance inspector requires 2,000 h of training. AR can be useful. It can help to provide knowledge and also help to understand maintenance processes faster irrespective of place and time [3].

7.3.3 Example 3: Application of AR for Maintenance Operations and Providing Complex Training in Aeronautic-Related Processes

There are difficult operations in different aeronautical processes which are connected to maintenance and training work and to transfer the knowledge of the difficult operation types of methodologies that are present. In [1], the authors have presented a differentiation of various types of these methodologies which include utilization of teaching techniques that are traditional and to perform a particular task of assembly requiring printed instructions and manuals as one of their methodologies. Another methodology whose differentiation is presented in [1] by the authors is the use of audiovisual tools for the purpose of providing additional information to operators. The next methodology presented is the use of AR application for the same purpose of utilizing virtual content to make the actual real-world environment better. The authors in [1] are analyzing a solution by utilizing AR. The solution is being utilized to improve the cognitive process of a maintenance operator in the business of aviation by utilizing AR. This technology is utilized in the assembly of a training kit of an RV-10 airplane. This airplane is sold commercially to be used for practicing the assembly operations of this aircraft. As a case study, the training tool kit for airplane RV-10 is presented. For 4 h, the assembly training of the RV kit utilizes a low-cost system which was created to guide the operator through each operation, which includes the preparation of tools, deburring holes, etc., and analysis results are offered. A comparison of results against other technologies tested in the author's research group is presented. So, the authors in [1] made an AR application. This application works in a normal laptop with results that are stable and give the user information which is used during the training period of 4 h. A simple statistical analysis was done to compare the results of the AR application. When the authors in [1] were writing their paper, during that time, a statistical study was is in process, and they have mentioned that they will present it in a future work, but the results that the authors obtained until the moment of writing their paper showed an excellent tendency for the AR technology compared to other teaching techniques [1].

7.3.4 Example 4: Application of AR-Based System and Knowledge-Based Systems in Aircraft Maintenance

Keeping in check and making sure of the safety of flight, training, and maintenance of aircraft are very vital. A number of components and knowledge of the maintenance procedures are included in the maintenance process.

To avoid making any operational errors, there are certain procedures which technicians have to follow in a maintenance process. Also, a lot of cost is involved in the maintenance work of an aircraft. In order to reduce operational errors and time-related costs, an intelligent augmented reality (IAR) system is proposed by the authors in [4]. The authors, with their proposed system, also aim to help out the technicians of the aircraft with difficult work by utilizing an UI/UX interface which is intuitive for the maintenance work.

The proposed system mainly consists of three important modules which are AR module and knowledge-based system (KBS) module, and the third one is between the AR and KBS modules. It is a unified platform with an integrated UI/UX module.

At Korea Air Lines (KAL) hangars, the IAR system is overall tested. As per the results obtained, the proposed system can be helpful for the technicians to be more accurate and effective in carrying out their tasks of maintenance [4].

7.3.5 Example 5: Application of VR in Aircraft Cabin Design Process

In the initial design stages of the design process of aircraft cabins, VR can be utilized. The authors have described this in their paper [5]. Via making the communication better between stakeholders and stakeholder levels through the use of immersive and real size imagery of different detailing levels, this paper [5] has its focus on enhancing the design process. A pilot was created and conducted, and three people were included in it. Each sketch was captured during simulations in VR, wherein one of the designers was sketching and the other was monitoring the process on the external screen. The results were promising, and VR technology seemed to be useful in the design process [5].

7.4 Conclusion

Nowadays, XR technologies are quite widely and efficiently being utilized across various sectors in numerous applications as XR technologies not only bring benefits or advantages but also help to simplify work in different ways—for example, in the aviation sector, employees can learn work, like maintenance-related work, and train themselves in a safe environment and be prepared to handle different situations. Similarly, in the aviation sector and other different work applications, XR technologies can be applied, and their application can provide great advantages to this sector. The aviation sector has its importance worldwide. There is a large-scale utilization of aircraft on a daily basis for both traveling and for the transportation of goods, so technologies like XR, which can truly help in aircraft related work processes as discussed in the chapter with the help of examples, can benefit the aviation sector as well as be a game changer for this sector.

XR technologies do seem to have a lot of potential for use in the aviation sector. Thus, as seen in the chapter, XR technologies can be utilized in the aviation sector for different applications, which have been briefly discussed in this chapter using examples from literature review, and it can be seen from the discussion done in the chapter that XR technologies' application can be very advantageous for the aviation sector.

References

1. Rios, H., Hincapié Montoya, M., Caponio, A., Mercado, E., Mendívil, E., Augmented Reality: An Advantageous Option for Complex Training and Maintenance Operations in Aeronautic Related Processes, vol. 6773, pp. 87–96, 2011, 10.1007/978-3-642-22021-0_11.
2. Cabero-Almenara, J., Barroso-Osuna, J., Llorente-Cejudo, C., del Mar Fernández Martínez, M., Educational Uses of Augmented Reality (AR): Experiences in Educational Science. *Sustainability*, 11, 4990, 2019.
3. Hincapié, M., Caponio, A., Rios, H., González Mendívil, E., An introduction to Augmented Reality with applications in aeronautical maintenance. *2011 13th International Conference on Transparent Optical Networks*, Stockholm, Sweden, pp. 1–4, 2011, doi: 10.1109/ICTON.2011.5970856.
4. Jo, G.-S., Oh, K.-J., Ha, I., Lee, K.-S., Hong, M.-D., Neumann, U., You, S., A Unified Framework for Augmented Reality and Knowledge-Based Systems in Maintaining Aircra. *Proceedings of the AAAI Conference on Artificial Intelligence*, vol. 28, pp. 2990–2997, 2014, https://doi.org/10.1609/aaai.v28i2.19023.
5. Moerland-Masic, I., Reimer, F., Bock, T.M., Meller, F., Nagel, B., Application of VR technology in the aircraft cabin design process. *CEAS Aeronaut. J.*, *13*, 1, 127–136, 2022, https://doi.org/10.1007/s13272-021-00559-x.
6. De Crescenzio, F., Fantini, M., Persiani, F., Di Stefano, L., Azzari, P., Salti, S., Augmented Reality for Aircraft Maintenance Training and Operations Support. *IEEE Comput. Graphics Appl.*, 31, 1, 96–101, Jan.-Feb. 2011, doi: 10.1109/MCG.2011.4.
7. Ostanin, M. and Klimchik, A., Interactive robot programing using mixed reality. *IFAC-PapersOnLine*, 51, 50–55, 2018.
8. Azuma, R., Baillot, Y., Behringer, R., Feiner, S., Julier, S., MacIntyre, B., Recent advances in augmented reality. *IEEE Comput. Graphics Appl.*, 21, 6, 34–47, Nov.-Dec. 2001, doi: 10.1109/38.963459.
9. Mujber, T.S., Szecsi, T., Hashmi, M.S.J., Virtual reality applications in manufacturing process simulation. *J. Mater. Process. Technol.*, 155–156, 1834–1838, 2004, https://doi.org/10.1016/j.jmatprotec.2004.04.401.
10. Fast-Berglund, Å., Gong, L., Li, D., Testing and validating Extended Reality (xR) technologies in manufacturing. *Procedia Manuf.*, 25, 31–38, 2018, https://doi.org/10.1016/j.promfg.2018.06.054.
11. Doolani, S., Wessels, C., Kanal, V., Sevastopoulos, C., Jaiswal, A., Nambiappan, H., Makedon, F., A Review of Extended Reality (XR) Technologies for Manufacturing Training. *Technologies*, *8*, *4*, 77, 1–20, 2020.

12. Kuleto, V., Stanescu, M., Ranković, M., Šević, N.P., Paun, D., Teodorescu, S., Extended reality in higher education, a responsible innovation approach for generation y and generation z. *Sustainability*, 13, 11814, 2021.
13. Wiederhold, M.D., Gao, K., Widerhold, B.K., Clinical use of virtual reality distraction system to reduce anxiety and pain in dental procedures. *Cyberpsychol. Behav. Soc. Netw.*, 17, 359–365, 2014.
14. Cipresso, P., Giglioli, I.A.C., Raya, M.A., Riva, G., The past, present, and future of virtual and augmented reality research: A network and cluster analysis of the literature. *Front. Psychol.*, *9*, Article 2086, 2018, https://doi.org/10.3389/fpsyg.2018.02086.
15. Hanson, R., Falkenström, W., Miettinen, M., Augmented reality as a means of conveying picking information in kit preparation for mixed-model assembly. *Comput. Ind. Eng.*, 113, 570–575, 2017, 2017/11/01/.
16. Bucea-Manea-Oni, R., Bucea-Manea-Oni, R., Simion, V.E., Ilic, D., Braicu, C., Manea, N., Sustainability in higher education: The relationship between work-life balance and xr e-learning facilities. *Sustainability*, 12, 5872, 2020.
17. Bala, L., Kinross, J., Martin, G., Koizia, L.J., Kooner, A.S., Shimshon, G.J., Hurkxkens, T.J., Pratt, P.J., Sam, A.H., A remote access mixed reality teaching ward round. *Clin. Teach.*, *18*, 4, 386–390, 2021, https://doi.org/10.1111/tct.13338.
18. Calabuig-Moreno, F., González-Serrano, M.H., Fombona, J., García-Tascón, M., The Emergence of Technology in Physical Education: A General Bibliometric Analysis with a Focus on Virtual and Augmented Reality. *Sustainability*, 12, 2728, 2020.
19. Strzys, M.P., Kapp, S., Thees, M., Kuhn, J., Lukowicz, P., Knierim, P., Schmidt, A., Augmenting the thermal flux experiment: A mixed reality approach with the HoloLens. *Phys. Teach.*, 55, 376–377, 2017.
20. Radianti, J., Majchrzak, T.A., Fromm, J., Wohlgenannt, I., A systematic review of immersive virtual reality applications for higher education: Design elements, lessons learned, and research agenda. *Comput. Educ.*, *147*, Article 103778, 2019, https://doi.org/10.1016/j.compedu.2019.103778.
21. Stylidis, K., Dagman, A., Almius, H., Gong, L., Söderberg, R., Perceived quality evaluation with the use of extended reality, in: *Proc. Design Soc., Int. Conf. Eng. Design*, vol. 1, no. 1, pp. 1993–2002, 2019.
22. Petrov, P.D. and Atanasova, T.V., The Effect of Augmented Reality on Students' Learning Performance in Stem Education. *Information*, *11*, *4*, 209, 2020, https://doi.org/10.3390/info11040209.
23. Radkowski, R. and Kanunganti, S., Augmented reality system calibration for assembly support with the microsoft hololens, in: *Proceedings of the International Manufacturing Science and Engineering Conference*, College Station, TX, USA, p. V003T02A021, 18–22 June 2018.
24. Kaščak, J., Teliskova, M., Torok, J., Baron, P., Zajac, J., Husar, J., Implementation of augmented reality into the training and educational process in order to support spatial perception in technical documentation, in: *Proc. IEEE 6th*

Int. Conf. Ind. Eng. Appl. (ICIEA), pp. 583–587, Apr. 2019, (write authors name again correctly here in this reference].

25. Olsson, T., Lagerstam, E., Kärkkäinen, T., Väänänen-Vainio-Mattila, K., Expected user experience of mobile augmented reality services: a user study in the context of shopping centres. *Pers. Ubiquitous Comput.*, 17, 2, 287–304, 2013.
26. Shin, D.H. and Dunston, P.S., Identification of application areas for augmented reality in industrial construction based on technology suitability. *Autom. Constr.*, 17, 882–894, 2008.
27. Seth, A., Vance, J.M., Oliver, J.H., Virtual reality for assembly methods prototyping: a review. *Virtual Reality*, 15, 5–20, March 01 2011.
28. Stark, E., Bisták, P., Kucera, E., Haffner, O., Kozák, S., Virtual Laboratory Based on Node.js Technology and Visualized in Mixed Reality Using Microsoft HoloLens, in: *Proceedings of the 2017 Federated Conference on Computer Science and Information Systems*, Prague, Czech Republic, pp. 315–322, 3–6 September 2017.
29. Nee, A.Y.C., Ong, S.K., Chryssolouris, G., Mourtzis, D., Augmented reality applications in design and manufacturing. *CIRP Ann.*, 61, 2, 657–679, 2012.
30. Mcmillan, K., Flood, K., Glaeser, R., Virtual reality, augmented reality, mixed reality, and the marine conservation movement. *Aquat. Conserv. Mar. Freshwater Ecosyst.*, 27, 162–168, 2017.
31. Syberfeldt, A., Danielsson, O., Gustavsson, P., Augmented reality smart glasses in the smart factory: Product evaluation guidelines and review of available products. *IEEE Access*, 5, 9118–9130, 2017.
32. Muñoz, A., Mahiques, X., Solanes, J.E., Martí, A., Gracia, L., Tornero, J., Mixed reality-based user interface for quality control inspection of car body surfaces. *J. Manuf. Syst.*, 53, 75–92, Oct. 2019.
33. Mazuryk, T., Virtual Reality History, Applications, Technology and Future, 1999.
34. Gong, L., Fast-Berglund, A., Johansson, B., A Framework for Extended Reality System Development in Manufacturing. *IEEE Access*, 9, 24796–24813, 2021, doi: 10.1109/ACCESS.2021.3056752.
35. Kaminska, D., Sapinski, T., Wiak, S., Tikk, T., Haamer, R.E., Avots, E., Helmi, A., Ozcinar, C., Anbarjafari, G., Virtual reality and its applications in education: Survey. *Information*, 10, 318, 2019.
36. De Ponti, R., Marazzato, J., Maresca, A.M., Rovera, F., Carcano, G., Ferrario, M.M., Pre-graduation medical training including virtual reality during COVID-19 pandemic: A report on students' perception. *BMC Med. Educ.*, 20, 1–7, 2020.
37. Borsci, S., Lawson, G., Broome, S., Empirical evidence, evaluation criteria and challenges for the effectiveness of virtual and mixed reality tools for training operators of car service maintenance. *Comput. Ind.*, 67, 17–26, 2015, 2015/02/01/.

38. Carmigniani, J., Furht, B., Anisetti, M., Ceravolo, P., Damiani, E., Ivkovic, M., Augmented reality technologies, systems and applications. *Multimedia Tools Appl.*, *51*, 341–377, 2010.
39. Kress, B. and Cummings, W., Towards the Ultimate Mixed Reality Experience: HoloLens Display Architecture Choices. *SID Symp. Dig. Tech. Pap.*, 48, 127–131, 2017.
40. Gerup, J., Soerensen, C.B., Dieckmann, P., Augmented reality and mixed reality for healthcare education beyond surgery: An integrative review. *Int. J. Med. Educ.*, 11, 1, 2020.
41. Noghabaei, M., Heydarian, A., Balali, V., Han, K., Trend Analysis on Adoption of Virtual and Augmented Reality in the Architecture, Engineering, and Construction Industry. *Data*, 5, 26, 2020.
42. Lucas, J.D., Immersive VR in the construction classroom to increase student understanding of sequence, assembly, and space of wood frame construction. *J. Inf. Technol. Construct.*, *23*, 179–194, 2018.
43. Coolen, B., Beek, P.J., Geerse, D.J., Roerdink, M., Avoiding 3D Obstacles in Mixed Reality: Does It Differ from Negotiating Real Obstacles? *Sensors*, 20, 1095, 2020.
44. Margetis, G., Apostolakis, K.C., Ntoa, S., Papagiannakis, G., Stephanidis, C., X-Reality Museums: Unifying the Virtual and RealWorld Towards Realistic Virtual Museums. *Appl. Sci.*, 11, 338, 2021.
45. Bahri, H., Krcmarik, D., Moezzi, R., Kočí, J., Efficient use of mixed reality for bim system using microsoft HoloLens. *IFACPapersOnLine*, 52, 235–239, 2019.
46. Eschen, H., Kötter, T., Rodeck, R., Harnisch, M., Schüppstuhl, T., Augmented and Virtual Reality for Inspection and Maintenance Processes in the Aviation Industry. *Procedia Manuf.*, *19*, 156–163, 2018, https://doi.org/10.1016/j.promfg.2018.01.022.
47. Milgram, P. and Kishino, F., A taxonomy of mixed reality visual displays. *IEICE Trans. Inf. Syst.*, 77, 12, 1321–1329, 1994.

8

Extended Reality Applications in Tourism Sector

Pedro Pablo Chambi Condori

Universidad Nacional Jorge Basadre Grohmann, Tacna, Peru

Abstract

In the circumstances of the COVID-19 pandemic, the tourism sector was one of the most worst-hit sectors. Tourism contributes directly and indirectly to job creation, and it also leads to economic development. Tourism also helps to introduce different cultures as well as locally made products of different places across the world. During the pandemic, the tourism sector faced a lot of losses. Its capacity to generate jobs was lost. Its development had stopped completely. After easing of the pandemic restrictions in the world, making up for the losses that the tourism sector faced during the pandemic, for the recovery of the tourism sector's capacity to generate jobs, and for the further development of the tourism sector, application of extended reality (XR) technologies in tourism can be helpful. It could also help in enabling tourism marketing and in the promotion and publicity of tour places. Overall, XR can be very useful for tourism. In this chapter, the different applications of XR technologies in the tourism sector are briefly discussed. Also, the various advantages of XR technologies in the tourism sector are discussed in the chapter.

Keywords: Tourism sector, extended reality, augmented reality (AR), virtual reality (VR), mixed reality (MR), travel, tourist

8.1 Introduction

There are different industries which are based worldwide like tourism for example. It includes a huge amount of information propagation [16].

Email: ppchc2007@gmail.com

Manisha Vohra (ed.) Introduction to Extended Reality (XR) Technologies, (143–156) © 2025 Scrivener Publishing LLC

Tourism is one such industry or sector which is quite well known. It is a prominent sector in the society. It holds a great value. In the tourism sector, various aspects need to be taken care of right from working on strategies for reaching out to the potential tourists to ensuring that the tourists have great overall experience of their entire stay at their tourist destination, each and every thing needs to be worked upon and looked after. The tourism sector contributes in different ways to a country, like economically, socially, etc. Tourism helps in promoting the different aspects of a country, for example, the rich cultural heritage of a country, the local products of a country, etc. The tourism sector generates jobs and provides employment opportunities to many people. The COVID-19 pandemic had an adverse effect on the entire world. The day to day lives of people in each and every work sector—everything—was affected. The tourism sector had come to a complete standstill. Only after the pandemic restrictions were lifted did the tourism sector reopen and start working again slowly. To get the tourism sector back to the pre-pandemic state and to help it recover the losses and grow, different approaches are essential. Approaches like inclusion of different technologies can be a great option. Even before the pre-pandemic period, the tourism sector was looking and moving toward various approaches to help it grow. In some places, the tourism sector had witnessed the implementation of certain approaches in a few cases for the overall betterment and growth, but the pandemic had hit this sector hard. Now, especially after the pandemic period, bringing different approaches becomes necessary for the betterment of this sector. In recent times, the tourism sector has witnessed various advances with the help of approaches like the inclusion of different technologies. The inclusion of technologies like XR technologies can truly be very advantageous for the tourism sector. Application of technologies like XR in the tourism sector and how it can be helpful for this sector will be discussed further on in this book chapter.

Tourism marketing is a key element in the tourism industry and is part of the strategy of all its companies, be it accommodation or other organizations related to leisure, travel, and catering. The tourism business is not entirely self-managed since many processes are carried out in different areas and departments, where experts carry out the work process of various kinds. Nowadays, everything from products to experiences is marketed, and in the marketing strategy, communication and advertising take center stage in order to reach as many audiences as possible. In addition, if the objective is to get closer to customers and improve sales, tourism marketing turns out to be the right tool to achieve it. XR technologies can help tourists in different ways by helping with local language translation, providing additional information regarding the place they are visiting, etc., and overall help in providing a great experience to the tourists. The positive experience different tourists have after visiting a tourist destination is very useful as it plays a great role in creating a good buzz for that particular tourist destination, which ultimately helps in tourism marketing.

8.2 Extended Reality (XR) Technologies

Extended reality (XR) is referring to the combination of virtual environments and real environments where human and machine interaction takes place via hardware and computer technology generated interactions. XR technologies consist of virtual reality (VR), mixed reality (MR), and augmented reality (AR) [14]. There are various technologies emerging. AR is one of them [11].

8.2.1 AR

Physical reality is enhanced by AR by the integration of virtual objects into the physical world. AR can overlap or mix computer-generated virtual objects with real-world scenes or objects [32]. AR is a technique that uses digital technology to superimpose information on the usual formats of image, video, or text; in other words, augmented reality superimposes digital elements on images of reality through applications that are executed through a computer, a smartphone, or a tablet device. It is a technological trend in which digital data merges with the real world. In this way, users can enjoy a different experience where reality and virtual merge. With AR, virtual objects can be introduced into the real world and interact with them, thanks to digital technology. By overlaying virtual information on a user's perception of the real world, AR merges the real world and the virtual world [10]. AR utilizes real world like a substrate and extends it. The extension is done by overlaying information which is generated by the computer [6]. So, AR is a novel interaction tool which enables an interaction between a human and a computer. On a real-world environment, AR overlays computer-generated information [22]. AR is a technology that is mature. AR has been utilized in different domains [6]. For areas like edutainment, education, or cultural heritage presentations, applications of AR have a great immersion potential [27].

The author in [34] has defined some properties of an AR system. An AR system brings together virtual objects and also real objects in an environment which is real. An AR system runs in real time and in an interactive manner. An AR system aligns virtual and real objects with each other [34].

A user's perception of the real world and interaction with the real world is made better by AR [24]. For the purpose of presenting content, new possibilities are brought by AR technology. This technology allows the user-observed content to be added to the real world. In natural dimensions also, AR lets us visualize objects which are located in distant locations—its 3D models. Computer-generated content, sounds, etc., is superimposed by AR to make the perception of observed objects better [9]. For making sure of efficiency in knowledge transfer for different processes and in different environments, AR mixes actual reality and virtual reality, making new tools available to the user [23], which is very useful. Users might see a live view of the world which is surrounding them, augmented with digital annotations, some information superimposed upon it, etc., by using a display like mobile phone or tablet. Where a particular product or item of interest is kept, when the device is pointed in that direction by a user, the system augments output with additional information regarding the environment. The additional information varies from information regarding points of interest to receiving real-time notifications related to a location, etc., [15]. Common examples of AR include Pokemon Go and Google Glass [29].

8.2.2 VR

In the past 5 years, VR has quickly leapt to the tangible world of living rooms of people, their playing fields, and beyond from the realm of fantasy and science fiction [29]. Undeniably, many people's interest in the past years has been attracted by VR. This technology provides such a manner of human–computer interaction which is powerful, easy, and intuitive. Without the requirement for learning how the complex user interface works, the users can view and even manipulate a simulated environment in the same manner that we act in the real world [19]. A computer-simulated environment is what VR is. which lets users manipulate 3D virtual models online. The physical world is experientially replaced by VR [32]. In other words, VR is where a user can interact and navigate in an environment which is computer-generated, triggering real-time simulation of the user's senses [33]. Many people can experience VR technology due to today's equipment of VR. In the case of sightseeing, for example, it is done by keeping the head in a desired direction during walking utilizing motion sensors or control stick. So, in this manner, the user experience is brought very close to reality, as close as possible by VR, making the user experience as if he is actually being transported to another location and time—namely, the virtual world—which is due to VR trying to occupy all human senses [17]. In various scenarios, applications and benefits of VR have been explored by researchers [8]. For example, using VR, different applications such as data visualization systems and flight simulators were the ones which were developed comparatively quick. Afterward, VR was applied as a teleoperating and collaborative medium, and it was applied in other different areas as well [19].

8.2.3 MR

Another XR technology is mixed reality (MR). In MR systems, users perceive the real environment around them, i.e., the physical environment and also the digital elements presented through MR systems. Semitransparent display utilization is one example. The users, when utilizing MR systems, are provided with the illusion that digital objects and physical objects are in the same space [35]. However, in this chapter, we will be discussing and understanding two XR technologies with application in tourism, i.e., AR and VR.

8.3 Application of XR Technologies in Tourism

Technology is used in different work sectors right from education, medical to tourism, etc. Technology does have an impact in each and every area of work where it is used. It has had a great impact on management and marketing of places [1]. In order to remain competitive in the tourism sector and to attract modern tourists, digital technology evolution has become a necessary thing in recent times. VR and AR are new forms of digital technology which are utilized in public space [2]. Both XR technologies VR and AR can be a great resource for the tourism sector's growth. In cultural heritage and tourism research, different new realities which include VR, AR, and MR have been getting more and more attention [25].

If AR and VR are noticed, then they have got the interest attracted of not only investors but also the general public in the past 5 years [3]. Furthermore, keeping focused on the aspect of visualization of information at indoor cultural spaces and outdoor cultural spaces, the combination of linked open data (LOD) and AR technologies is very interesting for the users on the sectors of cultural heritage and tourism, respectively [5]. VR and AR are both utilized in different sectors from consumer application to manufacturers, and they are providing great benefits via several applications [7].

If the tourism industry is viewed in today's time, it faces different challenges which include competitiveness of destinations and marketing [21].

It needs different technologies which can help it grow. XR technologies like VR and AR can be useful in the tourism sector. XR technologies' application in tourism can help in overcoming different challenges that the sector faces and can help it grow in different ways. In fact, people have already started using XR technologies in the tourism sector. According to the authors in [12], the pace of AR adoption in the tourism sector is growing. Recently, various organizations and destinations have either implemented this innovative technology or at least begun to have considerations regarding the opportunities that AR provides in order to bring enhancement in the experience of the visitor. The past few years have witnessed a huge number of scholars carrying out research on different aspects like AR acceptance and behavioral intentions, AR user requirements, and creating a tourism experience with AR as well as AR tourism gaming [12].

Attraction places for visitors, with the help of AR, get the ability of creating content which is engaging and is overlaid onto artworks or objects [13].

There are two types of augmented reality technology that are currently used:

- Marker based on augmented reality: It works through a 2D marker, similar to a QR code. When one of these markers is pointed with the device, the augmented reality experience is launched.
- Without augmented reality marker: With this version, you can use any place in the real world as a trigger to launch augmented reality. Typically, these triggers are usually images or locations. Applications that use this technology can use GPS information to generate the augmented reality launch when the device is in a certain location.

8.3.1 AR in the Tourism Sector

From tourism's point of view, in a first aspect, it is important to make potential tourists know the tourist attractions that a certain place offers, whose resource is advertised through the networks of travel agencies and the companies that operate in the tourism sector, and for this, the application of AR in the tourism sector can help.

The companies that operate in the tourism market require that their products, offers, etc., reach their customers in the best possible way, and to all markets, for which they carry out promotional and advertising activities through various means; and one of the modern means that has a potential to reach potential customers in a massive way is with the application or use of AR. With the help of AR, in a flexible way, the travelers can know information regarding the places to visit, hotels, typical food dishes, crafts, and the landscaped spaces that nature offers [30].

AR technology has the capability of revolutionizing the experience of the tourist. It does so by making the planning, preview and access possible of the location-based information of the holiday journey and destinations. All this is possible from different places in a simple and interactive way. Hotel can be previewed and booked by users, its information can be accessed by them while they are there. The users can also navigate around their destination. A user can also do a translation of written and spoken signs or conversations in locating dining and entertainment options. All this can all be done, thanks to AR, in a simple way via an app on a mobile device [30]. The first medium having the potential for introducing AR to mass market are smartphones, which have a significant impact for AR tourism applications [4].

The initial AR smartphone apps came out in the year 2009, utilizing AR technology for adding a layer of guidance, content, and entertainment to physical locations that are viewed via the smartphone's camera view. The very first app which was built particularly for tourism was an interactive and real-time guide aiming to enhance the experience of the visitor. The app was Tuscany+. Layering digital enhancements over an already existing real-life scenario or reality is made possible by AR technology [30].

Perspective guests can survey the rooms before booking them due to AR technology, which is a great advantage. For a guest to select a hotel, the particular hotel's locational advantage is considered to be one of the most attractive features. AR may enable the user to have a glance at the location of the hotel. It may also provide a view of historical events that are eminent and cultural experiences of the nearby destinations. During the time that the guests interact with their apps, AR may advertise more of its attractive features along with beautiful sightseeing [30]. These are some really useful advantages of the application of AR in the tourism sector.

Not just in this but also in many different ways can AR be helpful in the tourism sector. We will further understand how the application of AR can help in the tourism sector with the help of some examples which are as follows.

Quite meaningful insights can be provided by AR visualizations when applied in archaeological or historical parks or museums, for initiated visitor or specialist and also for the ones who are non-specialist or who are first-time visitors who have a difficulty in imagining how a site could have initially looked like [20].

The study done by the authors in [12] had the aim to find out the perceived value of stakeholders with respect to the implementation of AR so as to enhance museum experience at cultural heritage sites. As a case study, for this research, a museum in the UK was considered. A common agreement was found across stakeholder interviews and focus groups, and it was that AR implementation adds a number of various aspects of value to the museum as well as the visitor's experience [12].

In [18], the authors carried out a research in which, in order to enrich a visitor's enjoyment and learning while they are touring a culturally rich city, the authors [18] implemented an AR treasure hunt game. For this particular study, the authors [18] chose Valletta, the 2018 European Capital of Culture. To find out the effectiveness of an AR serious game which has built-in navigation tools, two prototype mobile applications were implemented and deployed. After the research, the conclusion obtained was that in providing city information and enriching the tourist's experience, AR was useful. Also, it is important to include GPS navigation as it is crucial to elicit interest and achieve a competitive advantage over traditional city tours [18].

A partnership between Manchester Metropolitan University (MMU), the Dublin City Council, and Dublin Institute of Technology (DIT) helped to emerge the Dublin AR Project. This project got its origin from the idea of supporting Dublin's brand development to become the "innovative city" in Europe. The aim of the authors in [15] is to find out the requirements of the tourists for the development of a mobile AR tourism application in urban heritage. Tourists visiting Dublin City, which included international as well as domestic tourists, were interviewed briefly, and a thematic analysis was utilized to analyze the interviews' findings. So, it was suggested from the findings that even though AR is past the hype stage, this technology is on the verge of being implemented in the tourism industry in a meaningful way. The findings also convey that it requires to be designed for serving a particular purpose for the user. The end result of this research aims to develop a mobile AR application for the tourism industry in Dublin [15].

Thus, AR can transform the tourism sector for the better in different ways as seen in the discussion above.

8.3.2 VR in Tourism

VR technology can benefit tourism planning and management. VR technology possesses unique testing capabilities, which is why it can benefit tourism planning and management very well. In the development of management plans, an extremely vital element is understanding of the visitors' patterns of space, place, and time, and this also includes shifting the burden from areas having heavy usage to those areas having limited usage. What is needed here are 3D visualizations as they are superb tools in doing so. VR technology is continuing to evolve, and the entertainment industry has got a way to make this evolution very useful with respect to marketing the different tourist attractions which are entertaining. The aim of the authors in [31] is to provide an insight regarding how recent trends in VR have changed the manner that the tourism and hospitality industry communicates their offerings and meets the tourists' needs. So, the approach by the authors in [31] is on the basis of literature review which they carried out systematically, where the relations between focal concepts are provided for the analysis of potential future developments regarding VR. This paper not only identifies but also analyzes how tourism and the hospitality industry are affected by VR technology through three main touch points. Those three points are marketing of tourism on the basis of technology, planning and management of future tourism, and potential of VR potential in changing consumer requirements. As a part of smart tourism, VR is being developed in order to give information regarding different destinations and attractions while showing its potential to become a new tourism service. However, this trend has proved to be very useful. VR is letting tourists gain the experience of a destination in advance, which is quite an advantage of VR application in tourism. It is also lets tourists get a preview of local attractions. Detailed VR navigations which are detailed, interactive, easy and realistic help the tourists in the process of planning of trip and activity [31]. VR thus has the potential and can transform the tourism sector for the better. VR will continue to advance, and as such, opportunities in the tourism sector will grow exponentially [31].

In tourism, the experience of the tourist when the tourist visits a particular place is of great importance. Tourist destinations aim to provide a great overall experience to the tourists. For this purpose, they work on various things—for example, some of them are ensuring that the tourists get to know the history and other important information regarding the place that they are visiting. Along with it, they also try to make sure that the tourist gets to experience the actual essence and culture of that particular place that the tourist is visiting, and similarly, there are many such things which are taken care of in order to provide a great overall experience to the tourists. XR technologies can be helpful here, and specifically talking about VR, it can be useful. For example, museums are one of the highly visited locations by tourists. In the context of a museum, various studies emphasize regarding the positive effect brought on from the cultural experience by the use of VR [26]. This is another great advantage of VR application in tourism.

Further talking about VR in tourism, the authors in [28] have written a paper regarding the utilization of VR as a tool in tourism destinations in order to develop the behavior perspective of tourists. The authors conducted a study in this context. An exploring research study was carried out by them. The study consisted of a certain number of respondents for identifying the role of VR in selecting a tourist destination and also the potential customers' expectations which could rekindle the tourism industry for a post-pandemic world [28].

The results pointed that VR applications that are highly utilized for destination marketing purposes aim toward the creation of a certain image for a tourist destination. It even aims to communicate this to the outside world in a manner which is consistent and coordinated. The findings also promote the importance of developing future scenarios for VR as a decisive factor for strategic planning in the sector of tourism [28].

So, as discussed above in this chapter, overall, VR application in the tourism sector, just like AR application in the tourism sector, is advantageous and can, to a great extent, be helpful for the sector, and these XR technologies can thus truly transform the tourism sector in different ways for the betterment and further development of the sector.

8.4 Conclusion

The tourism sector is a very important sector. This sector is a great contributor to a country in economic, social, etc., ways as stated previously. In this chapter, different applications of XR technologies are discussed along with its advantages. As seen from the discussion in the chapter, XR technologies can really transform the tourism sector for the betterment and further development of the sector. XR technologies are a boon for the tourism sector. It can provide different opportunities for the tourism industry. Overall, XR technologies can be very useful for tourism sector.

References

1. Jung, T.H. and tom Dieck, M.C., Augmented reality, virtual reality and 3D printing for the co-creation of value for the visitor experience at cultural heritage places. *J. Place Manag. Dev.*, *10*, 2, 140–151, 2017, https://doi.org/10.1108/JPMD-07-2016-0045.

2. Katkuri, P.K., Mantri, A., Anireddy, S., Innovations in Tourism Industry Development Using Augmented Reality (AR), Virtual Reality (VR). *IEEE Region 10 Annual International Conference, Proceedings/TENCON*, 2019-October (December), pp. 2578–2581, 2019, https://doi.org/10.1109/TENCON.2019.8929478.
3. Cipresso, P., Giglioli, I.A.C., Raya, M.A., Riva, G., The past, present, and future of virtual and augmented reality research: A network and cluster analysis of the literature. *Front. Psychol.*, *9*, Article 2086, 2018, https://doi.org/10.3389/fpsyg.2018.02086.
4. Kečkeš, A. and Tomičić, I., Augmented Reality in Tourism - Research and Applications Overview. *Interdiscip. Descr. Complex Syst.*, *15*, 1, 157–167, 2017, https://doi.org/10.7906/indecs.15.2.5.
5. Moraitou, E., Konstantakis, M., Kontaki, C., Aliprantis, I., Kalatha, E., Kalavrytinos, P., Tsigris, A., Tsougkrianis, P., Anagnostopoulos, C., Caridakis, G., Travelogue with augmented cultural and contemporary experience. *CEUR Workshop Proc.*, *2235*, 66–75, 2018.
6. Boboc, R.G., Băutu, E., Gîrbacia, F., Popovici, N., Popovici, D.-M., Augmented Reality in Cultural Heritage: An Overview of the Last Decade of Applications. *Appl. Sci.*, 12, 19, 9859, 2022, https://doi.org/10.3390/app12199859.
7. Yagol, P., Ramos, F., Trilles, S., Torres-Sospedra, J., Perales, F.J., New trends in using augmented reality apps for smart city contexts. *ISPRS Int. J. Geo-Inf.*, *7*, 12, 2018, https://doi.org/10.3390/ijgi7120478.
8. Radianti, Z., Majchrzak, T.A., Fromm, J., Wohlgenannt, A systematic review of immersive virtual reality applications for higher education: Design elements, lessons learned, and research agenda. *Comput. Educ.*, *147*, Article 103778, 2020, https://doi.org/10.1016/j.compedu.2019.103778.
9. Templin, T. and Popielarczyk, D., The use of low-cost unmanned aerial vehicles in the process of building models for cultural tourism, 3D web and augmented/mixed reality applications. *Sensors (Switzerland)*, *20*, 19, 1–26, 2020, https://doi.org/10.3390/s20195457.
10. Syberfeldt, A., Danielsson, O., Gustavsson, P., Augmented reality smart glasses in the smart factory: Product evaluation guidelines and review of available products. *IEEE Access*, 5, 9118–9130, 2017.
11. Cabero-Almenara, J., Barroso-Osuna, J., Llorente-Cejudo, C., del Mar Fernández Martínez, M., Educational Uses of Augmented Reality (AR): Experiences in Educational Science. *Sustainability*, 11, 4990, 2019.
12. Tom Dieck, M.C. and Jung, T.H., Value of augmented reality at cultural heritage sites: A stakeholder approach. *J. Destin. Mark. Manag.*, *6*, 2, 110–117, 2017, https://doi.org/10.1016/j.jdmm.2017.03.002.
13. Tom Dieck, M.C., Jung, T., Han, D.I., Mapping requirements for the wearable smart glasses augmented reality museum application. *J. Hosp. Tour. Technol.*, *7*, 3, 230–253, 2016, https://doi.org/10.1108/JHTT-09-2015-0036.

14. Doolani, S., Wessels, C., Kanal, V., Sevastopoulos, C., Jaiswal, A., Nambiappan, H., Makedon, F., A Review of Extended Reality (XR) Technologies for Manufacturing Training. *Technologies*, 8, 4, 77, 1–20, 2020.
15. Kourouthanassis, P., Boletsis, C., Bardaki, C., Chasanidou, D., Tourists responses to mobile augmented reality travel guides: The role of emotions on adoption behavior. *Pervasive Mob. Comput.*, 18, 71–87, 2015, https://doi.org/10.1016/j.pmcj.2014.08.009.
16. Kenteris, M., Gavalas, D., Economou, D., An innovative mobile electronic tourist guide application. *Pers. Ubiquitous Comput.*, 13, 103–118, 2009, https://doi.org/10.1007/s00779-007-0191-y.
17. Kuleto, V., Stanescu, M., Ranković, M., Šević, N.P., Paun, D., Teodorescu, S., Extended reality in higher education, a responsible innovation approach for generation y and generation z. *Sustainability*, 13, 11814, 2021.
18. Cauchi, M. and Scerri, D., Enriching Tourist UX via a Location Based AR Treasure Hunt Game, in: *2019 IEEE 9th International Conference on Consumer Electronics (ICCE-Berlin)*, Berlin, Germany, pp. 199–204, 2019, doi: 10.1109/ICCE-Berlin47944.2019.8966141.
19. Mazuryk, T., Virtual Reality History, Applications, Technology and Future, 1999.
20. Damala, A., Marchal, I., Houlier, P., Merging Augmented Reality Based Features in Mobile Multimedia Museum Guides, in: *Proceedings of the XXI International CIPA Symposium*, Athens, Greece, 01-06 October, 2007.
21. Jung, T. and Han, D.-I., Augmented Reality (AR) in Urban Heritage Tourism. *e-Rev. Tour. Res.*, 5, 1–5, 2014.
22. Nee, A.Y.C., Ong, S.K., Chryssolouris, G., Mourtzis, D., Augmented reality applications in design and manufacturing. *CIRP Ann.*, 61, 2, 657–679, 2012.
23. Hincapié, M., Caponio, A., Rios, H., González Mendívil, E., An introduction to Augmented Reality with applications in aeronautical maintenance. *2011 13th International Conference on Transparent Optical Networks*, pp. 1–4, 2011, doi: 10.1109/ICTON.2011.5970856.
24. Carmigniani, J., Furht, B., Anisetti, M., Ceravolo, P., Damiani, E., Ivkovic, M., Augmented reality technologies, systems and applications. *Multimed. Tools Appl.*, *51*, 341–377, 2010.
25. Trunfio, M., Campana, S., Magnelli, A., Measuring the impact of functional and experiential mixed reality elements on a museum visit. *Curr. Issues Tourism*, 23, 1990–2008, 2020.
26. Popovici, D.-M., Iordache, D., Comes, R., Neamtu, C.G.D., Bautu, E., Interactive Exploration of Virtual Heritage by Means of Natural Gestures. *Appl. Sci.*, 12, 4452, 2022.
27. Novotný, M., Lacko, J., Samuelčík, M., Applications of multi-touch augmented reality system in education and presentation of virtual heritage. *Procedia Comput. Sci.*, 25, 231–235, 2013.

28. Oncioiu, I. and Priescu, I., The Use of Virtual Reality in Tourism Destinations as a Tool to Develop Tourist Behavior Perspective. *Sustainability*, 14, 7, 4191, 2022, https://doi.org/10.3390/su14074191K.
29. Mcmillan, K., Flood, K., Glaeser, R., Virtual reality, augmented reality, mixed reality, and the marine conservation movement. *Aquat. Conserv. Mar. Freshwater Ecosyst.*, 27, 162–168, 2017.
30. Nayyar, A., Mahapatra, B., Le, D., Suseendran., G., Virtual Reality (VR) & Augmented Reality (AR) technologies for tourism and hospitality industry. *Int. J. Eng. Technol. (UAE)*, 7, 156–160, 2018, doi: 10.14419/ijet.v7i2.21.11858.
31. Pestek, A. and Sarvan, M., Virtual reality and modern tourism. *J. Tour. Futures*, 7, 2, 245–250, 2021, https://doi.org/10.1108/JTF-01-2020-0004.
32. Lu, Y. and Smith, S., Augmented Reality E-Commerce: How the Technology Benefits People's Lives, *Human Computer Interaction*, IntechOpen, Rijeka, Croatia, 2008, doi: 10.5772/6301.
33. Guttentag, D.A., Virtual reality: Applications and implications for tourism. *Tour. Manag.*, 31, 5, 637–651, 2010, doi: https://doi.org/10.1016/j.tourman.2009.07.003.
34. Azuma, R., Baillot, Y., Behringer, R., Feiner, S., Julier, S., MacIntyre, B., Recent advances in augmented reality. *IEEE Comput. Graphics Appl.*, 21, 6, 34–47, Nov.-Dec. 2001, doi: 10.1109/38.963459.
35. Costanza, E., Kunz, A., Fjeld, M., Mixed Reality: A Survey, in: *Human Machine Interaction. Lecture Notes in Computer Science*. D. Lalanne, J. Kohlas, (eds), vol 5440, pp. 47–68, Springer, Berlin, Heidelberg, 2009, https://doi.org/10.1007/978-3-642-00437-7_3.

9

Role of Augmented Reality and Virtual Reality in Medical Imaging

S.N. Kumar[1], A. Lenin Fred[2*], Ajay Kumar H.[2], L. R. Jonisha Miriam[2], I. Christina Jane[2], Parasuraman Padmanabhan[3] and Balázs Gulyás[3]

[1]Amal Jyothi College of Engineering, Kanjirappally, Kerala, India
[2]Mar Ephraem College of Engineering and Technology, Elavuvilai, Tamil Nadu, India
[3]Cognitive Neuroimaging Centre (CONIC), Lee Kong Chian School of Medicine, Nanyang Technological University, Singapore, Singapore

Abstract
The role of automation and artificial intelligence plays a pivotal role in the healthcare sector for disease diagnosis and surgical preplanning. Augmented reality and virtual reality have immense applications in the healthcare industry, and especially medical imaging enjoys fruitful outcomes. Augmented reality is a technology that couples real-world objects with virtual ones, while virtual reality generates a completely virtual environment. The AR and VR role is inevitable in radiology for proficient disease diagnosis and treatment planning. Radiology education has a new face change with the advancements in AR and VR. The 3D modeling of medical data helps doctors and physicians have an efficient understanding of the anatomy and anomalies. The AR and VR aid biomedical engineers in visualizing the internal circuitry of scanning equipment and facilitate the ease of repair, paving the way to propose a design for better proficiency. For troubleshooting scanning equipment, a service engineer utilizes AR and VR tools to discuss with the experts to find an optimum solution. The chapter organization is as follows: AR and VR technology and its impact in the health care sector, the role of AR and VR in medical imaging, different perspectives of AR and VR applications in radiology, and the future of radiology with AR and VR technology.

Keywords: Medical imaging, virtual reality, augmented reality, radiology

**Corresponding author*: leninfredip@gmail.com

Manisha Vohra (ed.) Introduction to Extended Reality (XR) Technologies, (157–172) © 2025 Scrivener Publishing LLC

9.1 Introduction

Virtual and augmented facts are taking an increasing number of the essential position in surgical training additionally to surgical care. R. Randall McKnight *et al.* give an opinion on the evolving nature of this education equipment and offer examples in their use and efficiency. Additionally, at present, they approximately mentioned the realistic and moral implications of incorporating this generation and its effect on each orthopedic surgeon and their patients. Head-installed displays (HMDs) constitute a probable adjunct to surgical accuracy and training. They concluded that AR and VR become mainstays of destiny education efforts. However, greater proof is needed to make a decision as to which education generation interprets to progress medical performance [1]. The role of XR in cardiothoracic surgery is highlighted in [2], also gaining prominence in surgical preplanning, simulation, and telemedicine. The embedded controller for 3D imaging and visualization using AR is highlighted in [3], which produces efficient results than the classical tracked controllers. The application of VR in CBCT scanning and radiography is put forward in [4]. An ophthalmology application of AR/VR, Holo Lens with the pupil lab eye tracker, was found to be proficient for surgical preplanning [5].

Augmented and combined reality are novel show technology which is capable of merging digital objects, in both two and three dimensions, with the particular world. With augmented or combined reality, clinical imaging could also be more easily available or displayed in the real 3D area during techniques to embellish guidance, at instances while this data is the maximum needed. In [6], the modern-state applications of the AR/VR applications in 3D visualization are highlighted. An open-source computer simulation toolkit completely included in one of the foremost extensively used clinical image visualization and evaluation software platforms is put forward in [7]. By integrating VR features in 3D Slicer, a longtime clinical image evaluation and visualization platform, Slicer VR, allows digital reality experience through one click. Slicer VR permits shared collaborative VR experience both regionally and remotely [7].

An in-depth review of the applications of augmented reality (AR) in three important fields where AR use is currently increasing like entertainment, medicine, and retail is highlighted in [8]. The VR-based 3D reconstructions of CT-scans in craniofacial malformations thereby fused CT and MR data [9]. The applications of 3D AR in medical image registration using 3D AR gadgets were put forward in [10]. The features of VR in anatomy education were stated in [11], the performance analysis was validated by comparing with the 2D techniques, and VR improves the proficiency in teaching of anatomy. An augmented reality platform was proposed in [12] for the extraction of the region of interest in medical images using 3D models, producing efficient results when compared with the manual and semi-automatic methods.

The effectiveness of digital reality (VR) as a tutorial device to supply immersive and experiential learning environments to biomedical engineering (BME) students was highlighted in [13]. This study administered scholar immersion using motion pictures of simulation-based medical settings to market BME scholar education in required conversation abilities while participating with healthcare professionals. This study concludes that the investment of your time and money to make VR videos and acquire VR sources was beneficial in developing an improved studying experience for BME students [13]. An overview of AR/VR applications in education, training, and patient care in radiology was put forward in [14]. The VR-based system enables cancer patients to understand how radiotherapy helps in curing cancer cells. The 3D simulation of radiotherapy patients enables the patients to understand the process of radiotherapy [15].

Section 9.2 highlights the specific applications of AR/VR in medical imaging and surgical preplanning. The future of AR/VR in the healthcare sector is also highlighted, and finally, a conclusion is drawn in Section 9.3.

9.2 Materials and Methods

The concept of augmented reality and virtual reality is depicted in Figure 9.1. Virtual reality helps the users to visualize real-world objects in a virtual environment as depicted in Figure 9.1(a). Figure 9.1(b) depicts the pass-through augmented reality, where real-world objects and virtual entities are visualized through a camera or specialized devices. Figure 9.1(c) depicts the see-through augmented reality through devices like Google glasses.

Virtual reality and augmented reality have immense applications in the medical sector. Figure 9.2 depicts the applications of VR/AR technology based on the clinician and patients as the user.

AR/VR technology plays a vital role in surgical preplanning especially in biopsy for cancer diagnosis. VR is an efficient clinical tool for clinical education and aids the medical personnel for a better understanding of the concepts. Contouring or annotation is a notable feature of VR technology in radiology and aids the radiologist in scanning report assessments. VR serves patient education and, especially in this current COVID-19

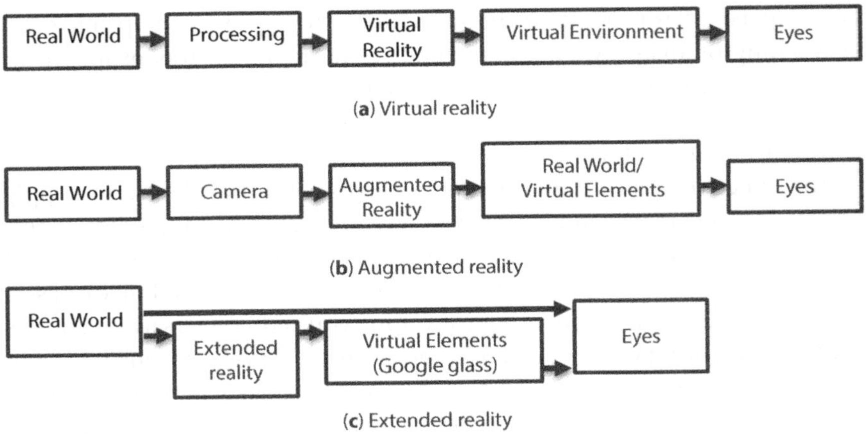

Figure 9.1 Concept of virtual reality and augmented reality.

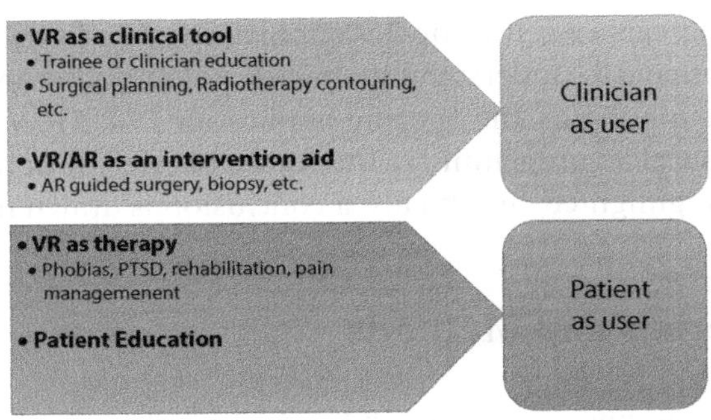

Figure 9.2 Clinician and patient as users of AR/VR technology.

scenario, helps the public to be aware of the health policies. VR therapy is gaining prominence in phobias, rehabilitation, pain management, and post-traumatic stress disorder (PTSD).

9.2.1 Role of Virtual Reality/Augmented Reality in Radiology

Virtual reality (VR) and augmented reality (AR) technologies can revolutionize healthcare, with numerous implications for radiology [16–18]. These technologies have found applications in a wide range of fields, including entertainment and gaming as well as the military, education, and sports. These technologies can model real-world entities in a better manner for improved understanding. Many medical specialties are now investigating how these tools can be applied to their respective fields.

9.2.1.1 *Improve the Radiology Training*

AR/VR technology improves active learner participation, and the research studies indicate that these technologies increase the attention of participation. Medical imaging has already revolutionized treatment procedures and aids for surgical pre-planning. The medical images are obtained in DICOM or Raw format and are converted into 3D entities. AR was already utilized for training radiologists in understanding the complex anatomy. VR finds its role in supporting the radiologist to react in specific situations like administering the contrast agents in the human body. AR/VR technologies also aid the trainee radiologist in better understanding the expert lecturers. The students utilize the stereoscopic viewers for a better understanding of the concepts. The operational procedures of the radiological equipment are also strengthened by AR/VR technology. Artificial intelligence relies heavily on AR/VR technology in better understanding of the concepts. The role of AR/VR in imparting improved knowledge in radiology is stated in [19, 20].

9.2.1.2 *Improve the Effective Communication Between the Radiologists*

Complex surgical procedures necessitate a thorough understanding of anatomic relationships to plan and execute them [17, 21]. There are several commercially available simulators for novice procedurals or surgeons. Three-dimensional models enable the physicians to perform surgical preplanning and play a vital role in complicated scenarios. VR/AR tools enable the radiologist to share the images with different users simultaneously, thereby performing annotation and helping in obtaining collective opinions from experts.

9.2.1.3 *Improve the Communication with the Patients*

In a variety of ways, virtual reality and augmented reality technologies can help with patient education. It makes interventional radiology procedures more comfortable for patients. Some patients are having fear in taking scans. VR tools enable the patients to understand the process of radiology workflow, thereby making them comfortable in taking scans and educating them what has to be done while entering a radiology department in a hospital, what the physicians will be doing, and the entire process like preparing the patients for taking scans to report after the acquisition of images. Immersive reality can also be used to simulate a procedure so that a patient is aware of the steps and what he or she will experience. The application of augmented reality and virtual reality technology in the treatment of patients has a lot of potentials. A detailed study on orthopedic rehabilitation using AR/VR technologies was highlighted in [22]. A systematic review was conducted in [23], highlighting the rehabilitation of stroke patients using AR/VR technologies. AR/VR-based games to relieve the stress of patients were highlighted in [23]. The patient-specific anatomical model was generated by using 3D printing technology based on AR/VR technology [24]. The AR-based electronic health record for patients was proposed in [25], AR/VR glasses with data gloves are also used for the 3D anatomical organ study. In [26], the AR-based platform for arachnophobia treatment was highlighted; the mental health care of the patients is given importance. The role of AR in teleconsultation was highlighted in [27]. Telemedicine gains prominence in the COVID-19 scenario.

9.2.1.4 Support for the Interventional Radiology Procedures

When performing interventional radiology procedures, doctors must always navigate needles, wires, and catheters to the desired location. The location of the lesion and its size are vital before surgery, AR tools aid the physicians in the investigation of lesion location and help efficiently in targeting the desired anatomical structure for treatment and drug delivery. AR has also been used to provide these types of intraoperative fusion images in open surgery neurosurgery and tracheostomy tube placement surgery, neurosurgery, and tracheostomy tube placement. The role of AR in interventional radiology is highlighted in [28]. The role of AR/VR in radiology education is highlighted in [20]. In [29], the advanced concepts of AR/VR in healthcare education were proposed; the challenges are also discussed in this work. The role of AR/VR in radiology education, training, and applications in healthcare is highlighted in [30]. The process of learning the anatomy of human organs by AR/VR is highlighted in [31], and the role of AR/VR in radiology workflow for better diagnosis of diseases is highlighted in [17].

9.2.2 Surgical Preplanning and Medical Image Analysis

The overview of AR/VR in the surgical application is put forward in [32]; the role of VR in spine endoscopic surgery was also stated in this work.

Depth perception is crucial in AR-based surgery; hence, in [33], the authors proposed an improved depth perception mechanism by switching from AR to VR technology. A review on the applications of AR, VR, and MR in spine surgery was investigated in [34]. The skill of visual reality has evolved, and VR and AR are increasingly being used in educational and surgical applications. The development of virtual reality technologies allows users to integrate medical knowledge, medical data, and graphical data. It can provide more precise information, allowing users to increase their safety and reduce their risk. Although virtual reality and augmented reality are not extensively employed in dentistry, they have made tremendous progress in other professions like neurosurgery and cranial surgery. On the head-mounted display (HMD), users can examine medical information and images connected to the procedure. It can also significantly lower surgical risk when compared to the regular visual data.

To properly incorporate AR or VR into a surgical procedure, surgeons must be able to call on intelligent augmentation in the appropriate format and at the appropriate time throughout the procedure. To achieve this goal, first, recover and understand the process, and then model and monitor it to design adaptive, dynamic user interfaces that are action- and workflow-driven. This is accomplished by obtaining as many key factors as possible during a series of identical treatments. Signals, such as endoscope pictures, ECG signals, or external sensors such as external cameras, RFID, or magnetic or inert sensors mounted to an operating gear or staff can be collected from within the operating room. The variable matrix length representing all signals recorded over time is represented for each procedure. Intraoperative signals allow us to anticipate current process status, and for every moment and task activate personalized visualization and user interfaces. At each stage of the surgery, this information changes depending on surgical actions and the current status of critical parameters in a surgical operation, such as patient monitoring data, endoscopic recordings, and active tools.

The immersive virtual environment has been produced in the Oculus Rivet CV1 with a pixel resolution of 1,200 × 1,080 per eye in Unity (version 2017.3.0f3), a multi-platform game engine. The head-mounted display had a diagonal field of view of around 110° and a frame rate of 90 frames per second. The original Oculus tracking system has a maximum recommended tracking space of 5 × 5 ft for the head-mounted display and two Oculus touch controls. Both the tracking position and orientation are permitted. The wide tracking space enabled fluid and realistic movements that encouraged users to move both themselves and the 3D model to monitor the anatomy better. A low-cost VR-based simulation was proposed in

[35] for oncology surgery procedures, and the recent innovative AR/VR techniques in spine surgery were investigated in [36]. The role of AR in neurosurgery was analyzed in [37], and the VR and 3D printing models' importance in surgery are stated in [38].

9.2.3 Virtual Reality Visualization of Segmented Radiological Images

3D visualization refers to the use of computer-aided algorithm for the formulation of 3D models from 2D images [12]. The workflow of 3D visualization is similar, with only a few differences in contrast to 3D printing and virtual reality. For 3D printing, a 3D model is formulated by standard tessellation language (STL), additive manufacturing file (AMF), or 3D manufacturing file (3MF) formats. However, these printing 3D models are not suitable for rendering 3D models or virtual reality; these models are converted with additional preferences like material properties such as color, shades, and triangles as wavefront or object (OBJ) files. In 3D printing, the anatomical organs are represented by the number of triangles, and rendering images for virtual reality requires huge computational power to visualize in two HD displays for each eye, which is precisely synchronized at a high refresh rate. It limits the number of triangles/vertices and directly depends on the hardware specification of the computer for the smooth rendering of the visuals. Virtual reality usually uses a fewer number of triangles in contrast with 3D printing and also relies on the software used for rendering. The hardware limitations and insufficient anatomical details are the major challenges for the smooth visualization and interactive real-time visualization for clinical studies. For smooth and high-definition visualization, a high-performance computer is used, which can overcome the current limitations.

The 3D rendering models are visualized with different light sources based on the scenes and are affected by different lighting and material parameters. The virtual reality models' visualization can be improved with a better selection of parameters like lightning, transparency, texture, color, and good material properties for the display model. The properties for the rendering are chosen wisely to display the object as smooth or flat and the effect of light in shading to look in a unique way in the rendering mechanism. The lighting effects are improved by increasing the number of triangles/vertexes to adjust the minor shade changes in the model. This is similar to the number of triangles in the STL models. The smoothness of the model can be achieved with a sufficient number of triangles, but in the low-detail models, smooth shading normals are used for better smoothness. The anatomical model visualized is reliable in the low detail models; still there is caution in the results.

In 3D printing, the segmented images are used for stable, fixed structures, and structures that are unclear or distracting are highlighted by clinicians. However, in virtual reality, the segmented models are altered in real time (resized, clipped, faded, or removed) by the clinicians interactively using the software. The real-time interaction feature permits the clinicians to decide the anatomical portion of the model to be included or excluded from the visualization model. The required segmented portion of the anatomical model will improve the performance of the rendering as it reduces the total number of triangles/vertexes. Eliminating the details that are less relevant to the segmented model will increase the overall response and interactive experience. Virtual reality is more flexible as it guides and accesses tissue selection to include 3D-printed models.

The 3D printer models have a compulsory prerequisite that they should not have any open faces or holes; all the sides should be closed with solid or porous material in the polygon mesh. However, in virtual reality, the polygon mesh is not mandatory. VR has the advantage of visualizing the cross-section of cutting planes in real time. In 3D models, the rendering engines, by default, do not render the inside surface of the anatomical structures to reduce the computational complexity. This technique is known as back-face culling. To know the different effects of illusion, the secondary color or material is used in the 3D models.

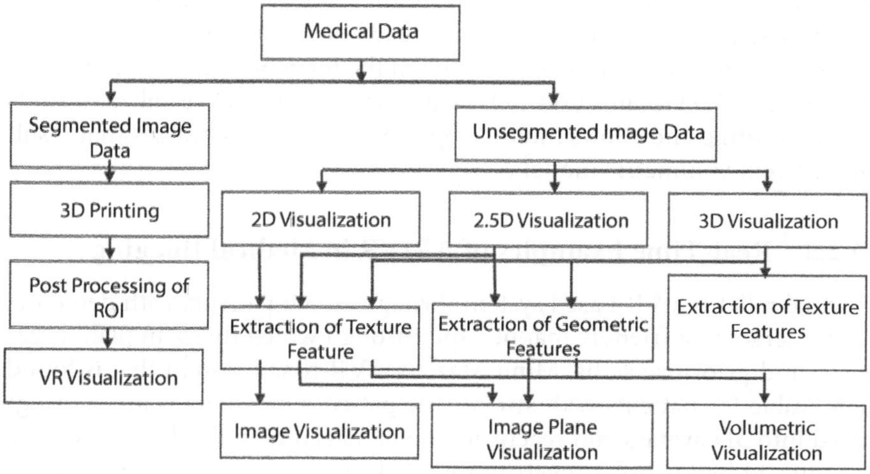

Figure 9.3 Radiological image viewing options using virtual reality.

The virtual reality visualization of segmented and unsegmented radiological images is depicted in Figure 9.3. In the segmentation, different image processing algorithms are there, and machine learning-based techniques are gaining prominence. The visualization of unsegmented images is categorized into three types: 2D, 2.5D, and 3D models. The characteristics of each model are also highlighted in Figure 9.3. The thresholding technique and VR were deployed for segmentation and 3D visualization of COVID-19 CT images [39].

9.2.4 Virtual Reality Visualization of Unsegmented Radiological Images

In the case of visualization of unsegmented radiological images, there are three techniques: 2D visualization [40, 41], 2.5D visualization, and 3D visualization [42, 43].

2D visualization: The spatial detail of 3D volume is not utilized in the 2D visualization. The medical images in DICOM format are converted into the image texture format. The rendering system utilizes the image texture in 2D format, and textures are in various formats. The CT image grayscale value is measured in terms of Hounsfield units, and during texture representation, full grayscale values should be utilized.

2.5D visualization: A moveable viewing plane that incorporates 3D spatial information and enables the users to choose oblique views of the images is utilized in this approach, allowing reorientation and reposition. The image in DICOM format is utilized here, and the texture information is generated. Here in the 2.5D visualization, 3D texture is used.

3D visualization: This is the widely used one, and it is also called volume rendering. The image is displayed in the form of a 3D object in space. Similar to 2.5D visualization, 3D texture is used here. 3D visualization aids in 3D printing and allows multiple options to choose iso-values that result in different volumetric models.

9.2.5 Real-Time Examples of AR/VR in Medical Imaging

Virtual relief is a VR-based system through which patients with dementia can interact in a friendly manner and through which they can plan, organize, and prioritize skills. Mind Maze is a VR-based system that is found applicable for patients with stroke. The patient's movements are transfigured into 3D avatars and reactivate the damaged neural cells. The studies conducted by Oxford University revealed that patients, when exposed to fear in virtual reality mode, reduce their anxiety. VR finds its role in surgery and other medical practices and helps to relieve the stress and anxiety of patients.

Brainpower is an AR tool that aids neurobiology using specialized software along with wearables such as Google glasses. It aids in teaching life skills to children and adults with autism. "Empowered Brain" is an improved version that aids children in developing their skills. Some people are having phobia in undergoing a blood test, they fear that nurses will not find the veins properly, and in many cases, little pain will also occur. AccuVien is an AR-based system that uses a portable scanner that traces the veins in blood vessels.

9.2.6 Future of AR/VR in Radiology

The development of more advanced technologies in the hardware and software industry will lead to the advancement of VR and AR that are suitable for medical and surgical applications [44, 45]. Nowadays, VR/AR technologies start implementing in society. The market statistics show that VR/AR technologies are increasing rapidly because of the emerging consumers in all domains. The development of AR/VR leads to robotic surgery with optimized operative pre-planning in the surgical fields. Using VR technology, the medical learning is improved by training in surgical simulations and enhanced visual–spatial learning [46]. In dental research, the digitization with AI/ML and AR/VR for personalized dental care is done by recording the natural motion of the patient and reconstruction with augmented intelligence for improved and cost-effective healthcare for patients. The enhancement of the CAD with machine learning techniques for the volume rendering of the medical data recognizes the anatomical structures and detects the abnormalities. VR and AR are potentially improving the visualization of the spatial and anatomical structures with the area of interest in the ultrasound images with the AI in the image understanding and robotic navigation [47]. AR and VR will make a way to medical televirtuality, virtual guidance for pre-planning surgery, patient study, and developing surgical simulators.

9.3 Conclusion

This chapter focus on the applications of AR/VR in medical imaging; the radiology sector plays a pivotal role in the healthcare industry for disease diagnosis and prediction. AR/VR aids the radiologist and physicians in using an improved and sophisticated technique to visualize the anatomical organs and understand their characteristics. AR/VR technology gains prominence in surgical preplanning and drug delivery for curing diseases. The medical education sector also has merits through the usage of AR/VR technologies. The future inventions in the healthcare sector rely heavily on AR/VR domain in generating fruitful outcomes for society.

Acknowledgments

The authors would like to acknowledge the support provided by Nanyang Technological University under NTU Ref: RCA-17/334 for providing the medical images and supporting us in the preparation of the manuscript. Parasuraman Padmanabhan and Balazs Gulyas also acknowledge the support from Lee Kong Chian School of Medicine and Data Science and AI Research (DSAIR) center of NTU (project number ADH-11/2017-DSAIR) and the support from the Cognitive Neuro Imaging Centre (CONIC) at NTU. SN Kumar would also like to acknowledge the support provided by Schmitt Centre for Biomedical Instrumentation (SCBMI) of Amal Jyothi College of Engineering.

References

1. McKnight, R.R., *et al.*, Virtual reality and augmented reality—translating surgical training into surgical technique, in: *Current Reviews in Musculoskeletal Medicine*, pp. 1–12, 2020.
2. Sadeghi, A.H., *et al.*, Current and future applications of virtual, augmented, and mixed reality in cardiothoracic surgery. *Ann. Thorac. Surg.*, 113, 2, 681–691, 2020.
3. Cordeil, M., *et al.*, Embodied axes: Tangible, actuated interaction for 3d augmented reality data spaces. *Proceedings of the 2020 CHI Conference on Human Factors in Computing Systems*, 2020.
4. Reymus, M., Liebermann, A., Diegritz, C., Virtual reality: an effective tool for teaching root canal anatomy to undergraduate dental students–a preliminary study. *Int. Endod. J.*, 53, 11, 1581–1587, 2020.
5. Lu, S., *et al.*, Integrating eye-tracking to augmented reality system for surgical training. *J. Med. Syst.*, 44, 11, 1–7, 2020.
6. Park, B.J., *et al.*, Augmented and mixed reality: technologies for enhancing the future of IR. *J. Vasc. Interv. Radiol.*, 31, 7, 1074–1082, 2020.
7. Pinter, C., *et al.*, Slicervr for medical intervention training and planning in immersive virtual reality. *IEEE Trans. Med. Rob. Bionics*, 2, 2, 108–117, 2020.

8. Parekh, P., *et al.*, Systematic review and meta-analysis of augmented reality in medicine, retail, and games. *Vis. Comput. Ind. Biomed. Art*, 3, 1, 1–20, 2020.
9. Bouaoud, J., *et al.*, DIVA, a 3D virtual reality platform, improves undergraduate craniofacial trauma education. *J. Stomatol. Oral Maxillofac. Surg.*, 122, 4, 367–371, 2021.
10. Andrews, C.M., *et al.*, Registration Techniques for Clinical Applications of Three-Dimensional Augmented Reality Devices. *IEEE J. Transl. Eng. Health Med.*, 9, 1–14, 2020.
11. Zhao, J., *et al.*, The effectiveness of virtual reality-based technology on anatomy teaching: a meta-analysis of randomized controlled studies. *BMC Med. Educ.*, 20, 1, 1–10, 2020.
12. González Izard, S., *et al.*, Nextmed: automatic imaging segmentation, 3D reconstruction, and 3D model visualization platform using augmented and virtual reality. *Sensors*, 20, 10, 2962, 2020.
13. Singh, A., *et al.*, Using virtual reality in biomedical engineering education. *J. Biomech. Eng.*, 142, 11, 111013, 2020.
14. Elsayed, M., *et al.*, Virtual and augmented reality: potential applications in radiology. *Acta Radiol.*, 61, 9, 1258–1265, 2020.
15. Wang, L.J., *et al.*, Virtual reality-based education for patients undergoing radiation therapy. *J. Cancer Educ.*, 37, 3, 1–7, 2020.
16. Douglas, D.B., Wilke, C.A., Gibson, J.D., Boone, J.M., Wintermark, M., Augmented reality: Advances in diagnostic imaging. *Multimodal Technol. Interact.*, 1, 4, 29, 2017 Dec.
17. Sutherland, J., Belec, J., Sheikh, A., Chepelev, L., Althobaity, W., Chow, B.J., Mitsouras, D., Christensen, A., Rybicki, F.J., La Russa, D.J., Applying modern virtual and augmented reality technologies to medical images and models. *J. Digit. Imaging*, 32, 1, 38–53, 2019 Feb.
18. Izard, S.G., Méndez, J.A., Palomera, P.R., García-Peñalvo, F.J., Applications of virtual and augmented reality in biomedical imaging. *J. Med. Syst.*, 43, 4, 1–5, 2019 Apr.
19. Mondal R., Role of augmented reality and virtual reality from the Indian healthcare education perspective–A systematic review. *J. Family Med. Prim. Care.*, 13, 8, 2841–28, 24 Aug 1.
20. Xu, X., Mangina, E., Kilroy, D., Curran, K.M., Healy, J.J., Campbell, A.G., Doctoral Colloquium—A Snapshot of the Future: Virtual and Augmented Reality Training for Radiology, in: *2020 6th International Conference of the Immersive Learning Research Network (iLRN)*, pp. 407–410, IEEE, 2020 Jun 21.
21. Le, D.N., Van Le, C., Tromp, J.G., Nguyen, G.N. (Eds.), *Emerging technologies for health and medicine: virtual reality, augmented reality, artificial intelligence, internet of things, robotics, industry 4.0*, John Wiley & Sons, India, 2018 Oct 16.
22. Berton, A., Longo, U.G., Candela, V., Fioravanti, S., Giannone, L., Arcangeli, V., Alciati, V., Berton, C., Facchinetti, G., Marchetti, A., Schena, E., Virtual

reality, augmented reality, gamification, and telerehabilitation: Psychological impact on orthopedic patients' rehabilitation. *J. Clin. Med.*, 9, 8, 2567, 2020 Aug.

23. Mubin, O., Alnajjar, F., Jishtu, N., Alsinglawi, B., Al Mahmud, A., Exoskeletons with virtual reality, augmented reality, and gamification for stroke patients' rehabilitation: systematic review. *JMIR Rehabil. Assistive Technol.*, 6, 2, e12010, 2019.
24. Wake, N., Alexander, A.E., Christensen, A.M., Liacouras, P.C., Schickel, M., Pietila, T., Matsumoto, J., Creating patient-specific anatomical models for 3D printing and AR/VR: a supplement for the 2018 Radiological Society of North America (RSNA) hands-on course. *3D Print. Med.*, 5, 1, 1–0, 2019 Dec.
25. Weng, M., Huang, L., Feng, C., Gao, F., Lin, H., Electronic medical record system based on augmented reality, in: *2017 12th International Conference on Computer Science and Education (ICCSE)*, pp. 753–756, IEEE, 2017 Aug 22.
26. Williams, R.M., Alikhademi, K., Drobina, E., Gilbert, J.E., Sutor, T., Augmented Reality for Rehabilitative Therapy: Patient experiences and Practitioner perspectives, in: *Proceedings of the Human Factors and Ergonomics Society Annual Meeting*, vol. 63, no. 1, pp. 748–752, SAGE Publications, Sage CA: LosAngeles, CA, 2019 Nov.
27. Anton, D., Kurillo, G., Yang, A.Y., Bajcsy, R., Augmented telemedicine platform for real-time remote medical consultation, in: *International Conference on Multimedia Modeling*, pp. 77–89, Springer, Cham, 2017 Jan 4.
28. Gurgitano, M., Angileri, S.A., Rodà, G.M., Liguori, A., Pandolfi, M., Ierardi, A.M., Wood, B.J., Carrafiello, G., Interventional Radiology ex-machina: impact of Artificial Intelligence on practice. *Radiol. Med.*, 16, 1–9, 2021 Apr.
29. McCarthy, C.J. and Uppot, R.N., Advances in virtual and augmented reality—exploring the role in health-care education. *J. Radiol. Nurs.*, 38, 2, 104–5, 2019 Jun 1.
30. Uppot, R.N., Laguna, B., McCarthy, C.J., De Novi, G., Phelps, A., Siegel, E., Courtier, J., Implementing virtual and augmented reality tools for radiology education and training, communication, and clinical care. *Radiology*, 291, 3, 570–80, 2019 Jun.
31. Duarte, M.L., Santos, L.R., Júnior, J.G., Peccin, M.S., Learning anatomy by virtual reality and augmented reality. A scope review. *Morphologie*, 2020 Sep 21.
32. Lohre, R., Wang, J.C., Lewandrowski, K.U., Goel, D.P., Virtual reality in spinal endoscopy: a paradigm shift in education to support spine surgeons. *J. Spine Surg.*, 6, Suppl 1, S208, 2020 Jan.
33. Choi, H., Cho, B., Masamune, K., Hashizume, M., Hong, J., An effective visualization technique for depth perception in augmented reality-based surgical navigation. *Int. J. Med. Rob. Comput. Assisted Surg.*, 12, 1, 62–72, 2016 Mar.
34. Sakai, D., Joyce, K., Sugimoto, M., Horikita, N., Hiyama, A., Sato, M., Devitt, A., Watanabe, M., Augmented, virtual and mixed reality in spinal

surgery: A real-world experience. *J. Orthop. Surg.*, 28, 3, 2309499020952698, 2020 Sep 8.
35. Groesbeck Parham, E.G., Cuevas, A., Fisher, B., Skinner, J., Mwanahamuntu, M., Sullivan, R., Creating a low-cost virtual reality surgical simulation to increase surgical oncology capacity and capability. *Ecancermedicalscience*, 13, 910, 2019.
36. Yuk, F.J., Maragkos, G.A., Sato, K., Steinberger, J., Current innovation in virtual and augmented reality in spine surgery. *Ann. Transl. Med.*, 9, 1, 94, 2021 Jan.
37. Gagandeep, S., Tejasvi, K., Nihal, M., Shubham, J., Anatoliy, V., Vadim, S., Prateek, P., Sunil, M., Long-term solutions in neurosurgery using extended reality technologies. *Neurosurg. Focus*, 51, 2, E2, 2021 Aug 1.
38. Reinschluessel, A., Fischer, R., Schumann, C., Uslar, V., Muender, T., Katzky, U., Kißner, H., Kraft, V., Lampe, M., Lück, T., Bock-Müller, K., Introducing Virtual & 3D-Printed Models for Improved Collaboration in Surgery, in: *Proceedings of the 18. Annual Meeting of the German Society of Computer- and Robot-Assisted Surgery*, vol. 18, O. Burgert (Ed.), pp. 253–258, 2019.
39. Benbelkacem, S., Oulefki, A., Agaian, S., Trongtirakul, T., Aouam, D., Zenati-Henda, N., Amara, K., Lung infection region quantification, recognition, and virtual reality rendering of CT scan of COVID-19. *Multimodal Image Exploitation and Learning*, vol. 11734, International Society for Optics and Photonics, p. 117340I, 2021 Apr 12.
40. American Association of Physicists in Medicine, Assessment of display performance for medical imaging systems. *Med. Phys.*, 32, 4, 1–156, 2005.
41. Norweck, J.T., Seibert, J.A., Andriole, K.P., Clunie, D.A., Curran, B.H., Flynn, M.J., Krupinski, E., Lieto, R.P., Peck, D.J., Mian, T.A., Wyatt, M., ACR-AAPM-SIIM technical standard for electronic practice of medical imaging. *J. Digital Imaging*, 26, 38–52, 2013.
42. Stegmaiert, S., Kieint, T., Stegmaier, S., Strengert, M., Klein, T., Ertl, T., A simple and flexible volume rendering framework for graphicshardware-based raycasting. *Fourth Int. Work. Vol. Graph*, pp. 187–241, 2005.
43. Ljung, P., Krüger, J., Groller, E., Hadwiger, M., Hansen, C.D., Ynnerman, A., Gröller, E., Hadwiger, M., Hansen, C.D., Ynnerman, A., State of the art in transfer functions for direct volume rendering. *Comput. Graph. Forum*, 35, 669–691, 2016.
44. Iwanaga, J., *et al.*, A review of anatomy education during and after the COVID-19 pandemic: Revisiting traditional and modern methods to achieve future innovation. *Clin. Anat.*, 34, 1, 108–114, 2021.
45. Hayre, C.M. and Kilgour, A., Diagnostic radiography education amidst the COVID-19 pandemic: Current and future use of virtual reality (VR). *J. Med. Imaging Radiat. Sci.*, 2021.
46. Clarke, E., Virtual reality simulation—the future of orthopaedic training? A systematic review and narrative analysis. *Adv. Simul.*, 6, 1, 1–11, 2021.
47. Von Haxthausen, F., *et al.*, Medical robotics for ultrasound imaging: current systems and future trends. *Curr. Rob. Rep.*, 2, 1 , 1–17, 2021.

Section 4

FUTURE DEVELOPMENTS OF EXTENDED REALITY

10

An Overview of Virtual Reality in Healthcare

Pavithra S.*, Vanithamani R. and Judith Justin

Department of Biomedical Instrumentation Engineering, Avinashilingam Institute for Home Science and Higher Education for Women, Coimbatore, India

Abstract

Virtual reality (VR) technology is very famous and is being employed in different application areas on a large scale. Modern healthcare knowledge is expanding quickly, and cutting-edge technology is being adopted at an incredible rate. VR is one of the cutting-edge technologies that can be included and employed in healthcare area. Through the utilization of VR, doors to new possibilities can be opened. VR can be used for providing lengthy and effective training sessions and can help in rehabilitation, planning operations, and much more which can be very useful. Examining VR applications in healthcare highlights the benefits, different possibilities with VR in healthcare, challenges, and future research potential.

Keywords: Virtual reality, healthcare, medicine, cardiac, surgery, dental, cerebral aneurysm

10.1 What is VR?

Virtual reality (VR) is a technology which is widely known. It is not just known but also widely used in different applications. Let us quickly go through some definitions of VR and understand what VR is. The VR industry is a global industry in which computer programs create 3D environments that can be navigated and interacted with by users for the purpose of simulating one or more of the user's five senses in real time [20]. In VR, information is displayed in a lifelike environment that stimulates

**Corresponding author*: pavithrasusi@gmail.com

Manisha Vohra (ed.) Introduction to Extended Reality (XR) Technologies, (175–188) © 2025 Scrivener Publishing LLC

the sense of touch and is stimulating the sense of sight [3]. Consequently, virtual reality is defined as a simulated or real environment in which a perceiver can experience telepresence, as defined by Jonathan Steuer in a scholarly article [10]. VR immerses the user in the 3D computer-generated environment. There are different definitions of VR available, but there are three common features of VR systems. The first common feature of VR systems is immersion. The second is perception—the perception of being actually present in an environment. The third common feature of VR systems is interaction; it is the interaction with that environment [vr1].

10.2 History of VR

It was in the late 1980s that VR was conceptualized, and the first VR tools were available for commercial use [1]. However, work on VR had started way before. Below is the description of the history of VR.

- Morton Heilig, in the years 1960 to 1962, worked on creating a multi-sensory simulator and created one which was "Sensorama". It was one of the first approaches of developing a VR system—a film in color and stereo which was prerecorded and augmented by binaural sound, wind, fragrance, and vibration experiences. A complete VR environment was created as the features of VR environment were present.
- Ivan Sutherland proposed "the ultimate virtual reality display" in 1965: an artificial world with interactivity, force feedback, sound, smell, and taste.
- The first fully realized virtual reality system, invented by Ivan Sutherland, "The Sword of Damocles", is considered the first head-mounted display (HMD) with correct head tracking. Stereo views were displayed correctly based on the position and orientation of the user's head.
- A force-feedback prototype "Grope" was developed in 1971 at the University of North Carolina (UNC).
- In 1975, a conceptual environment called the "Videoplace" was created by Myron Krueger. Cameras captured the silhouettes of users and displayed them on a large screen. Using image processing techniques that determined each participant's position on a 2D screen, the participants were able to interact with each other.

- A flight simulator "Visually Coupled Airborne Systems Simulator (VCASS)" was developed in 1982 by Thomas Furness at the US Air Force's Armstrong Medical Research Laboratories. Fighter pilots wore head-mounted displays that augmented their out-the-window views with graphics that indicated targeting or efficient flight paths.
- "Vived", a stereoscopic monochrome head-mounted display constructed at NASA Ames in 1984, was created with off-the-shelf technology.
- VPL manufactures the first commercially available VR devices, "DataGlove" (1985) and "Eyephone" (1988).
- "Boom" was commercially available since 1989 from Fake Space Labs. In Boom, two CRT monitors are contained in small boxes that can be observed through eye holes. As the mechanical arm measures the position and orientation of the box, the user can grab it, hold it by the eyes, and move through the virtual world.
- An architectural walkthrough application, "UNC Walkthrough Project", was developed at UNC in the second half of the 1980s. In order to improve this system, a pixel-plane graphics engine, HMDs, and optical trackers were developed.
- Using BOOM and DataGlove, NASA Ames developed the "Virtual Wind Tunnel" application in the early 1990s.
- "CAVE (CAVE Automatic Virtual Environment)" was introduced in 1992. Users must wear LCD shutter glasses to view the stereoscopic images instead of wearing an HMD. When compared to HMD systems, this approach provides better quality and resolution of viewed images as well as a wider field of view [8].

10.3 Introduction of VR in Healthcare

People's experience of the physical environment and the virtual environment has been changing due to the various developments in recent years [19]. VR is playing an important role in this. Today, in different areas of the lives of people, VR is being integrated. Right from videogames to various industry-based applications, VR is being utilized in it [2]. Health is an important aspect of our lives. A technology like VR can be helpful and highly effective when applied in healthcare. In recent years, digital technology has evolved quickly and enabled solutions which are creative and novel across clinical medicine in recent years. In this context, VR is a strong adjunct now in clinical medicine [11]. One of the greatly effective applications of VR is in the medicine area [6]. So, overall, with the application of VR, the healthcare area can benefit, and different possibilities with VR in healthcare can be explored. In fact, currently, VR is also making different things possible with its application. For example, it is being used in healthcare as an educational tool or training tool, etc. According to [11], VR creates "a sense of presence in an immersive, computer-generated, three-dimensional, interactive environment" through head-mounted displays, body-tracking sensors, and direct user-input devices.

The healthcare area has progressed dramatically over the past few years, including various technological advancements which even include the ones related to VR. Specifically talking about VR, then a VR system represents objects, spaces, and events using computer graphics. Multiple sensory channels are used to simulate and interact with the application, which mimics real-world situations in real time. The creation of a fully or partially virtual world can be done in a variety of ways at present. Computer technology is used to create an image of artificial reality almost entirely in three dimensions in VR, also known as phantomatics. An imaginary world is experienced as if it were real using virtual reality through a specialized system that delivers sensory information to the brain [7].

VR platforms come in many varieties. Many VR platforms, including those provided by HTC, Sony, and Oculus, work by replacing the field of vision of the wearer with high-resolution displays [5]. With advances in artificial intelligence and natural language processing, trainees and non-player characters can communicate more easily with each other and with their teammates [9].

Medical care has undergone a drastic change in patient awareness and perception in recent years. The combined effect of this process and the growing focus on patient safety has put traditional educational paradigms to the test in healthcare. Studies on surgical errors and healthcare costs, for instance, have contributed to an increased awareness of patient safety. There is always focus on constantly advancing medical training and education in order to make sure that the healthcare area gains benefit. When VR is applied for education and training purposes in healthcare, the application is time and case independent because the users can train and practice medical skills at any time. Also, during practice using VR, patients are not directly involved in the procedure; hence, surgeons can practice treatments under extreme circumstances without endangering the patient [12].

The advantage of VR lies in its ability to adapt to the specifics of different situations and to terminate the procedure as soon as possible. During the VR experience, we see a replica of the scene in the real world, predicting the sensory effects of our movements. Several types of VR hardware are used, while VR software is used to adjust the images on the user's display in response to changes caused by their movement in the virtual world [13].

10.4 Possibilities with VR in Healthcare

There are various possibilities with VR in healthcare. It can be used for different applications in the healthcare industry. Below are some examples from literature which will help you understand the different possibilities with VR in healthcare.

10.4.1 Possibility with VR for Cardiac Applications

Stanford Virtual Heart Project students learn about the heart using a virtual reality headset. Parents will be able to better understand their child's cardiac anatomy through this project. This improved depth of understanding should help parents better participate in their child's complex medical care. By using this application, Stanford medical students and trainees can see anatomy that is normal and abnormal. The students will also gain an understanding of how congenital anomalies affect the whole body. In order to gain a more comprehensive understanding of anatomy and physiology, students will use an immersive VR headset to inspect, manipulate, and walk through the models. In the library, trainees can find approximately two dozens of common congenital anomalies. A deeper understanding of these lesions' anatomical characteristics was obtained from these experiences. This will make it easier for us to understand and learn these abnormal physiologies and hemodynamic sequelae [5].

10.4.2 Possibility With VR for Surgery Applications

10.4.2.1 Example 1

The baseline psychomotor abilities of 16 surgical residents were assessed, followed by randomized treatment (MIST VR simulator diathermy task) until expert levels were achieved or a control group was formed. The attending surgeon was blind to the subjects' training status when they performed laparoscopic cholecystectomy. Using videotapes of gallbladder dissections, two independent investigators blinded to the identity of the subjects and their training scored each procedure minute for eight predetermined errors.

A comparison of baseline assessments between groups did not reveal any differences. A resident who received VR training was able to dissect the gallbladder 29% more quickly. The likelihood of non-VR-trained patients failing to progress was nine times higher as was the likelihood they would injure their gallbladders or burn nontarget tissue five times higher. The VR trained group had a sixfold lower rate of mean errors. In order to achieve specific target criteria during laparoscopic cholecystectomy, VR surgical simulation significantly improved resident performance [17].

10.4.2.2 Example 2

A critical objective of this research was to examine how Trochanteric Femoral Nail Advanced (TFNA™) could be applied as a complex surgical technique using IVR simulation. TFNA™ was evaluated in a Synbone® model during an advanced fracture treatment course by 10 residents. A VR simulator was used to practice the technique with five of the participants. During the course, all students applied the TFNATM and were asked to repeat it. A comparison was made between the two groups in terms of the time and number of steps it took them to complete the task. As a result, VR took 25.84 min, while the control took 31.6 min. Despite the VR group completing more steps and finishing earlier than the control group, there was no statistically significant difference between the two groups, but there was a tendency for the VR group to complete more steps and finish sooner than the control group. VR simulation could provide a more accessible way for participants to learn new surgical techniques in a safe environment. Progression-based training programs incorporating simulation and emerging technology are critical to developing proficiency-based programs with specific educational objectives. Validation studies that are larger, randomized, and internally and externally oriented are required [18].

10.4.2.3 Example 3

During a blind, randomized, controlled trial [21], orthopedic residents were assessed for their ability to perform total hip arthroplasty on cadavers. In addition, virtual reality simulation had a preferentially positive effect on surgical skills or knowledge. A pretest and total hip arthroplasty (THA) on a cadaver were administered to 14 post-graduate year 1 orthopedic residents for the purpose of establishing baseline knowledge and skills. Seven residents were then randomly assigned to a VR-THA simulation. Following that, all participants were asked to retake the test in order to determine whether their scores had improved. Score improvements on the test as well as cadaver THA scores were the primary outcomes. The testing results showed no significant difference between the VR and the control groups, respectively, in terms of improvement in test scores. The VR cohort's overall cadaver THA scores showed a significant improvement in multivariate regression analysis. There was a statistically significant difference between the VR cohort and the control group for every specific score category. However, this trend was having significance only for technical performance. In VR simulations, residents improve their surgical skills, but their medical knowledge does not change in a significant way. It was the technical skills that showed the most improvement. Further research is required to find out how best to utilize VR simulation as part of an integrated curriculum in orthopedic surgical education [21].

From the three examples above of possibilities with VR for surgery applications, it can be seen that VR is useful in surgery applications. However, more studies and research will be required in this direction as healthcare is a very important area. Further studies and research in this direction could also help in bringing about more development and improvement, and this could even lead to the generation of more possibilities with VR for surgery applications. However, VR use is growing. Commercial units of VR are rapidly becoming available, and technology holds the greatest potential for the future [14].

10.4.3 Possibility with VR for Gait Improvement in Patients Having Parkinson's Disease

As Parkinson's disease progresses, a person's gait is affected, resulting in shorter strides and slower walking speeds. The study in [22] examined the effects of dynamic visual feedback cues that respond dynamically to self-motion on patients with Parkinson's disease using a portable see-through virtual reality apparatus. There was a maximum of 20 participants. Residual effects were also measured in addition to on-line effects on walking speed and stride length. Without turning on the display, the visual feedback device had an estimated 2% effect on the patient. Patients who used the display improved their stride length and walking speed by 56%. After removing their devices and waiting for 15 min, 68% of patients improved their gait speed or stride length by 20%. Three-quarters of patients who performed their first test after 1 week showed significant improvements over their baseline performance. Despite imagining walking on tiles, they walked on them in reality. Using VR to provide feedback cues was examined to determine whether Parkinson's patients could improve their walking ability. It is recommended that a comprehensive treatment program be explored considering the residual effects of this strategy [22].

10.4.4 Possibility with VR in Dental Medicine

The authors in [15] reviewed clinical studies concerning AR/VR technology in dental medicine. They found that it was most used for motor skill training in university settings and for analyzing complex maxillofacial surgical protocols. A fast-computing device and supporting software will be required for translating AR/VR from the lab to the clinic. In addition to providing realistic outcome predictions and mitigating potential risks, AR/VR systems can also be used for preoperative planning and intraoperative navigation. Identified dental AR/VR clinical studies need to be interpreted as experimental in nature due to the fact that they may serve as training exercises with potential application to surgical protocols in the future. Particularly advantageous are intraoperative navigation to eliminate potential risks and preoperative preparation using AR/VR technologies to provide precise outcome predictions. The overlay pictures in this situation must coexist 3D, genuine, without delay, and with reliable correctness and precision. The rising amount of collected data needs intelligent handling. Although secured data anonymization is crucial, potential re-identification of individuals poses a variety of challenges: Advanced data analysis and interpretation techniques must be developed and enacted as well as sufficient security protocols [15].

10.4.5 Possibility with VR for Autism Spectrum Disorder (ASD)

ASD is a complicated neurodevelopmental illness that is marked by limitations in communication and social interactions as well as repetitive, limited norms of social. Although there is not a single, widely approved treatment for ASD at the moment, effective interventions in education, behavioral, social, and communication are seen to be a dependable way to improve people's lives. A recent study revealed that people with ASD play video games consistently. Long training sessions with therapists have been cut short by this technology-based technique. VR has shown to be the best option among all of these instructional technologies on the market for teaching neurocognitive abilities.

A total of 33 related studies were found through a systematic search. The findings showed that people who receive VR training were significantly better, with a Hedges *g* of 0.74 indicating a rather big impact size. It also turned out to be very successful to evaluate other abilities. The daily life skills effect was the strongest ($g = 1.15$). Other skills showed a moderate response to this impact, with *g* values of 0.45 for cognitive abilities, 0.46 for emotional control and recognition, and 0.69 for communications and social abilities. The study group was divided into age groups of 4–8, 8–12, 12–16, and older than 16 years to evaluate the effectiveness of the age intervention. Based on the mean age of their participants, each study fit within one of the following categories. We defined these four classification moderators for supplementary subgroup meta-analysis. Only VR-based training, not traditional training, was able to attain the significant effectiveness of everyday life abilities. Therefore, it makes sense to use VR to create rehabilitation services that concentrate on daily life skills in clinical settings. There is still potential for improvement in the design and use of VR technology for the other clinical purposes [24].

The study in [25] looked at a 3D virtual neurocognitive training program which affected how the social skills were developed in ASD kids. A total of 30 youngsters aged 7 to 16 and diagnosed with ASD participated in 10 1-h sessions spread across 5 weeks. Improvements were seen on tests of social attribution, executive function, and analogical thinking, according to the results. Many VR treatments are made to train adults, adolescents, or young children without discussing the consequences of using a single VR platform for all demographics [25].

10.4.6 Possibility with VR in Cerebral Aneurysm

In [16], the possibility with VR in the case of cerebral aneurysm was found out. Utilizing the ImmersiveTouch platform, an aneurysm clipping simulator with real-time sensory feedback was developed. Using computed tomography angiograms as a basis, a simulation of an aneurysm in the middle cerebral artery was developed. Approximately two-thirds of the residents had a close resemblance to real operative anatomy after being exposed to three-dimensional immersive anatomic details. Preoperative surgery rehearsal and neurosurgical training can benefit from simulation. Aneurysm surgery patients believed that the current technology provided realistic haptic feedback. Using patient-specific 3D multidimensional virtual images, aneurysms will be investigated and examined regarding their position, size, and direction as well as their connectivity to proximal vessels and other regions in the brain. By using this information, a surgical strategy can be established, including the best patient placement, the location and size of the craniotomy, the retraction of brain parenchyma, the avoidance of reactive brain regions, and the appropriate use of aneurysm clips [16].

10.5 Advantages of VR Use in Healthcare

VR use in healthcare makes it possible to gain practical, authentic experience without any risk. VR is getting popular in the healthcare industry and can become an important technology that training institutions may utilize to help students during their course of learning. Mentioned below are a few advantages of VR in healthcare:

- Helps in providing knowledge of medical procedures to students and trainees: Students and trainees can gain knowledge of medical procedures with great ease using VR. Without any risk, VR helps students and trainees to get the required knowledge.
- A better understanding of medical procedures for patients: In addition to helping students and trainees, VR can also help patients better understand the tests and procedures involved in a clinical trial. VR provides a visual experience that promotes a better understanding of the conditions experienced and decreases distractions or confusions, if any, by providing an interactive experience. So, overall, the medical procedures can be better understood by the patients using VR.
- Provides a feeling of being in control: By providing easy-to-understand information, virtual reality technology helps patients feel more in control, which, in turn, is helpful in relieving stress.
- Beating phobias: Certain phobias can be treated more effectively in virtual environments provided by virtual reality (VR) equipment [26]. Four 1-h exposure therapy sessions were held, on average, for the participants ($n = 23$) in the VR experimental group. As determined by a Fear of Spiders questionnaire, a Behavioural Avoidance Test (BAT), and severity ratings given by the clinician and a neutral assessor,

VR exposure was more successful in treating spider phobia than a control condition. Compared to 0% in the waiting list group, 83% of patients in the VR treatment group demonstrated a clinically significant improvement, and no patient discontinued the treatment [27].

- Medical imaging with greater detail: With EchoPixel's True 3D imaging system, doctors can view CT scans and MRI images in 3D, which means that this system makes VR medical imaging possible. This system helps the doctor better understand patients' structures and illnesses.
- Helps in rehab: MindMazeto's immersive virtual reality therapy can help stroke and brain injury victims regain motor and cognitive function more quickly. Physiotherapists can use virtual exercises and real-time feedback to determine if patients are ready to participate in everyday activities as well as motivate them to practice every day. Virtual reality offers the possibility of transferring part of rehabilitation to the home with the help of telecommunications [3].
- Management of chronic pain: Pain relief can also be achieved through VR. There are different approaches to treating pain, but the fundamental principle is the same. The primary goal is to identify the nerves that are generating the pain and then to implement the most appropriate treatment. There may be a series of therapies like muscle therapies or nerve therapies required for more complex procedures. In the meantime, VR is proving its own healing capabilities, reducing the need to use medications, which makes this an effective adjunct to other treatments. The use of VR in pain management has the potential to offer a viable alternative to standard narcotic therapy. Using distracting interventions for pain management may cause patients to perceive time more quickly [11].

  By incorporating virtual reality environments, it is anticipated that it will eventually be possible to assess temperamental traits, attitudes, and social adjustment using their environments [4].

This study in the chapter emphasizes the possibilities with virtual reality systems in the healthcare industry. Medical professionals and caregivers are always required, and mostly it is felt that there is shortage of them, so new technologies which can help them as well as the patients are being looked at with increasing amounts of hope every year. Electronic gadgets with huge computational capabilities, the rapid development of Internet infrastructure, and the expanding availability of quality gadgets are all factors that will lead to this field's development.

There are also several challenges that have arisen as a result of VR's growing use like cybersickness. It can sometimes leave the users with symptoms such as nausea, vertigo, headache, and disorientation. Inevitably, the severity of the illness will depend on the user's susceptibility. VR encounters can cause symptoms to manifest during and several hours afterwards. However, it is not just the use of VR but several other factors can also cause cybersickness [12]. Another challenge with VR is its high cost. VR therapy requires extensive software and hardware support as well as a great deal of time during therapy. Additional charges apply to high-resolution patient data. In order to store VR photos, ample file space is needed. So, this all increases its overall costing. Solutions are needed for these challenges. In order for VR to be largely included in healthcare, more thorough study and development will be required [23].

10.6 Conclusion

Virtual reality is gaining traction in the healthcare industry. VR is already being used in healthcare in several applications that are growing rapidly. It is expected that VR application will increase in hospitals over the next few years. Patients can benefit from their support. Virtual reality promises to help in some or other way in the course of the treatment process of patients. Learning procedural skills and interpersonal communication skills may be improved with VR modules in clinical education. As seen in the chapter, there are various possibilities with VR in healthcare, and it faces some challenges, too. There are many benefits of VR in healthcare as discussed in the chapter, but still there is a need for more study and development in this area for making sure that VR provides more benefits in the healthcare industry.

References

1. Cipresso, P., Giglioli, I.A.C., Raya, M.A., Riva, G., The Past, Present, and Future of Virtual and Augmented Reality Research: A Network and Cluster Analysis of the Literature. *Front. Psychol.*, 9, 2086, 1–20, 2018, doi: 10.3389/fpsyg.2018.02086.

2. Izard, S.G., Juanes, J.A., García Peñalvo, F.J., *et al.*, Virtual Reality as an Educational and Training Tool for Medicine. *J. Med. Syst.*, 42, 50, 2018, https://doi.org/10.1007/s10916-018-0900-2.
3. Rosen, J.M., Soltanian, H., Redett, R.J., Laub, D.R., Evolution of virtual reality [Medicine]. *IEEE Eng. Med. Biol. Mag.*, 15, 2, 16–22, March-April 1996, DOI: 10.1109/51.486713.
4. Whalley, J., Ethical issues in the application of virtual reality to medicine. *Comput. Biol. Med.*, 25, 2, 107–114, 1995, ISSN 0010-4825.
5. Silva, J.N.A., Southworth, M., Raptis, C., Silva, J., Emerging Applications of Virtual Reality in Cardiovascular Medicine. *JACC Basic Transl. Sci.*, 3, 3, 420–430, 2018.
6. Kim, Y., Kim, H., Kim, Y.O., Virtual Reality and Augmented Reality in Plastic Surgery: A Review. *Arch. Plast. Surg.*, 44, 3, 179–187, 2017, https://doi.org/10.5999/aps.2017.44.3.179.
7. Mazurek, J., Kiper, P., Cieślik, B., Rutkowski, S., Mehlich, K., Turolla, A., Szczepańska-Gieracha, J., Virtual reality in medicine: a brief overview and future research directions. *Hum. Mov.*, 20, 3, 16–22, 2019.
8. Mazuryk, T. and Gervautz, M., Virtual Reality-History, Applications, Technology and Future, 1999.
9. McGrath, J.L., Taekman, J.M., Dev, P., Danforth, D.R., Mohan, D., Kman, N., Bond, W.F., Using Virtual Reality Simulation Environments to Assess Competence for Emergency Medicine Learners. *Acad. Emerg. Med.*, 25, 2, 186–195, 2017, doi: 10.1111/acem.13308.
10. Muñoz-Saavedra, L., Miró-Amarante, L., Domínguez-Morales, M., Augmented and Virtual Reality Evolution and Future Tendency. *Appl. Sci.*, 10, 1, 322, 2020.
11. Pourmand, A., Davis, S., Lee, D., Barber, S., Sikka, N., Emerging Utility of Virtual Reality as a Multidisciplinary Tool in Clinical Medicine. *Games Health J.*, 6, 5, 263–270, 2017, doi: 10.1089/g4h.2017.0046.
12. Riener, R. and Harders, M., Introduction to Virtual Reality in Medicine, in: *Virtual Reality in Medicine*, pp. 1–12, 2012, doi:10.1007/978-1-4471-4011-5_1.
13. Riva, G., Wiederhold, B.K., Mantovani, F., Neuroscience of Virtual Reality: From Virtual Exposure to Embodied Medicine. *Cyberpsychol. Behav. Soc. Netw.*, 22, 1, 82–96, 2019, DOI: 10.1089/cyber.2017.29099.gri.
14. Szekely, G. and Satava, R.M., Virtual reality in medicine. *BMJ*, 319, 7220, 1305–1305, 1999, doi: 10.1136/bmj.319.7220.1305.
15. Joda, T., Gallucci, G.O., Wismeijer, D., Zitzmann, N.U., Augmented and virtual reality in dental medicine: A systematic review. *Comput. Biol. Med.*, 108, 93–100, 2019, ISSN 0010-4825.
16. Alaraj, A., Luciano, C.J., Bailey, D.P., *et al.*, Virtual reality cerebral aneurysm clipping simulation with real-time haptic feedback. *Neurosurgery*, 11, Suppl 2, 52–8, 2015.
17. Seymour, N.E., Gallagher, A.G., Roman, S.A., O'Brien, M.K., Bansal, V., Andersen, D.K., Satava, R.M., Virtual Reality Training Improves Operating

Room Performance: Results of a Randomized, Double-Blinded Study. *Ann. Surg.*, 236, 458–464, 2002.

18. Arroyo-Berezowsky, C., Jorba-Elguero, P., Altamirano-Cruz, M.A., Quinzaños-Fresnedo, J., Usefulness of immersive virtual reality simulation during femoral nail application in an orthopedic fracture skills course. *J. Musculoskelet. Surg. Res.*, 3, 326–333, 2019.
19. Flavián, C., Ibáñez-Sánchez, S., Orús, C., The impact of virtual, augmented and mixed reality technologies on the customer experience. *J. Bus. Res.*, 100, 547–560, 2019.
20. Guttentag, D.A., Virtual reality: Applications and implications for tourism. *Tour. Manag.*, 31, 637–651, 2010.
21. Hooper, J., Tsiridis, E., Feng, J.E., Schwarzkopf, R., Waren, D., Long, W.J., Poultsides, L.A., Macaulay, W.B., Papagiannakis, G., Kenanidis, E., Rodriguez, E.D., Slover, J.D., Egol, K.A., Phillips, D.P., Friedlander, S., Collins, M., Virtual Reality Simulation Facilitates Resident Training in Total Hip Arthroplasty: A Randomized Controlled Trial. *J. Arthroplasty*, 34, 10, 2278–2283, 2019.
22. Badarny, S., Aharon-Peretz, J., Susel, Z., Habib, G., Baram, Y., Virtual Reality Feedback Cues for Improvement of Gait in Patients with Parkinson's Disease. *Tremor Other Hyperkinet. Mov.*, 4, 1–5, 2014, DOI: 10.7916/D8V69GM4.
23. Javaid, M. and Haleem, A., Virtual reality applications toward medical field. *Clin. Epidemiol. Glob. Health*, 8, 2, 600–605, 2020.
24. Karami, B., Koushki, R., Arabgol, F., Rahmani, M., Vahabie, A., Effectiveness of Virtual/Augmented Reality–Based Therapeutic Interventions on Individuals With Autism Spectrum Disorder: A Comprehensive Meta-Analysis. *Front. Psychiatry*, 12, 665326, 2021.
25. Didehbani, N., Allen, T.T., Kandalaft, M., Krawczyk, D.C., Chapman, S., Virtual Reality Social Cognition Training for children with high functioning autism. *Comput. Hum. Behav.*, 62, 703–711, 2016.
26. Horváthová, D., Siládi, V., Lackova, E., Phobia treatment with the help of virtual reality. *2015 IEEE 13th International Scientific Conference on Informatics*, pp. 114–119, 2015.
27. García-Palacios, A., Hoffman, H.G., Carlin, A., Furness, T.A., Botella, C., Virtual reality in the treatment of spider phobia: a controlled study. *Behav. Res. Ther.*, 40, 9, 983–93, 2002.

11

Augmented and Mixed Reality in Education Sector

Prakash J.

Department of Computer Science and Engineering, PSG College of Technology, Tamil Nadu, India

Abstract

Education is one of the most significant part of each student's life. The education sector has a huge responsibility of ensuring that it is always making advances and progressing and also being up-to-date with the inclusion of different technologies feasible for application that can cause benefits to the sector. Extended reality (XR) technologies are feasible for application in the education sector and can provide benefits to the sector. XR technologies consist of augmented reality (AR), virtual reality (VR), and mixed reality (MR). This book chapter specifically talks about AR and MR in education. Examples of AR and MR applications are also discussed in the chapter. Also, some of the different benefits of AR and MR in education are mentioned.

***Keywords*:** Augmented reality (AR), virtual reality (VR), extended reality (XR), education sector, students, learners, virtual environment

11.1 An Introduction to Augmented Reality

Extended reality (XR) technologies are becoming popular day by day. XR includes or comprises of MR, AR, and VR [18, 46]. XR is getting more common in each day working life [43]. VR concept is not new [45]. It has been around for quite some time. It is quite popular now. AR and MR also have gained attention in the recent past. For the ergonomic improvement and economic improvement of many present industrial processes, the

Email: prakashera36@gmail.com

Manisha Vohra (ed.) Introduction to Extended Reality (XR) Technologies, (189–204) © 2025 Scrivener Publishing LLC

current emergence of new concepts, tools, and technologies of AR, VR, and MR opens a new scenario [8]. AR, VR, and MR have transformed many sectors. MR systems that vary in hardware, software, etc. are utilized everyday in different areas such as manufacturing, education and so on [13]. Now specifically talking about AR, then, to all our senses, including smell, touch, and hearing, AR can potentially apply to all senses [1]. The combination of real environments and virtual objects is AR technology. Onto the real world, computer-generated objects are overlapped [22]. Digital contents like information and objects in AR systems are overlaid in the real world, which means that users can actually still see and also interact with the surrounding environment while receiving the enhanced experience with digital details such as image and animation illustrations and text description [15]. In AR, the user is allowed to look at the real world with virtual objects composited with or superimposed upon the real world. AR does not completely replace reality; AR supplements reality instead [23]. Hence, instead of fully having a replacement of reality, AR supplements it. A digital overlay which sits on top of real environment is produced by AR [23].

AR gets into real-world computer-generated objects but only the user can see them. A combination of natural light and synthetic light is seen by the user when the user is utilizing AR applications. On top of a glass pair, overlaying images are projected, which enables the interactive virtual objects and images to be on top of a user's real-world view. AR applications are some of the things which can make AR accessible [16]. On the combination of the physical environment and virtual environment, AR systems are based [17]. In many AR experiences, the things that remain essential are graphics computers and software, displays, and trackers [19].

By bringing virtual information to the immediate surroundings of a user along with bringing the virtual information to also any indirect view of the real-world environment, such as live-video stream, AR aims at simplifying the life of the user [5]. AR no longer needs complicated hardware and software features. AR has become a common as well as increasingly widespread part of everyday life [11].

According to author in paper [23], a variation of virtual environments or virtual reality is AR [23]. Some of the AR platforms and the underlying concepts have been around since quite a long time [40]. In 2013 with the development of Google Glass, AR attracted attention of many people [41]. AR can be utilized in industrial applications. The authors in [42] discuss the support of manufacturing planning tasks with AR [42]. ARSG which is Augmented Reality Smart Glasses are quite popular and they are an important tool in smart factories [9]. Powerful tools for learning are AR systems as virtual information gets superimposed on actual physical environment that augments interaction and experience [44]. AR has the ability to provide a huge amount of knowledge without any paper required [47]. AR let's students carry out experiments in a safe environment [48].

As per a survey carried out by the author in [23], the survey defines that AR are systems having the three characteristics below:

1) Combining of real and virtual
2) In real time being interactive
3) Registration in 3D [23]

The different hardware components required for the applications of AR and the functions of the components are as follows:

➢ Computer
➢ Input devices
➢ Sensors
➢ Tracking system
➢ Display device
➢ Interaction tools

11.1.1 History of Augmented Reality

Thomas Preston Caudell coined the term Augmented Reality (AR) [41]. It was the time of 1990s, early 1990s to be accurate, when the term AR was coined, but the first completely functional AR system got built in the late 1960s. Ivan Sutherland was the one who had built this system along with his colleagues (1968). They built a mechanically tracked 3D see-through head-worn display through which computer-generated information mixed with physical objects, such as signs on a laboratory wall, could be seen by the person wearing it [35].

11.1.2 Augmented Reality Types

The different types of AR are listed below:

➢ Marker based AR
➢ Markerless AR
➢ Projection-based AR
➢ Overlap-based AR

11.1.3 Augmented Reality Interfaces

The different AR interfaces are listed below:

- Tangible AR interfaces
- Collaborative AR interfaces
- Hybrid AR interfaces
- Emerging multimodal interfaces

11.1.4 Augmented Reality Application Examples

In the manufacturing field and in other fields as well, AR has already been demonstrated to be a solution in many applications [10]. For supporting service technicians in maintenance, mobile augmented reality solutions are a promising technology [20]. AR can be utilized in kit preparation for mixed-model assembly as a means of conveying picking information. This is explained in [12] by the authors. So, in [12], the authors have provided information regarding how AR can be utilized for supporting kit preparation in the context of material supply to assembly [12]. Let us go through some applications of AR which are discussed in the following section.

11.1.4.1 Augmented Reality in Manufacturing and Repair

There are various places where AR can be utilized. AR has application in various places. For example, one category of AR application is assembly maintenance and complex machinery repair. It might be simpler to understand the instructions if they were available not as manuals with texts and pictures but instead as 3D drawings superimposed upon actual equipment, showcasing tasks which are required to be done step by step and even showcasing how it requires to be done and how to do those tasks. To make the directions further explicit, the superimposed 3D drawings can be animated [23].

11.1.4.2 Augmented Reality in Healthcare

Due to the immersion capabilities, AR/VR technologies have been receiving a lot of attention in the healthcare industry [14]. By superimposing the virtual organ onto the surgeon's view of the patient, the 3D volume of the organ can be seen; tissue that needs to be treated can be identified, and sensitive healthy areas can be avoided [32]. There are different possibilities and opportunities with AR and MR in the education sector. AR and MR can revolutionize the education sector. Let us discuss regarding this further as follows.

11.2 Augmented Reality in Education Sector

The current society is getting reshaped by AR which is emerging as a technology, and specifically, the fields of business and economics (B&E) is getting reshaped by AR [21]. However, not just these fields but also the field of education is experiencing the presence of AR and getting reshaped.

There is an increased pressure faced by educational organizations for providing experiences of learning which are outstanding, and these learning experiences are to be delivered to an increasingly diverse student population. Also, there is pressure to deliver exceptional technology-enhanced teaching (TEL) [4]. In the recent years, technology-enhanced learning (TEL) research has increasingly focused on emergent technologies like AR, mobile learning, ubiquitous learning, etc.; in the recent years, TEL has increasingly focused to improve the satisfaction and experiences of users in enriched multimodal learning environments. In the past few years, there has been an increasing interest for applying AR to create unique educational settings [6]. Due to the diverse possibilities that AR offers, it is one of the emerging technologies which have been rapidly incorporated in the education sphere [2]. AR could actually considerably ease the execution of complex operations; such kind of a breakthrough technology it is [3]. What has attracted the researchers' and developer's attention in several industry areas is AR's main function, which allows users to see real-world scene and virtual objects together [7].

As mentioned earlier, it has been found that, recently, there has been an increased interest in creating a special type of settings in the sector of education by the utilization of AR [6], and one of the reasons for this is that the advantages AR can provide in the education sector can be helpful like, for example, providing interactive learning experience for the students, etc., which will be discussed further in the chapter. In order to make the current models of teaching more better, different universities are longing for exploiting different new methods of visualization, and for this case, AR technology is actually a very nice promising technology [25]. The user, with the help of AR technology, will get a better view, which means that the user, with the help of AR technology, will get an enhanced view of the environment.

There are so many possibilities with AR in the education sector. AR can be utilized in education in different ways. It can be helpful for the students. Learning with the help of AR can become interesting and interactive.

AR has the power of engaging a learner in different kinds of ways that are interactive and which have not been possible previously. From computer-generated 3D models and environments, AR can provide every individual user, learning with the help of AR, with their unique path of discovery with rich content. Along with this, in the educational settings, for students, applications of AR are stimulating, attractive, and exciting. For the users, they provide support which is cost-effective [31].

Student-centered learning is improved when augmented reality (AR) is included in textbooks and educational software. Experiential learning is the best method for learning new abilities because it combines abstract thinking, introspective observation, testing based on meaningful experiences, and experimenting in novel locations and activities. AR technology offers a digital layer of information overlaid onto the physical environment, enriching the students' learning experiences. Within an AR learning environment, students are fully immersed in the educational content, including videos, audios, or games. This immersion allows them to perceive educational content in their surroundings and engage with it by moving around and altering perspectives. AR facilitates these intuitive interactions, thereby diminishing the cognitive burden on students. The proficiency level needed for users to access such content via natural interactions is minimal, leading to a more seamless interface between students and educational material. Market participants in this sector are prioritizing efforts to innovate products accessible to both mid-range consumers and enterprises. AR technology fosters increased interaction among students and between students and learning materials, thereby facilitating experiential learning. It enhances communication and interaction between teachers and students, providing visual support for learners to grasp intangible concepts. AR aids learners in visualizing abstract concepts or imperceptible phenomena, such as electron movements or magnetic fields [34].

AR is such a technology which makes possible generating virtual environments that overlap a real environment in either direct way or indirect way, allowing the interaction of reality with visualization of virtual graphics [16].

With AR games, the educators have the opportunity of utilizing a new, highly visual, and highly interactive form of learning. Even though AR gaming seems to have potential to be helpful in the education area, AR gaming is still in its infancy [30]. So, a lot of exploration and research will be required in this direction to ensure that AR games benefit the learners.

It also needs to be ensured that there are no ill effects of the use of AR games in education; only then can it be utilized in learning and only then can it be fruitful completely. It needs to be remembered that even though AR is not new, it is still in infancy, especially regarding its educational applications. There are still many problems to overcome and issues to explore in order to optimize existing AR applications and technologies for use in education [30].

11.3 Example of Augmented Reality Application in Education

11.3.1 Example: Integrating Augmented Reality Technology to Enhance Children's Learning in Marine Education

Multifaceted and rich issues are what marine education consists of. New materials of learning need to be developed in order to raise awareness of marine environments. For designing a marine learning program which is innovative, consisting of integration of AR for students who are in the primary (lower) grade, this study has adapted concepts from digital game-based learning. There is integration of virtual and physical learning materials by a proposed activity which encourages students to be engaged in a learning environment that is interactive, which thus makes learning interesting and fun.

Taiwan's water resources and marine ecology are introduced by the program. A total of 51 students in Taiwan who were in primary school participated in a quasi-experimental research design for accessing the engagement of the learners.

Indications received from the results are as follows:

1) The students viewed learning activities satisfactorily and were having high confidence by the learning activities.
2) The target knowledge was acquired by the students.
3) For the ones who are low academic achievers, this innovative learning program specifically helps them bring improvement in learning performance [33].

11.4 Benefits of Augmented Reality in Education Sector

- AR applications provide many options for reshaping routine lessons. The traditional method of teaching students in a classroom with the help of blackboard and chalk or of board and marker can be reshaped with the interactive AR learning sessions.
- Interactive AR learning sessions may have a huge positive impact on the students. These engage the students throughout the sessions and make studying entertaining and interesting which can lead to an increase in attention, concentration, and motivation of the students.
- Collaboration can increase and teamwork skills can improve through interactive AR classes in which all the students are able to easily participate in the learning process.
- Providing professional training to students using AR, in addition to teaching different concepts theoretically, can greatly benefit the students. For example, accurate reconstruction of in-field circumstances might benefit in developing the practical abilities required for a particular career.

11.5 An Introduction to Mixed Reality

When digital world and real world combine together, this combination is called MR. Physical objects and digital objects co-exist in MR in real time as well as interact with each other. Thus, through immersive technology, it encompasses AR as well as augmented virtuality.

MR experience is one where the user is placed in an interactive setting which is either real with virtual asset augmentation, or virtual with real-world augmentation [26].

The users in MR systems perceive the physical environment which is around them and also perceive the digital elements presented through—for example, the use of semitransparent displays.

Designing of MR systems is done to provide users with the illusion that digital objects are in the same space as physical objects.

Digital objects require to be precisely positioned into real environment and aligned with real objects in real time for this coexistence illusion. MR includes systems in which virtual aspects are dominant as well as the systems in which physical reality is dominant; MR includes them both.

With the help of MR applications, the viewing audience can be provided with experiences which are immersive and have real content and virtual content. For this specifically, MR-based applications can actually be developed, thereby helping the creators by relaxation of the requirement of modeling [38]. For the user, innovative interfaces can be designed where digital artifacts as well as physical artifacts exist together in the same computer-based environment utilizing MR as it comprises of technologies and concepts that help in this [24].

11.5.1 Mixed Reality Displays

There are different displays utilized in MR environments. Some of the most commonly used displays in MR environments are as mentioned below.

These are head-mounted displays (HMDs), hand-held displays, hand-held projectors, etc.

11.5.2 Mixed Reality Device HoloLens

A head-mounted MR device that is commercially available, known as the HoloLens2™, was developed by Microsoft Corporation (Redmond, WA, USA) [18]. The very first untethered MR system is the HoloLens, leading the road towards ultimate MR experience for the consumer as well as the enterprise [39]. HoloLens utilizes Simultaneous Localization and Mapping (SLAM), which are a set of algorithms that the HoloLens utilizes. The combination of real world and digital world is called MR, which is a development of importance, allowing for more natural interaction progressively, and this interaction is with both real content and digital content.

To describe differently in other and simple words, HoloLens is a pair of perspective holographic glasses. HoloLens basically includes a holograph processing unit for the purpose of handling real-time spatial mapping and processing, a graphics processing unit, and a central processing unit. The functions of HoloLens in comparison to conventional AR equipment are far more advanced like spatial sound design, gaze design, stereoscopic 3D display, etc. [37].

11.5.3 Mixed Reality Application Examples

MR can be used in different applications. For example, in [8], for car body surfaces' quality control inspection, a MR-based user interface has been proposed by the authors in [8] in order to improve the ergonomics and also the productivity of the workers [8].

Another example of MR application is its use for interactive robot programming. In an industry, the number of robots is increasing every year. They are utilized to automate various processes. For an intuitive and effective interaction between a robot and a human, it is necessary to create a system. The authors in [36] present a system based on MR for interactive programming of industrial robots [36].

These are just a few examples of MR application. MR can be used in different sectors, including the education sector, and can provide benefits to the sector. MR is useful not just for the education area but also for other different areas like architecture and construction. It provides opportunities for this industry as well [49]. Talking specifically about education sector, now we will discuss the application of MR in the education sector in the following section.

11.6 Mixed Reality in Education Sector

With MR, there are also different possibilities in the education sector. Learners can control their learning with MR by manipulating objects that are not real in an augmented environment in order to achieve understanding and knowledge.

From a combination of theoretical learning and practical learning with 3D virtual elements from MR applications, they can pool the benefits.

By allowing individuals to be engaged mentally, MR supports the learning process, and in low-spatial-ability learners, it develops interest. Hence, it is believed that this MR technology might be particularly useful for students having a low spatial ability in their learning while picturing science-related diagrams [29].

11.7 Example of MR Application in Education

11.7.1 Example: MR in the Education of Geometry

For geometry education, the authors in [27] have presented a MR environment. The system proposed in [27] was checked in different secondary schools in Greece, and the results obtained showed that the ones who utilized the system found it quite satisfactory in regard of making a provision of a learning approach which is more efficient [27].

11.8 Benefits of MR in Education

The different benefits of MR in the education sector are as follows:

- Learners can control their learning with MR [29].
- MR supports the learning process by allowing individuals to be engaged mentally, learning is supported by MR, and it develops interest in low-spatial-ability learners [29].
- The effectiveness and capabilities of remote learning are expanded by MR [28].

11.9 Conclusion

AR and MR are XR technologies which are useful in different sectors. The education sector can truly benefit from AR and MR application. In this chapter, AR and MR in education were discussed. With examples, the applications of both AR and MR in the education sector were also discussed. The benefits of AR and MR application in education were also stated.

References

1. Azuma, R., Baillot, Y., Behringer, R., Feiner, S., Julier, S., MacIntyre, B., Recent advances in augmented reality. *IEEE Comput. Graphics Appl.*, 21, 34–47, 2001, doi: 10.1109/38.963459.
2. Cabero-Almenara, J., Barroso-Osuna, J., Llorente-Cejudo, C., del Mar Fernández Martínez, M., Educational Uses of Augmented Reality (AR): Experiences in Educational Science. *Sustainability*, 11, 4990, 2019.
3. Hincapié, M., Caponio, A., Rios, H., González Mendívil, E., An introduction to Augmented Reality with applications in aeronautical maintenance. *13th International Conference on Transparent Optical Networks*, pp. 1–4, 2011, doi: 10.1109/ICTON.2011.5970856.
4. Kuleto, V., Stanescu, M., Ranković, M., Šević, N.P., Paun, D., Teodorescu, S., Extended reality in higher education, a responsible innovation approach for generation y and generation z. *Sustainability*, 13, 11814, 2021.
5. Carmigniani, J., Furht, B., Anisetti, M., Ceravolo, P., Damiani, E., Ivkovic, M., Augmented reality technologies, systems and applications. *Multimed. Tools Appl.*, *51*, 341–377, 2010.
6. Bacca, J., Baldiris, S., Fabregat, R., Graf, S., Augmented reality trends in education: a systematic review of research and applications. *J. Educ. Technol. Soc.*, 17, 133, 2014.

7. Shin, D.H. and Dunston, P.S., Identification of application areas for augmented reality in industrial construction based on technology suitability. *Autom. Constr.*, 17, 882–894, 2008.
8. Muñoz, A., Mahiques, X., Solanes, J.E., Martí, A., Gracia, L., Tornero, J., Mixed reality-based user interface for quality control inspection of car body surfaces. *J. Manuf. Syst.*, 53, 75–92, Oct. 2019.
9. Syberfeldt, A., Danielsson, O., Gustavsson, P., Augmented reality smart glasses in the smart factory: Product evaluation guidelines and review of available products. *IEEE Access*, 5, 9118–9130, 2017.
10. Nee, A.Y.C., Ong, S.K., Chryssolouris, G., Mourtzis, D., Augmented reality applications in design and manufacturing. *CIRP Ann.*, 61, 2, 657–679, 2012.
11. Kascak, J., Teliskova, M., Torok, J., Baron, P., Zajac, J., Husar, J., Implementation of augmented reality into the training and educational process in order to support spatial perception in technical documentation, in: *Proc. IEEE 6th Int. Conf. Ind. Eng. Appl. (ICIEA)*, Apr. 2019, pp. 583–587.
12. Hanson, R., Falkenström, W., Miettinen, M., Augmented reality as a means of conveying picking information in kit preparation for mixed-model assembly. *Comput. Ind. Eng.*, 113, 570–575, 2017, 2017/11/01/.
13. Borsci, S., Lawson, G., Broome, S., Empirical evidence, evaluation criteria and challenges for the effectiveness of virtual and mixed reality tools for training operators of car service maintenance. *Comput. Ind.*, 67, 17–26, 2015, 2015/02/01/.
14. Noghabaei, M., Heydarian, A., Balali, V., Han, K., Trend Analysis on Adoption of Virtual and Augmented Reality in the Architecture, Engineering, and Construction Industry. *Data*, 5, 26, 2020.
15. Gong, L., Fast-Berglund, A., Johansson, B., A Framework for Extended Reality System Development in Manufacturing. *IEEE Access*, 9, 24796–24813, 2021, doi: 10.1109/ACCESS.2021.3056752.
16. Petrov, P.D. and Atanasova, T.V., The Effect of Augmented Reality on Students' Learning Performance in Stem Education. *Information, 11*, 4, 209, 2020, https://doi.org/10.3390/info11040209.
17. Gerup, J., Soerensen, C.B., Dieckmann, P., Augmented reality and mixed reality for healthcare education beyond surgery: An integrative review. *Int. J. Med. Educ.*, 11, 1, 2020.
18. Bala, L., Kinross, J., Martin, G., Koizia, L.J., Kooner, A.S., Shimshon, G.J., Hurkxkens, T.J., Pratt, P.J., Sam, A.H., A remote access mixed reality teaching ward round. *Clin. Teach.*, 18, 4, 386–390, 2021, https://doi.org/10.1111/tct.13338.
19. Van Krevelen, D. and Poelman, R., A survey of augmented reality technologies, applications and limitations. *Int. J. Virtual Real.*, 9, 2, 1, 2010.
20. Quandt, M., Beinke, T., Freitag, M., User-Centered Evaluation of an Augmented Reality-based Assistance system for Maintenance. *Procedia CIRP*, 93, 921–926, 2020.

21. Teles Roxo, M. and Brito, P., Augmented Reality Trends to the Field of Business and Economics: A Review of 20 years of Research. *Asian J. Bus. Res.*, 8, 2, 94–117, 2018, 10.14707/ajbr.180051.
22. Kim, K., Lee, H., Hwang, J., Zo, H., Understanding augmented reality applications continuance, in: *2013 International Conference on ICT Convergence (ICTC)*, Jeju, pp. 189–190, 2013, doi: 10.1109/ICTC.2013.6675336.
23. Azuma, R.T., A Survey of Augmented Reality. *Presence: Teleoperators Virtual Environ.*, 6, 4, 355–385, 1997, doi: https://doi.org/10.1162/pres.1997.6.4.355.
24. Müller, D., Bruns, F.W., Erbe, H., Robben, B., Yoo, Y., Mixed reality learning spaces for collaborative experimentation: A challenge for engineering education and training. *Int. J. Online Eng.*, 3, 4, 15–19, 2007.
25. Liarokapis, F. and Anderson, E., Using augmented reality as a medium to assist teaching in higher education, in: *Proceedings of the 31st annual conference of the European association for computer graphics (Eurographics 2010)*, Norrköping, pp. 9–16, 2010.
26. Hughes, C.E., Stapleton, C.B., Hughes, D.E., Smith, E.M., Mixed reality in education, entertainment, and training. *IEEE Comput. Graphics Appl.*, 25, 6, 24–30, 2005, https ://doi.org/10.1109/MCG.2005.139.
27. Nikolakis, G., Fergadis, G., Tzovaras, D., Strintzis, M.G., A mixed reality learning environment for geometry education, in: *Methods and applications of artificial intelligence.* SETN 2004. Lecture notes in computer science, vol. 3025, G.A. Vouros and T. Panayiotopoulos (Eds.), Springer, Berlin, 2004, https://doi.org/10.1007/978-3-540-24674 -9_11.
28. Kolecki, R., Pręgowska, A., Dąbrowa, J., Skuciński, J., Pulanecki, T., Walecki, P., van Dam, P.M., Dudek, D., Richter, P., Proniewska, K., Assessment of the utility of Mixed Reality in medical education. *Transl. Res. Anat.*, 28, 2022, doi: 10.1016/j.tria.2022.100214.
29. Weng, C., Rathinasabapathi, A., Weng, A., Zagita, C., Mixed Reality in Science Education as a Learning Support: A Revitalized Science Book. *J. Educ. Comput. Res.*, *57*, 3, 777–807, 2019, https://doi.org/10.1177/0735633118757017.
30. Yuen, S.C., Yaoyuneyong, G., Johnson, E., Augmented Reality: An Overview and Five Directions for AR in Education. *J. Educ. Technol. Dev. Exch. (JETDE)*, *4*, 1, 119–140, 2011, https://doi.org/10.18785/jetde.0401.10.
31. Lee, K., Augmented Reality in Education and Training. *TechTrends*, 56, 2, 13–21, 2012, 10.1007/s11528-012-0559-3.
32. Tang, S.-L., Kwoh, C.-K., Teo, M.-Y., Sing, N.W., Ling, K.-V., Augmented reality systems for medical applications. *IEEE Eng. Med. Biol. Mag.*, 17, 3, 49–58, May-June 1998, doi: 10.1109/51.677169.
33. Lu, S.-J. and Liu, Y.-C., Integrating augmented reality technology to enhance children's learning in marine education. *Environ. Educ. Res.*, 21, 4, 525–541, 2015, DOI: 10.1080/13504622.2014.911247.
34. Shoikova, E., Nikolov, R., Kovatcheva, E., Smart digital education enhanced by AR and IoT data, 2018, 10.21125/inted.2018.1392.

35. Höllerer, T.H. and Feiner, S.K., Mobile Augmented Reality, in: *Telegeoinformatics: Location-Based Computing and Services*, H. Karimi and A. Hammad (Eds.), Taylor & Francis Books Ltd., Boca Raton, Florida, USA, 01/2004.
36. Caruso, G. and Re, G.M., AR-Mote: A wireless device for Augmented Reality environment. *2010 IEEE Symposium on 3D User Interfaces (3DUI)*, 20–21 March, pp. 99–102, 2010.
37. Park, S., Bokijonov, S., Choi, Y., Review of Microsoft HoloLens Applications over the Past Five Years. *Appl. Sci.*, 11, 7259, 2021, https://doi.org/10.3390/app11167259.
38. Sankaran, N.K., Nisar, H.J., Zhang, J., Formella, K., Amos, J., Barker, L.T., Vozenilek, J.A., LaValle, S.M., Kesavadas, T., Efficacy Study on Interactive Mixed Reality (IMR) Software with Sepsis Prevention Medical Education, in: *2019 IEEE Conference on Virtual Reality and 3D User Interfaces (VR)*, IEEE, pp. 664–670, 2019.
39. Kress, B. and Cummings, W., 11-1: Invited Paper : Towards the Ultimate Mixed Reality Experience: HoloLens Display Architecture Choices. *SID Symp. Dig. Tech. Pap.*, 48, 127–131, 2017, 10.1002/sdtp.11586.
40. Bahri, H., Krcmarik, D., Moezzi, R., Kočí, J., Efficient use of mixed reality for bim system using microsoft HoloLens. *IFACPapersOnLine*, 52, 235–239, 2019.
41. Arena, F., Collotta, M., Pau, G., Termine, F., An Overview of Augmented Reality. *Computers*, 11, 28, 2022, https://doi.org/10.3390/computers11020028.
42. Doil, F., Schreiber, W., Alt, T., Patron, C., Augmented reality for manufacturing planning, in: *Proceedings of the workshop on Virtual environments*, ACM Press, New York, pp. 71–76, 2003.
43. Minna, V., Sami, P., Vetoshkina, L., A Systematic Literature Review on Extended Reality: Virtual, Augmented and Mixed Reality in Working Life. *Int. J. Virtual Real.*, 21, 2, 1–28, 2021, 10.20870/IJVR.2021.21.2.4620.
44. Gavish, N., Gutiérrez, T., Webel, S., Rodríguez, J., Peveri, M., Bockholt, U., Tecchia, F., Evaluating virtual reality and augmented reality training for industrial maintenance and assembly tasks. *Interact. Learn. Environ.*, 4820, November 2014, 1–21, 2013.
45. Stylidis, K., Dagman, A., Almius, H., Gong, L., Söderberg, R., Perceived quality evaluation with the use of extended reality, in: *Proc. Design Soc., Int. Conf. Eng. Design*, vol. 1, no. 1, pp. 1993–2002, 2019.
46. Doolani, S., Wessels, C., Kanal, V., Sevastopoulos, C., Jaiswal, A., Nambiappan, H., Makedon, F., A Review of Extended Reality (XR) Technologies for Manufacturing Training. *Technologies*, 8, 4, 1–20, 77, 2020.
47. Dini, G. and Mura, M., Application of Augmented Reality Techniques in Through-life Engineering Services. *Procedia CIRP*, 38, 14–23, 2015, 10.1016/j.procir.2015.07.044.

48. Bucea-Manea-Oni, R., Bucea-Manea-Oni, R., Simion, V.E., Ilic, D., Braicu, C., Manea, N., Sustainability in higher education: The relationship between work-life balance and xr e-learning facilities. *Sustainability*, 12, 5872, 2020.
49. Huang, Y., Shakya, S., Odeleye, T., Comparing the Functionality between Virtual Reality and Mixed Reality for Architecture and Construction Uses. *J. Civ. Eng. Archit.*, 13, 409–414, 2019.

12

The Growth of Extended Reality

Venkatesh Iyengar[1]*, Vanishree Pabalkar[2] and Samaya Pillai[3]

[1]*Symbiosis Institute of International Business, Symbiosis International (Deemed) University, Pune, Maharashtra, India*
[2]*Symbiosis Institute of Management Studies, Symbiosis International (Deemed) University, Pune, Maharashtra, India*
[3]*Symbiosis Institute of Digital and Telecom Management, Symbiosis International (Deemed) University, Pune, Maharashtra, India*

Abstract
Extended reality (XR) technologies is a universal term inclusive of several immersive learning technologies, such as virtual reality (VR), augmented reality (AR), and mixed reality (MR). Extended reality is also represented in short as "X Reality" or sometimes called "cross reality". It is understood to be a convergence of the real physical world around us and a digital world or space. In today's connected world, XR technologies have the potential to improve and diversify the way businesses and associated communication are conducted. In fact, it can benefit different industries including medicine, education, and many others. As XR technologies evolve and develop further, there are growing opportunities and possibilities widening with it. The book chapter discusses important developments in the concept of extended reality. It also discusses the current players in the XR technologies domain, highlighting different real-world application areas of XR technologies, and with the help of some examples from the literature review, it further discusses the growth of the XR technologies. Different XR technologies apps are also discussed in the chapter. Summarizing multiple discussions about the exponential growth of XR technologies, there are clear indications that XR technologies can continue to grow in the future.

Keywords: Extended reality (XR) technologies, digital world, augmented reality (AR), virtual reality (VR), mixed reality (MR)

**Corresponding author*: rivenkys@gmail.com

Manisha Vohra (ed.) Introduction to Extended Reality (XR) Technologies, (205–218) © 2025 Scrivener Publishing LLC

12.1 Introduction

XR technologies are rapidly making its way into different industries and supplementing human reality in unimaginable ways. Augmented reality (AR), virtual reality (VR), and mixed reality (MR) offer a wide range of revolutionary immersive experiences, and these technologies are powering the popularly known extended reality (XR) technology. The XR technology is bridging distances and providing whole new experiences. Whether it is workforce training, day-to-day productivity, or immersive customer experiences, extended reality offers the opportunity to redesign work without the limiting factor of distance. "Extended reality" is the term that is used to refer to the complete combinations of environments ranging from virtual to real. This is a term that is commonly used for referring to aspects that include a perfect combination and communication of humans with that of machines. The term X here is the variable that could be applicable to computing technological advancements.

12.2 What is Extended Reality?

Extended reality creates a blended environment with a combination of the real, physical, and digital virtual worlds. Extended reality (XR) technology includes augmented reality (AR), virtual reality (VR), and mixed reality (MR)—meaning, that all these technologies converge into the XR technology umbrella. In other words, XR technology is like a huge umbrella technology term for all the technologies like augmented reality (AR), virtual reality (VR), and mixed reality (MR), and we can also consider those that are yet to be conceptualized or developed. By fusing the virtual and real worlds to create a mixed experience, all of these technologies increase the scope of the reality we see. XR is also called X reality or extended reality. Here X represents any present spatial computing technology or future spatial computing technologies like AR, MR, VR, and the areas interpolated among them. XR refers to all real and virtual combined environments and human–computer interactions that are generated by computer technology and wearable sensors [19]. According to [2], XR is explained or defined as a form of MR environment. From the fusion of ubiquitous sensor/actuator networks and shared online virtual worlds, this environment comes.

XR technologies encompasses the real and the virtual environments, wherein the interactions are seen happening between machines and humans. Extended reality technologies comprise the virtual reality (VR), mixed reality (MR), and augmented reality (AR). A set of data that can be shared by way of immersive sensory experiences is nothing but the concept of XR. It defines the process to overlay the real-time data in the user's view and the reality that is transcending the way businesses are now conducted [3]. XR is an area that includes the main concepts like virtual reality (VR), augmented reality, and mixed reality. This provides the user with a better understanding of the world in an extensive manner. The sectors like education, healthcare, etc., are some significant domains that can gain benefit from XR technologies. The authors [5] suggest that the reality-to-virtuality continuum, or XR, is a superset that contains the full spectrum. Mixed reality (MR) not only overlays but anchors virtual objects to the real world. Virtual reality (VR) immerses users in a fully artificial digital environment. Augmented reality (AR) overlays virtual objects in the real-world environment. When it comes to mixed reality, the user is in a position to directly interact and can manipulate physical and virtual items and the connecting environments. This can be achieved by modifying the most recent sensing and imaging technologies. The user has the possibility to independently combine the actual and virtual worlds thanks to mixed reality. It offers a platform so that the user can literally have one hand in the real world and the other in an imaginary setting, allowing for the literal application of the terms real and imagery.

12.2.1 Augmented Reality (AR)

Virtual information, objects, and digital details form the fundamental blocks for augmented reality (AR) technology. This enhances the real world with digital specifics like images, animation, etc. The user interface is the dominant aspect of AR. Devices like screens, tablets, glasses, and smartphones are an integral part of this technology. Augmented reality is the environment where the virtual world is associated with that of the real world. The user has the option to have a view of the real environment as well as can access the information that is generated via a computer. The users' view of reality can be augmented by AR [2]. AR hardware components include input devices, sensors, etc. Input devices let users interact with AR systems. Sensors are useful in tracking mechanisms. The display is also one of the useful AR hardware components. They let users interact with the AR system. Their examples are head-mounted displays (HMDs), monitors, and wearable devices like glasses, gloves, etc. [18]. In augmented reality, virtual content is displayed in two ways. The first is virtual things/objects are inserted into actual environments, making it difficult for users to tell them apart from actual ones. An example is the popular mobile game Pokemon GO. The second is that virtual information is made available to users to aid in their comprehension of the real world and the provision of the required support, such as real-time maps, notations, and sensory data. For instance, real-time augmented reality navigation data can be shown to help drivers. The famous example of this technology, as mentioned above, is the Pokémon GO game that overlays digital creatures in the real world, the other example being the Snapchat filters that attach digital objects such as hats or glasses to the users. Some of the commonly known AR devices are Google ARCore, Apple ARKit, etc. AR's presence is growing in different areas. For example, in the last decade, AR's presence has considerably grown in the automotive market [12]. Similarly, in various other areas, AR's presence is growing and AR is being utilized in various sectors.

12.2.2 Virtual Reality (VR)

Virtual reality (VR) and virtual environments (VE) are used in the computer community interchangeably. These terms are the most popular and most often used, but there are many others. Just to mention a few most important ones: synthetic experience, virtual worlds, artificial worlds, and artificial reality. All these names mean the same [6]. If the last 5 years of VR presence is viewed, then in the last 5 years, it can be seen that it has very quickly leapt to a tangible world of people's living room, their fields for playing, and even beyond it from the realm of fantasy and science fiction [21]. In virtual reality (VR), the user's vision is often altered from the real world to an identical or somewhat different virtual environment. In virtual reality (VR), the users are fully involved in the virtual world. The users in the case of VR are completely immersed in a virtual world. They cannot view the real world surrounding them [1]. The history of VR technology's history is quite longer than it might seem. The VR concept was formulated in the 1960s. The very first commercial tools of VR appeared in the late 1980s [20]. The dominant device used in this technology is the headgear or headset which gives a head-mounted display. The head-mounted display gives a 360° view of the virtual, i.e., artificial, world. The users are completely in the make-believe world, almost shutting out the real world, giving the experience of traversing the moon, swimming beneath the sea, etc. The novel domain of the gaming industry was among the early adopters of this technology. Now, other industries like healthcare, construction, engineering, etc., have also started embracing this technology. Some examples of VR devices are the HTC VIVE, Oculus Rift, and Google Cardboard.

The users can actually look around the artificial world, move around in it, and interact with virtual features or items. Let us go through the basic components of VR immersive applications. The user has an HMD, tracker, and manipulation device which is optional. When a person starts actions like walking or head rotating, then data that describes the person's behavior is fed to the computer. It is fed from input devices. In real time, information is processed by the computer and appropriate feedback is generated, which is passed back to the user. It is passed back through output displays. Input devices are responsible for interaction, output devices for the feeling of immersion, and software for proper control and synchronization of the entire environment. How to communicate with a computer is determined by input devices. Presenting the virtual environment and its phenomena to the user is done by output devices. They contribute to generating an immersive feeling at most. These include visual, auditory, or haptic displays. After input hardware and output hardware, underlying software is the one which is responsible for playing an important role. It has to look after the management of I/O devices, analyze incoming data, and generate proper feedback [16].

VR systems can be described as follows according to the immersion level it offers to the user:

- Desktop VR
- Fish tank VR
- Immersive systems

Desktop VR—It is sometimes known as window-on-world (WoW) systems. Desktop VR is the simplest type of VR application, and it uses conventional monitors to display images of the world. Any other sensory output is not supported.

Fish tank VR—It is the desktop VR's improved version. Head tracking is supported by these systems and hence improves the feeling of "being there". This is possible due to the motion parallax effect. Still a conventional monitor is used by these systems but, generally, sensory output is not supported by them.

Immersive systems—It is VR systems' ultimate version. With the help of a head-mounted display (HMD) which supports a stereoscopic view of the scene as per the user's position and orientation, these systems allow the user to completely immerse in a world that is computer-generated. By using audio, haptic, and sensory interfaces, these systems may be enhanced [16].

12.2.3 Mixed Reality (MR)

In mixed reality, both the digital and the physical entities coexist. Additionally, they engage in live interactions with one another. The real-world environment and the unreal one both merge together. This is the latest upgrade in technology and is also called “hybrid reality”. It also uses devices like a headgear. Compared to VR technology or AR technology, the MR headset has more computing power. “Microsoft’s HoloLens” is a working example of this technology, wherein users can interact with both physical and digital objects in real space.

12.3 Growth of XR Technologies

In the recent decade, the growth of XR technologies encompassing VR, AR, and MR has witnessed continuous growth. It finds useful applications across different industry domains. In different application areas, it is being well integrated to provide immersive experiences to its users. Continued developments in the area of XR technologies can witness the expanded use of its applications even further and impact several aspects of our personal and professional lives.

Some of the real-world application areas of XR technologies include the following:

- Entertainment and gaming
- Education, training, and development
- Healthcare
- Manufacturing and industry applications
- Tourism and hospitality
- Real estate management
- Marketing

All these real-world applications are discussed below as follows:

- Entertainment and gaming: The domain of video gaming has been around for many years now. In the current times, the virtual reality gaming and entertainment industries are one of the largest users of such XR technology. While virtual reality can provide immersive gaming experiences, augmented reality technology allows for the blending of the real physical world with virtual elements, thereby enhancing the gaming experiences.

- Education, training, and development: XR technologies can assist and can be quite useful in the creation of simulated environments. Simulations for training the learners for different situations and developing skills by learning from it can be very useful. Virtual learning environments such as VR-based classrooms having interactive content can be implemented for students. training development, interactive content, and virtual language immersion.
- Healthcare: Virtual simulations can assist in training medical students to understand complex surgical procedures. It can also help in the virtual exploration of human anatomy. VR can be used for anxiety reduction, pain management, and even physical rehabilitation. Furthermore, XR technologies can assist in providing interactive health education to students, conducting 3D representations of human anatomy, etc.
- Manufacturing and industry applications: AR and VR applications are quite useful in training assembly line workers through simulation and AR overlays for maintenance and repair of machinery and equipment. The manufacturing industry can largely benefit with the use of XR technologies for design and 3D prototyping, virtual prototyping, collaborative designing, assembly line optimization, carrying out simulations, providing remote assistance, helping with inventory visualization, etc. In the automotive industry, XR technologies like AR technology, for example, can be extremely useful, and hence its presence has grown considerably in this industry in the last decade as rightly mentioned by the authors in [12].
- Tourism and hospitality: Tourists can gain benefits by using these XR technologies. The tourism and hospitality sector can get a lot of help using XR technologies. For example, there can be virtual hotel tours provided to the tourists with XR technologies, easy language translation can be availed by tourists with XR technologies-based apps, etc. From booking hotels to visiting and exploring tourist destinations, different XR technology-based apps can be helpful and make things simpler.

- Real estate management: Giving a real feel and simulation of the real estate property and enhancing the customer experience using XR technologies can bring strong business opportunities and better success rates. XR technologies can assist the real estate industry with VR property showcasing, architectural visualization, AR building overlays, VR interior designs, AR furniture placements, interactive site planning, etc.
- Marketing: XR technology can provide the try-before-you-buy approach aspect which could give the customers a great experience and convert the prospective customer to a confirmed buyer. The marketing industry can utilize XR technologies for product demonstrations, reality advertisements, etc.

In the literature review, various examples of the inclusion of XR technologies in different application areas were found. For example, some of these are mentioned as follows: The authors in [7] created a VR simulation for the purpose of pump maintenance. It was developed with the goal of educating beginners. The authors in [8] examined the efficacy of head-mounted display (HMD)-based training transfer for assembly operations in a study using augmented reality. They carried out a study using two groups. The results of the study demonstrate that integrating the real and virtual assembly phases bolstered the case for training transfer and demonstrated that the succeeding group had made fewer mistakes. The study conducted by the authors in [4] evaluated the utilization of VR platforms. For industrial training and maintenance systems, the VR platform is an integrated part of a digital factory. For providing industrial training and maintenance services, an efficient tool can be a VR platform which is digital factory-based as a VR platform gives an intuitive and immersive human–computer interface. The results from the study gave the suggestion that, for training and maintenance of industrial tasks that are complex, the utilization of VR platforms should be encouraged and the utilization of VR platforms for purposes should be evaluated further. In the case of marketing and sales, VR is widely in today's time in marketing and sales case by companies in order to experience their products with potential customers and to understand them better. In order to create order-picking instructions that are independent of language, the authors in [9] used augmented reality, considering that the instructions are not always in the local tongue and taking into account the inputs from the users of the instructions. In such cases, textual inputs are collected from the users using AR-based instructions and also instruction in other languages. It was seen that the users who use language-independent visual AR are able to wind up the activities much faster when compared to the ones using other language-based instructions. The authors in [10] had come up with a mixed reality setup. This included the see-through cameras that were then combined with the head-mounted display (HMD). This was further checked in the system in implementing the process of manufacturing an aircraft maintenance door. The outcome was that the level of knowledge procured in the mixed reality and the knowledge procured in the conventional face-to-face process did not have any significant difference as such, which means that the mixed reality setup was useful. As suggested in [11], sight, hearing, touch, smell, and taste are the five fundamental senses on which humans base their perception of actual objects. It appears that a virtual thing does exist if it can provide the same synthesized perceptions as a genuine object. Digital technologies are used to create virtual content [11].

In the application area of sports, AR can enhance the audience's quality of experience and athlete performance. Athletes can get real-time AI support with AR eyewear. In order to increase the success pass percentage, for instance, the ideal pass route might be shown in the soccer players' glasses. The audience can view details that were not previously available, like the participants' names, rankings, and background knowledge. For instance, spectators near the rear of a large stadium cannot see players clearly. The names and performances of players near the relevant player can be added to their perspective to enhance it [11].

In the application area of automotive industry, AR is crucial to all aspects of the design, production, sales, maintenance, etc., of motor vehicles. AR can aid designers in making decisions; it can allow clients to change the car model they choose. For drivers who utilize overhead-mounted displays (OHMDs), AR has been employed to give collision warning, driver assistance, navigation, and lane departure warning [11, 12]. Due to their lack of formal training, drivers frequently find it difficult to recognize automotive faults. AI can recognize and display issues using AR devices. Additional details, such as neighboring auto repair businesses or contact details, can also be displayed [11].

In the case of historical architecture, recent studies and research on cultural monuments have demonstrated how using the most recent advancements in the fields of 3D survey, 3D modeling, building information modeling (BIM), and extended reality can increase awareness of architectural history [13]. The authors in [13] have discussed various case scenarios for the "Lombard monuments—the Basilica of Sant'Ambrogio in Milan" using AR–VR to understand and appreciate this historical architecture. This kind of research requires a high degree of information sharing from multiple disciplines and industries like restoration, geomatics, 3D virtual museums, and serious gaming; this digital workflow demands a vast amount of data sources and a holistic approach. This research displays the key findings from the generative process of digital environments aimed to increase the degree of information and enhance the contents derived from the informative models, together with entertainment software and games [13].

In the healthcare area, specifically talking about cardiology, it is found that due to recent advancements results, new classes of devices like 3D VR and AR displays have surfaced. The cardiology field, where spatial reasoning is important, is benefitted from these tools. Additionally, a lot of these technologies make use of fresh input paradigms that enable interventionists to operate software interfaces in sterile settings where it was previously impossible to communicate with computers. The advantages of XR technology that are most easily accessible come in the form of 3D anatomical representations and real-time displays of anatomy and tools. XR devices have been applied to education and pre-procedural planning. It has also been applied to cardiac interventions. Where using traditional devices is difficult, these devices excel in settings. For example, cardiac catheterization lab. The XR technology is improving, and as it is improving, new applications of XR in cardiology will continue to emerge. The XR technology hardware market is evolving quickly. Future hardware developments should enhance user comfort and visual realism. Haptic feedback integration with XR technology systems could be a significant development for interventional procedures [14].

The authors in [15] conducted a thorough search for projects utilizing XR technology in the Internet of Things (IoT) settings, both in commercial applications and scholarly studies. The most cutting-edge application they had ever seen, according to the authors, involved an elevator manufacturer using HoloLens to assist its technicians with elevator repair and maintenance. Initial cloud system uploads by the elevator company included sensor data and elevator systems. Elevator data was recorded and saved by the cloud system service. It also contained information about the motor's temperature, the shaft's alignment, the speed of the cab, and the operation of the doors. Rapid component identification and failure diagnosis were made possible by real-time data visualization in the cloud.

In their research study, the authors in [16] have discussed the pros and cons of using XR in research. They conducted a survey to understand what opportunities XR can provide with what kind of loss. The survey results they received make it obvious that the respondents think remote XR technology research has the potential to be a fruitful research strategy [16].

Similarly, in another research, the authors in [17] discussed various models related to the acceptance of technology by the common man. The technology AR–VR–XR is the newest on the block and also needs to be adopted by all people; in this context, the authors summarized most theories related to technology acceptance [17].

12.4 Current Companies Dealing in the XR Technology Domain

The global extended reality market includes major companies working in the XR technology domain, such as the following:

- Microsoft
- Meta
- Apple
- Google
- HTC
- Samsung Electronics and many more

Below are examples of some XR technology-based devices/products:

- Amazon Echo Frames smart glasses
- Bosch Light Drive BML500
- Jio Glass
- Epson Moverio BT-300
- Google Glass
- Lenovo Lightweight AR Glasses
- Nreal Mixed Reality Glasses
- Ajna Lens
- ACER AH101
- Aryzon
- ASUS HC 102
- Avegant AG101 VR Video Headsets
- Canon MREAL MD-20
- Lenovo Explorer
- Lenovo ThinkReality A6

- Lenovo Mirage VR S3
- Microsoft HoloLens

12.5 Examples of XR Technology-Based Apps

XR technology can be accessed easily with many apps, which can be deployed on our smart phones.

Below are examples of some XR technology-based apps:

- ➢ Google Lens
- ➢ Amikasa
- ➢ Mondly
- ➢ SketchAR

Google Lens: If an AR-based app needs to be experienced by users, this particular app can be tried. It is available on Android, iOS, etc. It requires just pointing the camera at an object or image with Google Lens, then the app searches the Internet for the same. It can translate the text, and it can also provide you with information regarding the object that you are pointing your camera at.
Amikasa: This is an AR-based app which is helpful especially for architects, interior designers, and contractors. It can support design and measuring floor plans. It can help in the creation of floor plans by using a phone's camera, and it also enables adding of different photos. It is available on iOS devices.
Mondly: It is an app that supports learning a new language. It can teach 33 languages. This app enhances the user's experience of language learning with the help of AR and VR along with the use of other technologies and features it provides. It is available on both Android and iOS.
SketchAR: It is an app that helps you learn drawing and make yourself better in drawing. One of the important features about this app is that it includes AR technology to help provide users a great learning experience.

12.6 Conclusion

XR technologies are transforming the way we live. XR technologies have the capability to change the way we shop, we do business, we learn, we connect with others, and also how to entertain ourselves. XR technologies can help simplify tasks, aid productivity, and enhance creativity in different tasks.

There are many areas of applications of XR technologies. It is being applied in various applications and even studied and considered for use in different applications as seen in the examples discussed in the chapter. There are many different XR technology-based apps available that are very useful. It can be said that based on the discussion regarding XR technologies in the chapter, which includes application areas of XR technologies, examples from literature review, discussion on XR technologies apps, etc., there is visible growth of XR. Based on all of these discussions, there is a probable indication that, in the future, XR technologies are set to grow further, and it can be more frequently and widely used in different applications if it continues to develop further and keep on providing various benefits to its different areas of application, be it industrial area of application or healthcare and so on. Thus, it seems that, moving into the future, XR technologies have a great chance of continuing to grow further.

References

1. Fast-Berglund, A., Gong, L., Li, D., Testing and validating Extended Reality (XR) technologies in manufacturing. *Procedia Manuf.*, *25*, 31–38, 2018.
2. Pavlik, J.V., Experiential media and transforming storytelling: A theoretical analysis. *J. Creative Ind. Cult. Stud.-JOCIS*, 3, 046–067, 2018.
3. Bellini, H., *Episode 93: Beyond VR & AR: Extended Reality to Transform Our Lives as Consumers*, J. Siewert (Interviewer), Goldman Sachs Exchanges Podcast, New York, NY, 2018, [Accessed 24 October 2023]. Available at: https://www.goldmansachs.com/insights/podcasts/episodes/05-18-2018-heather-bellini.html.
4. Shamsuzzoha, A., Toshev, R., Vu Tuan, V., Kankaanpaa, T., Helo, P., Digital factory–virtual reality environments for industrial training and maintenance. *Interact. Learn. Environ.*, *29*, 8, 1339–1362, 2021.
5. Milgram, P., Takemura, H., Utsumi, A., Kishino, F., Augmented reality: A class of displays on the reality-virtuality continuum, in: *Telemanipulator and telepresence technologies*, vol. 2351, Spie, pp. 282–292, 1995, December.
6. Mazuryk, T. and Gervautz, M., Virtual Reality - History, Applications, Technology and Future, 1999.
7. Winther, F., Ravindran, L., Svendsen, K.P., Feuchtner, T., Design and evaluation of a VR training simulation for pump maintenance, in: *Extended Abstracts of the 2020 CHI Conference on Human Factors in Computing Systems*, pp. 1–8, 2020, April.
8. Werrlich, S., Nguyen, P.A., Notni, G., Evaluating the training transfer of Head-Mounted Display based training for assembly tasks, in: *Proceedings of*

the 11th Pervasive Technologies Related to Assistive Environments Conference, pp. 297–302, 2018, June.
9. Murauer, N., Müller, F., Günther, S., Schön, D., Pflanz, N., Funk, M., An analysis of language impact on augmented reality order picking training, in: *Proceedings of the 11th Pervasive Technologies Related to Assistive Environments Conference*, pp. 351–357, 2018, June.
10. Gonzalez-Franco, M., Pizarro, R., Cermeron, J., Li, K., Thorn, J., Hutabarat, W., Tiwari, A., Bermell-Garcia, P., Immersive mixed reality for manufacturing training. *Front. Rob. AI*, *4*, 3, 2017.
11. Akyildiz, I.F. and Guo, H., Wireless extended reality (XR): Challenges and new research directions. *ITU J. Future Evol. Technol.*, *3*, 2, 1–15, 2022.
12. Merenda, C., Kim, H., Tanous, K., Gabbard, J.L., Feichtl, B., Misu, T., Suga, C., Augmented reality interface design approaches for goal-directed and stimulus-driven driving tasks. *IEEE Trans. Visual Comput. Graphics*, *24*, 11, 2875–2885, 2018.
13. Banfi, F., Brumana, R., Stanga, C., Extended reality and informative models for the architectural heritage: from scan-to-BIM process to virtual and augmented reality. *Virtual Archaeol. Rev.*, *10*, 21, 14–30, 2019.
14. Andrews, C., Southworth, M.K., Silva, J.N., Silva, J.R., Extended reality in medical practice. *Curr. Treat. Options Cardiovasc. Med.*, *21*, 1–12, 2019.
15. Andrade, T. and Bastos, D., Extended reality in iot scenarios: Concepts, applications and future trends, in: *2019 5th Experiment International Conference (exp. at'19)*, pp. 107–112, IEEE, 2019, June.
16. Ratcliffe, J., Soave, F., Bryan-Kinns, N., Tokarchuk, L., Farkhatdinov, I., Extended reality (XR) remote research: a survey of drawbacks and opportunities, in: *Proceedings of the 2021 CHI Conference on Human Factors in Computing Systems*, 2021, May, pp. 1–13.
17. Chuah, S.H.W., Why and who will adopt extended reality technology? Literature review, synthesis, and future research agenda. *Literature Review, Synthesis, and Future Research Agenda (December 13, 2018)*, 2018.
18. Arena, F., Collotta, M., Pau, G., Termine, F., An overview of augmented reality. *Computers*, *11*, 2, 28, 2022, [Accessed 24 October 2023]. Available at: https://doi.org/10.3390/computers11020028.
19. Doolani, S., Wessels, C., Kanal, V., Sevastopoulos, C., Jaiswal, A., Nambiappan, H., Makedon, F., A review of extended reality (XR) technologies for manufacturing training. *Technologies*, *8*, 4, 77, 2020, [Accessed 24 October 2023]. Available at: https://doi.org/10.3390/technologies8040077.
20. Cipresso, P., Giglioli, I.A.C., Raya, M.A., Riva, G., The past, present, and future of virtual and augmented reality research: a network and cluster analysis of the literature. *Front. Psychol.*, 9, 2086, 2018, doi: 10.3389/fpsyg.2018.02086.
21. Mcmillan, K., Flood, K., Glaeser, R., Virtual reality, augmented reality, mixed reality, and the marine conservation movement. *Aquat. Conserv. Mar. Freshwater Ecosyst.*, 27, 162–168, 2017.

Index

Printed and bound by CPI Group (UK) Ltd, Croydon, CR0 4YY

17/09/2026

14964274-0001